Media Reception Studies

Media
Reception
Studies

Janet Staiger

NEW YORK UNIVERSITY PRESS
New York and London

NEW YORK UNIVERSITY PRESS
New York and London
www.nyupress.org

Library of Congress Cataloging-in-Publication Data
Staiger, Janet.
Media reception studies / Janet Staiger.
p. cm.
Includes bibliographical references and index.
ISBN 0–8147–8134–9 (cloth : alk. paper) —
ISBN 0–8147–8135–7 (pbk. : alk. paper)
1. Mass media—Audiences. I. Title.
P96.A83S73   2005
302.23—dc22   2005000998

New York University Press books are printed on acid-free paper,
and their binding materials are chosen for strength and durability.

Manufactured in the United States of America
c 10 9 8 7 6 5 4 3 2 1
p 10 9 8 7 6 5 4 3 2 1

To my students, who have taught me so much.

Contents

Acknowledgments

Beyond the bibliography, which lists many colleagues with whom I have enjoyed conversations over the years about these matters, I want particularly to note with gratitude the Faculty Research Assignment from the University of Texas, which allowed me to begin this project, and the University of Texas Libraries, which have been the most efficient and helpful libraries for which one can hope.

1

Introduction

The history of reception studies begins at the moment speakers attempted to figure out what listeners might understand about messages. Hoping to influence, persuade, or merely enlighten their audiences, speakers needed to know whether or not their intentions matched interpretations and whether those interpretations would produce the hoped-for outcome in the other people. Rhetorical studies provides an excellent survey of theories and tactics for communicating ideas to narrow the gap between expectations and consequences. Literary studies has as well a history of speculation about these desires.

This book will present the dominant theories and findings in contemporary media studies focused primarily on fictional film and television, although these theories and findings have application to nonfictional texts and, with some revisions, to other media such as popular music, literary texts, and comics. This book's purpose is to provide one mapping of the field that might give directions for travel to others attracted to the landscape. Centuries of humanistic thought about oral and written communications have influenced what media studies offers. The introduction of social scientific approaches to individuals in a communications environment also has produced a variety of theories and approaches to audience analysis. Yet, because of both the addition of moving images to messages and the mass commodification of very powerful combinations of audiovisual materials, media studies has been a magnet during the past century for contemplation around questions of audiences and effects of communication.

In turn, media studies has influenced rhetorical, literary, and social scientific scholarship with its research on implications of the gaze, representations of sexuality and violence, and easy access to images and texts by children and all classes and cultures. Every few years from at least 1915 in the United States, individuals have sought at a federal level to regulate

1

moving images. This drive to control exists in every country (see, for instance, Kuhn, 1988). In discussing moral panics, Martin Barker (1998:137) points out that concerned citizens tend to create "others" for portions of the society. These others are "incomprehensible and dangerous"; they are vulnerable (and need protection) or monstrous (and require control).

Obviously, media reception is an area of public policy that requires thoughtful research and wise counsel to balance free speech rights with social needs. This brief introductory chapter will provide some initial terminology and concepts that will interweave throughout the rest of the book. While some of these definitions and schemata may seem far from the most pertinent issue of what spectators do with media (or media do to them), I hope you will bear with me.

Definitions and Implications of Reception Studies

Terry Eagleton refers to reception studies as "a social and historical theory of meaning" (1983:107), while Jonathan Culler, describing one theorist's approach, explains that it "is not a way of interpreting works but an attempt to understand their changing intelligibility by identifying the codes and interpretative assumptions that give them meaning for different audiences at different periods" (1981:13). As Wolfgang Iser puts it in one of my favorite characterizations, "The 'stars' in a literary text are fixed; the lines that join them are variable" (1972:282).

All these definitions of the field underline that reception studies is not a hermeneutics or truth-finding of the meaning of the text. The enterprise it engages is historical and theoretical. It asks, *How* does a text mean? For whom? In what circumstances? With what changing values over time? Reception studies does not presume a meaning as an essence to be extracted by an insightful critic. Such a position is *not* to suggest that a text does not exist: stars are there. Nor does asking about *how* a text is meaningful to various readers imply that texts do not have effects on their readers or viewers. What the meanings are for readers may be quite pertinent to their behaviors, attitudes, and beliefs. So reception studies asks, What kinds of meanings does a text have? For whom? In what circumstances? With what changes over time? And do these meanings have any effects? Cognitive? Emotional? Social? Political?

In this book, I will use *spectator, reader, viewer,* and *audience* interchangeably. Other scholars have debated the implications of each of these terms (Bennett, 1996; Blumer, 1996:100–101). Vocabulary matters, but in casual usage I will treat the terms as compatible. Most of the research and debate does not hinge on distinctions among these words.

What does matter is the value of this research for the social world. Klaus Bruhn Jensen (1987:23) emphasizes that research on media audiences is of consequence to political and socioeconomic research. Moreover, the question of media meanings and effects is particularly one of judgment and evaluation. I would ask, Why is it that almost always it is "bad" effects that consume public attention and policy? Perhaps we should pay more attention to the apparent good effects of media, such as teaching young children reading at an early age or marshaling youth to care about civil rights or informing all citizens about political controversies. Indeed, the evaluation of effects is significant for all social and political views. Both conservative and progressive individuals want to know about outcomes from engagements with movies and television. For instance, Étienne Balibar and Pierre Macherey declare, "'The least one can ask of a Marxist theory is that it begin to produce real transformations, practical effects, either in the means of production of literary texts and art works, or in the manner in which they are socially consumed'" (quoted in Kuentz, 1976:92).

Implications of reception studies research also include related judgments about valuable (or not) texts. Once reception studies theorized variable meanings, it also "open[ed] the door to rewriting literary history and to redefining the literary canon" (Silberman, 1984:250). No natural, universally "worthwhile" texts exist. All interpretations are subjective, and all texts have political and social meanings and values—"positive" or "negative," "reinforcing" or contrary to the beliefs of their various readers.

Reception studies scholarship also points out that these variable tastes and the canons of the laudable must be debated in new ways. Lawrence Levine has written an extremely influential study of the division of taste cultures into highbrow and lowbrow in which he notes that this split in American culture in the 1880s produced a "sacralization," a reverence for some works (such as Shakespeare's plays), and "increased the distance between amateur and professional" (1988:139). Audiences with education in certain sorts of culture learned particular ways to engage that culture, often deemed "correct," versus the "untutored" audiences who either had no skills to access that culture or responded in ways the educated audiences considered inadequate.

While earlier divisions (regional, class, and so forth) among American citizens were significant, any division has political implications. As Ian Angus explains, any division of culture produces two issues for all democracies: "the monopolization of access to relevant social knowledge" and "the inability of listeners to transform themselves into speakers" (1993:233). Thus, in a situation in which owners and managers of culture industries have monopolies by which to express themselves and to be labeled the "professionals," Angus argues that we must insist that the "right to speak" be equal to the "right to be heard." So-called amateurs can be closed out of the public sphere, with their tastes and values diminished as secondary to the preferences of only part of the social formation. Free speech is now being argued as necessarily including equal access to make heard the speech of the listeners.

Thus, reception studies is not just about the consumption of media messages but also about access to producing them. As I shall discuss in chapters about fans and minorities, the articulation of personal reactions to mass media is part of the field of research. Reception studies matters for our individual and our social and political lives. It is a particularly pragmatic field even if at times reaching specific conclusions is difficult.

General Theories beneath Media Reception Studies

Media reception studies turns to the same sorts of theories for human behavior and history as do most social sciences. It looks to political science and linguistics. It relies heavily on psychological and sociological propositions developed during the past century. Throughout this book, I will refer occasionally to these theories as underpinning a more detailed proposition about media reception and effects. While I believe my understandings of these theories are typical, a short outline of what I mean will probably facilitate communication. I turn first to psychological theories and then to sociological ones.

Three lines of psychological research have dominated twentieth-century psychology. Although Wilhelm Wundt's introspectionism turned philosophical investigation of the mind into experimental science, the first strong contender for a theory of how the individual responds to the social world is **behaviorism**. While most people associate behaviorism with the work of the Russian physiologist Ivan Pavlov, his theory involved certain mental categorizing. Rather, behaviorism uses the notions of conditioning and of stimulus and response to found a positivist approach usually attributed to J. B. Watson. Successors include B. F. Skinner and Albert Bandura. Behaviorists argue that because scientists have no direct access to the individual's mind or experiences, we should investigate behavior that is observable. Thinking and affect are interpreted as implicit behavior. What is considered is visible stimulus-response behavior. The proposition is that a stimulus (S) produces a feeling or attitude (Rf) that produces an action response (Ra). Conditions exist for responses. The stimulus has to be at a threshold for the subject to perceive it. Factors can contribute to or interfere with an S/R relation. Repetition should improve the response rate. Contradictory stimuli decrease the probability of a response. Systems may be self-regulating.

This point-to-point model is atomized, as if the world were always in a simple mode. It also easily permits statistical output. One of the main problems with behaviorism is that it has no large-scale theory of learning complex ideas. However, some communication theorists have used it. As I shall discuss in chapter 2, post–World War II mass communication scholars applied it to argue that fears of threats from propaganda were exaggerated. Changing people's opinions was not an easy task. Behaviorism has also underpinned much of the social science research on possible media effects from watching violence or sexually explicit materials (see chapter 7).

The second major psychological theory is **psychoanalysis**. This is a depth model of the individual. A simple depth thesis would assume that the individual has a consciousness. However, psychoanalysis is a complex depth model because it holds that individuals develop an unconscious as well. Moreover, distortions in associations of ideas exist, although these distortions are organized in relation to an individual's experiences with the social world. Scholars widely use Sigmund Freud's story of the typical development of a heterosexual male in Anglo-European culture as a touchstone for how such an unconscious develops and what might be characteristic distortions (castration anxiety, fetishisms).

The usual complaints about psychoanalysis are the difficulty in verifying the individual's unconscious representations, the generalization of the typical story, the negative portrayal of women (as inferior to men), and the unclear theorization of same-sex desires for men and women. Still, the power of the theory to explain bodily symptoms, affective responses, and (at least) heterosexual male actions in an Anglo-European context has made it a favorite of communication scholars, with the theory dominating film studies for several decades (see chapter 3).

Cognitive psychology is the third psychological theory. Coming out of research in Gestalt psychology, Soviet psycholinguistics, and artificial intelligence, this approach has improved in power over the past forty years as a theory of human consciousness. Employing the proposition that individuals develop schemata (mental scripts, frameworks, prototypes, templates) from social experience, cognitive psychology has recently attempted to overcome the criticism that it focused nearly entirely on thinking and had little to contribute to understanding affect. With an increased attention to emotion, cognitive psychology is a strong competitor with psychoanalysis. Some individuals see the two theories as potentially able to be merged (Rosenfield, 1985; Damasio, 1994). Scholars in both social sciences and cultural studies use cognitive psychology (see chapters 2 and 3).

The other major theories are sociological ones that focus on the individual within a social group. Ultimately, this is much like any figure/ground problem. In looking at the optical illusion of a woman or a vase, what one sees depends on which is foregrounded: here, the social unit or the individual. In social theory, scholars analyze both institutional and informal groups for how they come together, are maintained, or dissolve and how individuals function within such groups. The rules governing the behavior in the group (norms), the relative status and duties of the group members (roles), the kind and amount of control that members have over each other (power), the degree of attachment (cohesion) to the group, and the degree of agreement (consensus) are typical matters for attention.

Two major perspectives typify social theory: functionalist and conflict theory, characterized by their views of the fundamental nature of society. **Functionalist** theory assumes that society is primarily harmonious. Homogeneous values produce a basic consensus. Shared culture shapes social structures. Functionalists focus on what produces stability and continuity in a society. **Conflict** theory (often produced out of a Marxist or other radical perspective) operates from the premise that society is conflictual. Heterogeneous values exist, primarily because individuals are not equal in power or do not have equal material resources. Dominant and subordinate groups battle over norms and resources, with dominant groups seeking to engineer consent through producing representational systems that may attempt to convince subordinated individuals to adopt beliefs and perspectives that ultimately are not in their best interest (hegemony). Conflict theory focuses on what produces change or alterations in society.

These theories produce recurring debates. These debates include claims about:

- Inherent, essential, or innate processes versus learned or ideological ones.
- Universal processes versus group processes versus individual processes. Group processes include the issues of "identities," which are complexly organized for some theorists into "communities" with possible sociological hierarchies and functions for the individuals within the group or for others in "matrixes of domination."
- The spectator being "active" or "passive," "normative" or "resistant"; or generally around questions of "agency" (who or what is in control or has what kinds of power).
- Whether the individual or the text explains the meanings made and any effects. This debate produces four models of the individual/text relation: education, reinforcement, mediation, and power (see chapter 2).
- Sources of causality. The four models of the individual/text relation produce different subquestions about foundational causes for the relation. In the case of those models that assume great influence from the text, scholars focus on what the nature of the text is and what the viewers will do as a consequence. When the models give some or great agency to individuals, researchers consider what the source of the readers' power is and how variable the readers may be. For theorists who consider historical context as well, research broadens into what contextual factors in history produced the features of spectators.
- The place(s) of cognition and emotion in the process.
- Metaphors to describe the interpretive event. These metaphors imply specific theories.
- Methodological maneuvers.

These recurring debates generally reduce to differences in theories of the psychological individual and the individual in society. The theories also tend to associate with particular methods. Consequently, although in the next chapters I will not address every one of these debates for every theory of meaning-making and effect, I will try to summarize notions of (1) the psychological individual, (2) the social individual, and (3) the preferred methods of research.

Media communication research is a history of debates over not only functionalist versus conflict sociological perspectives and theories of the psychological individual but also the philosophical premises about research that underpin inquiry. Empiricism, positivism, materialism, idealism—each of these epistemologies also produces schisms and debates. As I shall discuss in chapter 2, these psychological and social theories employ four different models of the relation between individuals and media representations. No simple correspondence exists among the theories. Psychoanalysis has been combined with both functionalism and critical sociology, and so on. Yet all researchers are seeking to explain media reception and effects. What is the place of how we think of our selves as individuals and our imagined communities in our media experiences? How does our engagement with media provide an ability to reflect on culture and society, and our continuity with or distance from them? Do we have agency in our media consumption, our reception, and our actions? If so, how? All these questions matter for public policy, as I shall discuss particularly in chapters 6 and 7.

The Methods of Research and Textual Analysis

Certainly one of the earliest and still the most prevalent method for finding evidence about the reception of media texts is scholarly analysis of written and oral texts from which the critics then make claims about what readers do. (Readers always make the meanings that the critics want them to turn out!) Initially applied to novels, poetry, speeches, and theatrical performances, the textual methods of literary and rhetorical analysis have the common attribute of considering a speaker's or writer's expression of words to audiences of one or many. Beyond this common research method of textual analysis, many differences exist.

As I outlined in *Interpreting Films* (1992), presumptions about how meaning is determined can vary from theses that the texts' characteristics are the most important feature to propositions that the readers or the context is what matters when people experience media. Examples of contemporary "text-activated" theorizing are found in the work of textual critics as seemingly diverse as Roland Barthes, Umberto Eco, Gérard Genette, Michael Riffaterre, Meir Sternberg, Stanley Fish, and Wolfgang Iser. I include in the "reader-activated" category the scholarship of Norman Holland and David Bleich. In the "context-activated" group are writings by Hans Robert Jauss and Jacques Leenhardt (Staiger, 1992).

In this book, I consider thinking about meaning-making and media effects using four models of individual/text relations: education, reinforcement, mediation, and power. In this schema, texts and textual analysis still matter. All theorists to be considered in the following chapters use textual analysis as their method of finding evidence about features of the messages. *More important, however, these researchers also use textual analysis for depicting all their evidence of individuals' interpretations.* Thus, surveys, reports of focus group discussions, questionnaires, and so forth are subjected to the same methodological tools used to characterize the message being interpreted. Often, scholars assume their evidence of meaning-making is straightforward material without considering that it, too, is subjected to some sort of textual analysis, with all the methodological concerns that textual analysis involves.

Because this book is not a survey of methods of textual analysis, I can only briefly explicate several of the major methods; however, researchers in media studies should become familiar with them. The debates to be encountered are disagreements among social and psychological theories. Yet to make distinctions between the arguments coming into play, it will be valuable to discriminate among the methods of marshaling evidence of the objects seen (the media texts) and of internal states of thinking, interpreting, and feeling (the individuals making meaning). That is, various theories of media texts and individuals tend to employ specific (and different) textual methods. Thus, noting these possibilities becomes important.

Aristotelian and neo-Aristotelian criticism derives from Aristotle's *Rhetoric* and *Poetics,* which considered tragedies (at least) as having six parts: a fable or plot, characters, diction, thought (which was best analyzed as rhetoric), spectacle, and melody. Because Aristotle considered the plot to be the most important aspect of tragic texts, he devoted much attention to the possible arrangements of plot in terms of peripety (changes in states of things to the opposite—what might be called "turning points"), discovery, and suffering. The influence of Aristotle on nineteenth-century dramatic criticism, and by extension analysis of literature, produced standard plot summaries that emphasized segmenting the text into exposition, precipitory events, rising action, climax, and denouement. Twentieth-century literary studies has extended this work not only into individual studies of texts but also into modes and genres. Examples of the continuing use of this basic textual method exist in the heritage of R. S. Crane, John Cawelti, and the Chicago school. Neo-Aristotelian criticism typically focuses on the setting, situations, complications, characters, discoveries, and thoughts or themes of the text or a group of texts. A good example of this method's application in media studies is Horace Newcomb's *TV: The Most Popular Art* (1974).

Rhetorical criticism may add to Aristotelian criticism a consideration of the text's appeals (ethos, logos, and pathos) and elements of the textual situation (speaker, subject, and audience). Kenneth Burke, for example, created a major new line of rhetorical analysis when he posed dramatism as a framework for analysis. John Louis Lucaites and Celeste Michelle Condit (1985) argue for just such a rhetorical revision of classical Aristotelian studies of media narratives, which they claim tend to focus on poetics without sufficient regard to dialectical (truth) or rhetorical (persuasion) analysis.

A third major approach to text criticism has been **phenomenology**— an attempt to turn impressionist criticism into a method. Phenomenology focuses on how the interpreter engages with the text. The interpreter has a self-consciousness, but the object has its own properties. Often phenomenology involves pulling themes out of a mass of evidence and then re-sorting the material into groups, checking on the validity of the groupings through the interpreter's encounter with the primary documents. Iser's approach to reception aesthetics is a prominent instance of this method (Iser, 1972, 1976).

Content analysis eventually becomes a very popular textual method in media reception studies because it seems so able to quantify textual information. Locating and counting some preselected features of texts seems to have occurred at least by the 1700s, when people accused a group of hymns of undermining Swedish clergy, but a comparative study of "symbols" in a standard hymnal versus the new one seemed to prove the allegations false (Krippendorff, 1980:13). A methodologically valid content analysis will not assume a meaning to any unit of the text but will consider the unit's meaning as determined by the context. Behavioral communication analyses of media, especially studies of sexually explicit materials and violence, use this method and, as I shall discuss later, occur in the earliest social scientific approaches.

American New Criticism is a variant on Aristotelian analyses but with very particular features that proved anticipatory of later methods. Arguing that form and content are inseparable, New Critics look not only at formal structure but also at rhetorical structures of levels of meaning, symbolizations, clashes of connotations, paradoxes, and irony. As this list from Cleanth Brooks's *Well Wrought Urn* (1947:218) suggests, oppositions are important because it is through the resolution of apparent oppositions that the best poems present a universal truth. A remarkably faithful example of American New Criticism in film studies is David Bordwell's analysis of *Citizen Kane* (1971).

American New Criticism came out of, but also was superseded by, **Russian formalism, neoformalism,** and **narratology.** The Moscow Linguistic Circle (Roman Jakobson, Osip Brik, Boris Tomashevsky), the *Opoyaz* group (Victor Shklovsky, Boris Eichenbaum, Yury Tynjanov), and Czech structuralism (a relocated Jakobson, Jan Mukařovský, Rene Welleck) constitute founders of this procedure for studying texts. Formalism does not assume that texts are comparable to sentences, with "grammars." Rather, formalists consider textual structures to exist, formed by devices that have functions such as presenting plot and character information (compositional motivations), providing a sense of verisimilitude (realist motivations), conforming to generic expectations (generic or intertextual motivations), and supplying aesthetic play (aesthetic motivations). Analyzing the transformation of materials in the text through the ordering and selection of devices becomes the task for the critic. Often part of formalism is the notion of normative structures and conventional uses of devices as background for the production and reception of any text. Thus, contextual norms and specific textual deviations are privileged concerns for the analyst. Important scholars developing narratology include Genette, Sternberg, and Seymour Chatman. Bordwell and Kristin Thompson (1979) are most recognized for introducing this application into film studies, although, as I shall note in chapter 3, they combine this analytical method with a cognitive psychology theory of how individuals process information.

An early example of **linguistic** and **semiotic analysis** is the scholarship of Vladimir Propp. Differing from his formalist contemporaries, Propp conceptualizes folktales as having minimal units that build into a story much as words create a sentence (1928:15). This grammatical analogy occurs often through the twentieth century, but the influence of Ferdinand de Saussure (1916) in the 1950s and contemporary linguistic theories by Noam Chomsky and others produce the impetus for story grammars by A. J. Greimas, Claude Bremond, and Barthes and semiotic explorations by Eco. These linguistic and semiotic approaches to texts are so powerful that they nearly overwhelm other textual methods in media studies between 1970 and 1985. Indeed, I will expand on this method in chapter 3 in the account of the history of theories of audience reception.

Connected to the impact of Saussurean linguistics and semiotics is **structuralism,** in which individuals such as Claude Lévi-Strauss find in Saussure's linguistic theory a model of language acquisition that matches Hegelian dialectical philosophy. Focusing less on syntax and semantics (linguistics) or syntagms and paradigms (semiotics), structuralist criticism seeks deep binary oppositions informing texts as subterranean structures. Ironically, not unlike American New Criticism's fascination with oppositions, structuralism offers not only a textual method but an anthropological and philosophical theory about its speakers and listeners. Attraction by midcentury scholars to structuralism makes great sense. In film studies, Noël Burch's *Theory of Film Practice* (1969) provides a good media application.

Occurring from the very earliest attempts to analyze a text, **symptomatic criticism** supplants traditional **hermeneutics** when Sigmund Freud provides a psychological theory for why subtexts for any message might exist. Although symptomatic criticism has similarities to structuralist criticism in that both of these methods look at surface features to discover deep structures that are knowable by repetition, symptomatic criticism assumes the cause for the configuration is latent content due to repression of energies, suppressed by the creator of the text. The function of repetition is not to make a myth's binaries apparent (as in structuralism) or the denotation of a sign clear (as in linguistics or semiotics) but to attempt to fix a private association to a content unit. Distortions are inevitable. All sorts of scholars use symptomatic criticism to plumb the text: Marxists examine messages for hidden statements about class; feminist, gay and lesbian, and queer theorists consider sex, gender, and sexuality; and scholars of racism read for race and ethnicity.

Poststructuralism might be considered a variant of symptomatic criticism in that it assumes that distortions exist between surface features and what produces those features. What distinguishes it is its insistence on analyzing how the text reveals within its own surface information about what it attempts to argue is outside itself. Unlike structuralism which assumes a "final," static, self-contained object (the text), poststructuralism sees the object (the work) as connected to all other discourses as a production. The task is redefined from seeking a hidden meaning to be translated. Now the analyst's job is to trace the productivity of the work and to locate the gestures toward the unsaid. Barthes's *S/Z* (1970) is a key example of this critical method, but Barthes takes much from Pierre Macherey's *Theory of Literary Production* (1966); both books provide excellent instances of poststructural literary criticism. In media studies, the *Cahiers du Cinéma*'s analysis of John Ford's *Young Mr. Lincoln* (1970) is exemplary. A variant on this method is Jacques Derrida's **deconstructionism**.

As I suggest, critical methods for analyzing written and spoken texts show up in every scholarly attempt to describe what happens in an event of reception. However, writers have very distinct ideas about that engagement. While some textual methods imply a theory (such as a linguistic method implies a "reading" process), the association of various textual methods with particular theories of reception is not necessary. Indeed, a chart of options could be produced, with theories of spectators running in one direction and methods of analyzing the relation between the text and individuals in the other direction.

Readers might have noted that I have provided media examples of these various textual methods. In no case have I provided a method that is specific to moving images because, as far as I am aware, no such method exists. Although scholars of media have called for critical methods that would address the special qualities of moving images, none has appeared. Attempts to apply some of these methods to film and television have proved troublesome; as I will discuss in chapter 3, the effort to apply semiotic theory to images is one good instance of this.

Cautions about Methodologies

No approach to meaning-making and effects avoids doing textual analysis of something: movie reviews, ethnographic notes, individuals' statements, focus group remarks, statements about memories, the objects spectators are looking at and listening to. This is ironic, since to study meaning-making, scholars have to interpret. Every approach has the same basic problem of researchers eventually interpreting evidence they have gathered in some way. This is why I have described various ways of doing textual analysis. Of course, scholars debate the adequacy in terms of scope and coherence and the felicity of these methods.

For one thing, tribulations exist over how evidence of reception is gathered for subsequent textual analysis. Finding evidence for reception that has taken place in the past is difficult. Lack of evidence is usually the case; audiences watched movies and television programs but left no material traces of their thoughts or feelings. One of the most widely praised recent methods for searching out audience effects and meaning-making is ethnography, which, however, also has a strong record of criticism. Throughout their book, John Tulloch and Henry Jenkins (1995) discuss problems with investigating audiences and fans, including the power differential between ethnographers and their subjects and more specific matters such as leading audiences and interviewees toward answers that the interviewers desire. Factoring in the influence of being aware of being studied is necessary. Research from the 1920s notes that individuals who know they are being observed behave accordingly—although how that may affect their behavior is not predictable.

More recently, people have been using their own experiences as evidence. Matt Hills (2002) provides an excellent example of how to produce an autoethnography, a tool to consider for scholars who may also be fans. Still, autoethnographies are by no means any sort of random, unbiased source of information about audiences and interpretations of media.

Once evidence is at hand, debates over the best critical method occur. Some people argue that with content analysis, "The content categories are not allowed to emerge from the text, as is the case in naturalistic observation and in [other] textual analysis" (Newcomb and Hirsch, 1983:45). Perhaps this is so, but "naturalistic observation" and other textual methods are no more "objective." Each textual method has advantages and deficits, but these advantages do not include objectivity. Acknowledging the genre of the evidence is important. Texts such as reviews are produced for one reason and appropriated by reception scholars for another. Reviews, interviews, and ethnographies have conventions that must be dealt with in the textual analysis of the material.

This scholarship also faces its own production back into new texts as it reports its results, and thus self-reflection is necessary. As in the case of the new anthropology (Clifford and Marcus, 1986), reflexivity in engaging the object of study must occur. For instance, metaphors for activities occurring during the reception process should be read symptomatically to see what sort of assumptions underlie the theory (Lakoff and Johnson, 1980). The language in a theory reveals much about the theory's implicit propositions. As an example, the notion of audiences "poaching" on mass-produced texts is a widely used concept, derived from work by Michel de Certeau (1984). Recently Hills (2002) has questioned what exactly is implied by "poaching" and how far any propositions should go about fans as poachers escaping a capitalist system of media production. Among my travels in reception studies, I have noted the following tropes of the reception process, all of which need to be considered carefully for what they claim about the individual/text relation: activation, bricolage, commodity fetishism, erotics, flaneur-walk, game, inoculation, infantile regression, nomadic travel, nostalgic complacency, poaching, repetition compulsion, and window shopping.

Still, one cannot escape language, and I, for one, would not wish to do so. Nor would I encourage closing down too abruptly the observations of dedicated scholars of media. Certainly, through this book, it will be apparent where my current sympathies lie in terms of preferences in the debates. Still, I believe that as I have aged in studying media, the values of some sorts of research have become more apparent. I have included in this book work that is worth thinking about. I have undoubtedly also missed some scholarship that merits consideration. Any map misses details unless it is that mythical map which is completely isomorphic with what it represents. The shortness of this text indicates that this book is certainly not one of those mythical maps. My hope is that it can at least locate a scholar within a general region, from which the pleasures of self-discovery will then emerge.

I have arranged the theoretical framings in the next two chapters to permit me to follow historically several debates. Although histories sometimes suggest teleological developments, and my commentary may at times also imply a certain progress to the theorizing, at this moment almost all these theories are still widely employed within the field of reception studies. This will be most evident when I review the research in chapters 4 through 8.

Chapters 2 and 3 are somewhat historical surveys of major theories of media reception and effects, introducing the four models of individual/text relationship and comparing the various theories within those terms. Chapter 4 covers fans and fan behaviors. Chapter 5 considers various sorts of audiences that are drawn to stars or who engage in particular viewing activities around cult movies, camp, art cinema, or avant-garde texts. Chapter 6 focuses on minorities as viewers of film and television. Chapter 7 is an analysis of fears of effects as played out in debates about representations of violence, horror, and sexually explicit material. Chapter 8 covers memory and its place within personal and social reception.

2

Social Scientific Theories

This chapter surveys the major approaches within social scientific reception studies from the beginnings of cinema through the early 1980s. It attempts to draw some lines of comparison through what often appears to be very different approaches to the questions of interpretation and effect.

Although from the beginnings of textual analysis the interpretation of texts mattered, especially in biblical hermeneutical study, the potential effects of an engagement with a text might have psychological and social consequences. When this was a one-to-one matter, simple punishment of wicked behavior seemed feasible. However, the dissemination of texts into large groups of disenchanted peasants or workers, or libertines, was a larger threat. Thus, mass media engrossed social critics and reformers. As Roddy Reid discusses, with the construction of the concept of the nuclear "family" in France in the mid–eighteenth century, "discourses of domesticity, urban pathology, and colonial disorder operated in a manner that fully implicated them in a reciprocally authorizing relationship" (1993:63–64). What better disorder to worry about than the arrival into the household of reading and viewing materials that differ from those authorized by the state or religion? Or, equally in such a reciprocal arrangement, a member of the familial household who erupts into criminal behavior that threatens civil and state stability? As Reid notes, any deviation from the norm sets up a "discursive machine for moral panics and social paranoia" (65).

Scholars of such alarms have postulated waves of attention from the social body as a whole to a very specific kind of individual. In an overview of 150 years of these discourses, Graham Murdock (1997:70–73) argues that early tropes about readers stressed crowds out of control, but by the late 1800s, discourses associated these unruly crowds with the spread of visually graphic material in the new popular journalism and cinema. In

1874, James Greenwood in *The Wilds of London* attacked the penny dreadfuls that were believed to seduce not only pre- or semiliterate masses but also children. These children initially were imaged as innocents preyed upon by the media imagery, but new theories of adolescents also represented them as emotional to the point of being unable to control their own passions. Hooligans, working-class boys, were particularly of concern.

Thus, when social sciences—psychology, sociology, anthropology, and history—developed as disciplines in the mid-1800s, their intellectual foci directed themselves toward broad ranges of individual (but, ironically, never institutional) behavior to ascertain causalities among these inter-connected features: the family, urbanity, colonialism. Perhaps as well, the disarray in these entities also produced the social sciences. Moreover, two areas of individual human behavior were particularly threatening: sexual deviance and violence.

Cecilia von Feilitzen (1998) describes four "basic" causal relations that social sciences have asserted about those areas of human behavior, although I am interested here in the general formulation of causal hypotheses about the individual and media. The first relation assumes that watching media occurs as "cultural learning and/or frustration." Media is assumed to be a primary learning site. This relation does not contend, for instance, that learned aggression is innate or a natural instinct. Rather, the individual is assumed to be a somewhat "empty" vessel into which knowledge and experiences flow. I shall label this causal hypothesis the **education** model. A second relation social science theory has imagined is that media reflect culture and society and may function conservatively in "maintaining social order" (von Feilitzen, 1998:93). Both critical and liberal social theorists assert this **reinforcement** thesis.

Conceptualizing the individual as having developed attributes of some sophistication from the social context, the third relation asserts that the individual responds to the world based on those contextual, personal differences and uses media as a mediated access to that world. This **mediation** model appears in social science work on rituals (e.g., cultural studies), mood regulation (e.g., fantasy theory), and "uses and gratification" theory. Finally, the fourth basic relation is that of **power**. Individuals may have some self-resources in the face of media, yet media are so overwhelming as both to insist on their influence and also to fascinate. Equally, conservatives and radicals often envision media's relation to individuals in this way—either making good citizens into liberals or libertines (the conservatives' view) or repressing progressive urges or movements (the radicals' opinion).

These four basic theories or models about the relation between individuals and media require distinct conceptualizations of the individual to make sense. Both the education and reinforcement theses tend to imagine the individual as fairly malleable; the mediation and power theses conjecture a person as having agency and willpower separate from the particular situation of an encounter with media; in the case of the power thesis, however, the individual loses out in the contest. Additionally, theories of children need consideration here. As with many others before him, David Gauntlett (1996:39–48) notes that researchers have tended to treat children as different from adults; hence, the postulation is that they are particularly susceptible to media effects. Gauntlett indicates that the "empty vessel" thesis of the individual is a characteristic of the dominant theory—Piaget's model of the child's developmental stages functions from a premise of a prestructured automatic response to environmental stimuli. However, other theories of children's cognitive and emotional changes are gaining ground. Using these, Bob Hodge and David Tripp (1986) argue that children have many viewing skills, which places these scholars' work into the mediation group.

These basic views of the relation, however, do not really matter. What matters is the *effect* of the encounter. More important, what matters is a *bad* effect. I seriously doubt that all the hoopla about media would have occurred if people thought only what they judged to be good effects were coming from an experience with media. As I shall discuss later (and particularly in chapter 7), the definition of an effect can range from simply comprehending an image to reproducing images in real life. Reproduction of images can be benign (copying the hairstyle of Bette Davis) to lethal (reenacting a mass slaughter of family members). As Leo Handel (1950:175–76) neatly outlines this, a number of distinctions must be made: (1) What is the entity producing the effect? Movies in general? A specific type of film such as a crime film? A single film or even a single scene? (2) What is the nature of the effect? Broad social attitudes? Acceptance of "facts"? Personal gratification? (3) Is the causal relation the most likely or even possible? Does credible evidence of actual contact between the cause and the individual exist? Can the researcher discredit other possible causes? And so forth. David Buckingham notes that it is probably useful to distinguish between "emotional responses, behavioral effects (such as imitation) and longer-term ideological influences"

(1996:6). These sorts of distinctions will trouble all social scientific research. Moreover, all sorts of contradictions will occur. As John Hartley wryly observes, "Watching television causes violence and passive behavior (all at once!)" (1996:226).

Still, no matter how researchers theorize the individual, the fact remains that people do encounter texts and the world, and parts of these encounters make differences in lives. Hence, to discount radically the experiences of media would be obstinate. Even the most cynical debater with "effects" theories probably holds contravening theses about media, such as that people learn values from media, and "values are the basis of a people's identity, their sense of particularity as members of the human race" (Ngugi wa Thiong'o quoted in Couldry, 2000a:27). What is often at stake in these debates are (1) the relative merits of the effect and (2) the variable agency of the individual in contrast with the force of the text.

Reid's remarks about moral panics matter to this history because certain events seem to have precipitated the various waves of social scientific research on media effects. In fact, private and state funding with specific agendas also encouraged waves of research. Social reformers gathered funds from Progressive thinkers to produce the Payne Fund research in the late 1920s (Rowland, 1983:41–86); post–World War II concerns about external enemies (once the Nazis, now the Communists) and internal disarray (juvenile delinquents, minorities in urban areas) encouraged state funding in the late 1940s through the present (Rowland, 1983; Glander, 2000); and shifting attitudes about sexuality, as well as social movements such as feminism and gay/lesbian/bisexual/transgender rights, also stimulated state-supported research from the late 1960s. Major targets of this funded research have been images of violence and sex.

Through the last century, various social scientific theories have attracted enough attention and scholarship to become identifiable as lines of argumentation. Several useful typologies exist: Durkin (1985:15–18, 36–53), McQuail (1987:252–54), Cumberbatch and Howitt (1989:3–12), Frissen (1996:57), Renckstorf and McQuail (1996:9–11), Linné and Wartella (1998:105–14), and Livingstone (1998:237–55). I shall draw heavily on all these typologies to trace a history of (primarily) U.S. social scientific approaches to media effects, but I am responsible for the following mapping.

Early Mediation and Education Theories: The Chicago School,
Early Psychological Applications, and the Payne Fund Studies

Early local U.S. censorship and self-regulation of the movies formed from
presumptions of possible ill effects on viewers (see Staiger, 1995). Primarily using education models of the relation between viewers and the
medium, early middle-class advocates for control of film images argued
that individual images or scenes were potent conveyors of information
about how to commit crime or enjoy luxuries. In fact, vivid evidence existed that movies could produce not only petty crime or licentious living
but also riots. When the black heavyweight fighter Jack Johnson beat the
"Great White Hope" Jim Jeffries in 1910, interracial conflicts broke out
and "at least eighteen African Americans were killed" (Streible,
1996:182).

Other middle-class people, however, defended films as potentially con-
tributing positively to society (e.g., providing information about other
cultures and news of national concern). These people proposed a holistic
view of the filmgoing experience and believed that the entire narrative
story might teach moral lessons about individual responsibility and
agency. So even if a film contained images of violence or sexual immoral-
ity, the rule for acceptable narration was a particular twist on poetic justice: narrative rewards were to be "contingent upon the individual's behavior *after* knowing what the stakes of a choice are" (Staiger, 1995:83).
Such a proposition required the character to learn through experiences;
hopefully, a spectator did as well. This "pointillist" versus "total-picture"
(79) opposition regarding movie effects continues to the present as an important research question: Do viewers of films process scenes in isolation
or scenes within contexts, and what does the answer to this imply about
possible behavior?

Social scientific research on people, particularly working-class immigrants and their children, increased in the late 1800s as part of a desire by
parts of the middle class to organize the populace into groups that would
continue to support a middle-class political and cultural hegemony.
Threatened by the power of urban associations that appealed to newly
enfranchised workers, intellectuals sought explanations for class differences and group behavior as a result of those differences, especially where
deviancy in work ethics or sexuality confronted their normative expectations. Out of this concern rose early social scientific approaches to group
mores and norms that formalized the research agendas into disciplines

and the first departments of anthropology and sociology (Thornton, 1997:11–15). As Sarah Thornton presents it, Harvard scholars took the lead in theory, Columbia researchers preferred statistical investigations, and University of Chicago sociologists advocated "qualitative empirical research" and "urban micro-sociology," with Robert E. Park's model as a prime example of what these methods could offer. Chicago's Department of Sociology and Anthropology, founded in 1892, was the first sociology department anywhere.

Although much anecdotal analysis of who went to movies and why appears through the early trade press for movie exhibitors, audience studies grounded in social scientific theory and method appeared by the mid-teens. In 1915 William Healy published *The Individual Delinquent*, in which he used case evidence to argue a relation between films and juveniles' behavior (Jowett, Jarvie, and Fuller, 1996:26). Ray Leroy Short earned a master's degree in 1916 based on questioning one thousand Iowa City schoolchildren about their movie preferences. In 1914 the president of Reed College and in 1919 the Reverend J. J. Phelan, as part of his graduate work in Toledo, Ohio, completed similar surveys. Garth Jowett (1985:23–27) reports that the latter three studies broke the respondents into age groupings and linked them to film genre preferences, with some questions about stars as well.

By the 1920s, such demographic work used age categories but moved into new identity variables. In the famous Middletown studies, a portion of the material investigated attendance rates by age and announced that in 1923 Middletowners preferred the genres of "comedy, heart interest and adventure," and their favorite stars were Harold Lloyd, Gloria Swanson, Thomas Meighan, Colleen Moore, and Douglas Fairbanks (Lynd and Lynd, 1929:266). In expository fashion, however, Robert Lynd and Helen Lynd described how the Middletowners used the films within their social and leisure world. Thus, the Lynds were following Chicago school methods and were proposing a mediation model, since they assumed that individuals' specific identity features and personal needs produced preferences in media use.

Other research of the 1920s also takes a mediation model as the working hypothesis when constructing surveys and questionnaires. George Potamianos (1998) summarizes a survey conducted by a Sacramento, California, newspaper that split its respondents by sex and occupation. In the late 1920s, Harold Ellis Jones and Herbert S. Conrad surveyed preferences in rural New England using multiple identities—"age, sex, geographical location, economic and social status, intelligence, educational level, and the degree of sophistication" (1930:419)—and discovered, among other things, that the respondents had a strong preference for westerns. In 1926, Alice Miller Mitchell (1929) surveyed ten thousand Chicago schoolchildren, breaking them into three groups: an uncontrolled sample, children in juvenile delinquent institutions, and children in Boy Scout and Girl Scout organizations. Considering not only age but also sex, she studied "how children used the movies as socializing devices, the role of the movies as part of the 'normal' life of the child and what the patterns of preferences were for the various groups" (Jowett, 1985:26). Among her findings, which were published by the University of Chicago Press, were that both sexes used newspapers to decide which films to see. Mitchell's work is significant because it tries to place the functions of movies within the broader cultural life of adolescents and their dating and social development.

Alongside these Chicago-style and sociology-based studies of audiences and their preferences was some psychological research that evinces both mediation and education models of causality. Using his own experiences of watching movies as his evidence (a standard approach in psychological studies used by theorists as varied as the introspectionists and Sigmund Freud), Hugo Münsterberg (1916) applied Gestalt psychology to the problem of watching films. Münsterberg concluded that a person's "natural" mental processes of perception, cognition, memory, imagination, and emotion explained his or her experiences of the film. Working as it does from an abstract conceptualization of general spectatorship, his theory does not attempt to account for individual differences, but Münsterberg does assume that "natural" workings of the already established mind restructure textual information. Thus, his account is a mediation theory.

In 1922 Karl S. Lashley and John B. Watson published a government-funded study that examined whether movies could be used to inform people and change their behaviors about sexually transmitted diseases. Watson was a prominent U.S. proponent of behavioral psychology, which at this point assumed the individual's mind was a blank slate upon which stimuli produced responses that then became associations, causing learning to occur. Lashley and Watson secured a $6,600 grant from the U.S. Interdepartmental Social Hygiene Board for their psychology lab at John Hopkins University to study the potential of using film for educational campaigns about venereal disease. They began their research with an assumption that to change short-term or long-term behavior would require both information and emotional associations with that information. The researchers were somewhat skeptical about the project for a number of reasons; for example, they thought people were fairly "passive" (Lashley and Watson, 1922:5) when watching films because people considered films entertainment. Nevertheless, they proceeded to structure a laboratory experiment (the methodological preference for most behavioral studies) in which they surveyed their subjects' knowledge before and after seeing narrative educational films about venereal disease (surveys coded through content analysis methods). Using the movie *Fit to Fight* (1919), which had appealed to emotions, including pride, shame, sentiment, and fear, Lashley and Watson compared retention of material with a follow-up study about subjects' later behavior. While postviewing evidence indicated that some people who saw the film did go to doctors or clinics to find out if they had a sexually transmitted disease, little evidence existed that men planned to alter their sexual behavior, especially in terms of increasing abstinence. Thus, while the individuals may have learned something, at least this film did not produce any changes in actions.

Certainly the Payne Fund research has attracted the most attention for its intervention into national public discussion about possible media effects. Actually a collection of different types of studies, this research employed both mediation and education models and both sociological and psychological theory. Jowett (1971, 1985; Jowett, Jarvie, and Fuller, 1996; also see Rowland, 1983:41–51), along with several collaborators, has been the primary historian of this project. According to Jowett, the Payne Fund research was the idea of the Reverend William H. Short, who hoped to influence legislation for state regulation of films. Short and others believed that such legislation would never be passed by lawmaking bodies unless advocates provided scientific proof that films produced harmful effects. Thus, the managers of the project turned to the most respected social scientists to undertake rigorous research. Eventually scholars published thirteen monographs reporting various research projects. Among the findings were that movie watching changes sleep behavior, that a child sees scenes but not necessarily in larger narrative contexts, that attitudes can change at least for the short term, and that children imitate movies in their play.

However, other studies were less supportive of the original founders' hopes. Two early studies (1928–29) involved children's "intake and retention of information" (Jowett, Jarvie, and Fuller, 1996:66). As Jowett and colleagues summarize the research of a before-and-after documentary on dental hygiene, the children remembered a lot about the importance of brushing teeth, but their behavior did not alter. In fact, the control group's rate of brushing teeth increased more than that of those who viewed the educational documentary. Overall, the researchers "reached cautious conclusions that emphasized limited, indirect models of media influence" (58) and noted that other factors—such as society and culture —could moderate an individual's beliefs and behavior.

In fact, one researcher, Paul Cressey (who had recently completed a famous study of taxi dancers, women earning money from dancing with men) reversed his presumptions of effects from movies midway through his research and began to consider all sorts of other aspects of audience use of movies. Studying young male offenders, Cressey heard them tell that although the movies showed lawbreakers receiving their just deserts, the boys could point out real-life criminals who were successful. As Cressey summarized matters, "'Instead of being considered a unilateral force whose influences can be described as a "contribution" or "effect" . . . the motion picture is seen as one whose influence is everywhere modified by differentials in community and personality'" (Cressey in Jowett, Jarvie, and Fuller, 1996:87). Moreover, like Mitchell, Cressey's inversion of causality from the impact of movies on people to people's choice-making about movies produced detailed analyses of the theater environment. Cressey came to believe that it was the theater that drew the youth more than any specific movie: "In this ghetto [the theater], where traditional authorities had long been superseded, movie theaters were social centers, places for tough gangs to gather, for prostitutes to make assignations, and for young teens to test sexual and cultural boundaries" (87; see Cressey, 1932:171–80). Other studies were behavioral in their foundations. Jowett et al. point out that the researchers' "methods ranged from physiological studies (using such devices as the psychogalvanometer and the wired bed; . . .) through questionnaires, to open-ended interviews, autobiographies, content analysis and statistically standardized tests" (5).

As the Payne Fund research proceeded, its results split into data that the original promoters believed supported their views that movies had impact on viewers and other findings that differed from that position. Although Short attempted to moderate the official public relations summary of the research, its author, Henry J. Forman, believed strongly that films should be regulated. Thus, the popularized representation that he produced in *Our Movie Made Children* (1933) drew rebuttals. A major one was the rejoinder by Mortimer J. Adler in his *Art and Prudence* (1937). Adler criticized the research for making assumptions that became embedded in the tools of analysis; moreover, he posited that even if the data were accurate, "it did not follow that any particular course of action was thereby recommended" (Jowett, Jarvie, and Fuller, 1996:8). Jowett and colleagues indicate that beyond Adler's and others' responses, three paradigms superseded the Payne Fund research: the critical response of people such as Paul Lazarsfeld and members of the Frankfurt school who moved to the United States during the 1930s; the structural-functionalist sociology of Talcott Parsons and Robert K. Merton; and the "depth-psychology" response of psychoanalytical theories (118–21).

Still, the Payne Fund research is a major assemblage of 1930s approaches to sociological and psychological theory applied to film audience research. Richard Butsch (2000:233–34) notes that by 1933 the Payne Fund also supported research on radio audiences. Among its questions was whether the medium overstimulated its listeners, resulting in "neurotic" effects. This was a new issue within the problem of possible causal effects—a medium itself could affect its users. Yet more significantly, researchers such as Cressey acknowledged that their collected data did not fit their prior assumptions, and they rethought original causal relations. Cressey's and others' mediation theory of audiences and movies would eventually need further discussion in terms of developing the aspects of individuality in use and response to mass media.

While the Payne Fund organizers failed in their original agenda to prove that effects resulted from the content of films, Progressives still sought social solutions to the potential threat of watching films. From the earliest period of film, Progressives cautioned against state-regulated censorship but did support self-regulation of movies (Staiger, 1995:86–115). In the 1920s they encouraged children's matinees, with "safe" films. However, during the late 1920s and early 1930s, Progressives also championed teaching critical viewing skills so that where industrial self-regulation might be avoided, individual self-regulation might succeed. The film education movement of the 1930s produced film appreciation courses in public schools (Jacobs, 1990; Smoodin, 1998; also see Glander, 2000:4–5). These courses looked a lot like a literature class, and some books considered film aesthetics and " 'director's ability' " (Smoodin, 1998:31). Of signal interest, however, was training children and less-educated adults (i.e., the working class [Butsch, 2001]) to ask about the social value of the film.

Thus, researchers applied social scientific and psychological theory to the problem of film reception and possible effects very much in parallel with the developments in the disciplines. If the theory was there, someone used it to study movies and audiences. Because the basic theories assumed education and mediation hypotheses, the mass media research displays those propositions.

Early Power Theory: The Soviets, the Frankfurt School, and Other Intellectuals and Radicals in the 1920s and 1930s

The consequence of t ie worldwide depression beginning abroad in the 1920s but striking the United States in the late 1920s and accelerating in the early 1930s reinforced Marxist and other radical social views that capitalist systems could not protect vast numbers of people. Moreover, the dominant economic and political systems bound up the media through ownership or state-sanctioned laws that favored capitalist rather than proletariat interests. In the new Soviet Union, Sergei Eisenstein and others (e.g., Lev Kuleshov, Dziga Vertov) analyzed cinema for its potential effects on audiences. Likewise in Germany, intellectuals associated with, or part of, the Frankfurt school and the Institute of Social Research were critical of mass media as were some commentators in the United States.

Eisenstein produced at least two models of spectatorship; one appears to be a reinforcement proposition, and the other is a power one. Working in an era and nation in which Vladimir Lenin's copy theory epistemology produced a strict materialist line, Eisenstein's initial theory in the mid-1920s assumed cinema's function was to produce effects in spectators: "The work of art . . . is above all a tractor, plowing up the psyche of the spectator in a given class direction" (1924:18). Eisenstein's research problem about how to achieve a plowing up that would produce the good Soviet citizen was complicated, however, in that the contemporary thesis operating within Pavlovian psychology (the approved theory at the time) argued that spectators came already conditioned to the cinema. While the materialist psychology started with the view that stimulus and response created human reactions, sophisticated responses such as attending to, interpreting, and enjoying films were reflexes well channeled into adult behavior patterns. Eisenstein confronted this problem when he acknowledged that a czarist soldier may not respond to images the same way that a peasant might. Indeed, "shocks" to the system might dislodge the spectator from a theater seat, but shocks alone could not ensure a proper reorganization of conditioned associations. Even dialectically organized stimuli met conditioned barriers. Thus, Eisenstein's early theory grapples with the intransigence of an adult mind. At most, cinema might reinforce (or unsettle) beliefs, but finding ways to change those views could be difficult. Eisenstein faced the might of formed spectators, and his theory confronts its own assumptions that the film medium had little to no power to transform already conditioned individuals. At most, Eisenstein's early theory contains a reinforcement model of causality.

During the 1930s, Eisenstein turned to a newer materialist psychology advanced by A. R. Luria and Lev Vgotsky (Staiger, 1992:52–54). Vgotsky conceptualized children as initially social beings who transform dialectically into individual entities (reversing the development model proposed by Piaget). As mental and verbal growth occurs, individuals create private associations of public symbols, sensualizing, as Eisenstein viewed it, the concrete world into a richly textured, private realm of meanings. Again, Eisenstein's project was to consider how to construct his cinema to reform spectators. Moving from a stimulus (shock) thesis, he believed that he needed to reorganize individual private associations by reconstructing those associations. Once this adjustment of symbolic meaning was completed, he could present his message with all its sensual, emotional, and rational connotations. Should this succeed, the individual would be brought around to his view of matters. This model of the relation between cinema and spectators is more akin to a power model: assuming Eisenstein did this right, the already formed individual's worldview would be reorganized to the position articulated in the movie.

Intellectuals from Germany were involved as well in considering the consequences of mass media for social change, although in their case the problem was not transforming workers into Soviet citizens but preventing the bourgeoisie from becoming fascists. Theodor Adorno, Max Horkheimer, Otto Kirchheimer, Leo Lowenthal, Herbert Marcuse, Erich Fromm, Wilhelm Reich, and Walter Benjamin were all concerned with explaining the rise of the authoritarian state (Jay, 1973; Arato and Gebhardt, 1978; also see Rogers, 1994). When Horkheimer took over the chair of the Institute of Social Research in 1931, he restated a commitment to materialist theory that would be supplemented by empirical research, including "public statistics and questionnaires backed up by sociological, psychological, and economic interpretation of the data" (Jay,

1973:26). However, increasingly straightforward Marxism failed to explain the escalating threat of Nazism, and, in general, the question of how an oppressive mode of production remained in place occupied these scholars. For the Italian Marxist Antonio Gramsci, the answer was hegemony (Arato, 1978:7). The Frankfurt group sought another explanation.

One key theme these scholars had derived from traditional Marxism was the causal claim that a massification of culture and fetishization of commodities produced the decline of individual critical thinking. By the late 1920s, several of them incorporated Freudian psychological theory into their original Marxist explanations of social organization. Horkheimer considered Freud's theory of internalization. As Martin Jay discusses Fromm's version of this, the dominant class provides "'symbolic satisfactions to the masses, guiding their aggression into socially harmless channels'" (Fromm, 1931, quoted in Jay 1973:91). This model of the effects of entertainment implies a power theory of media in relation to audiences. It assumes that circumstances create an intent in individuals, or at least a desire, to react aggressively to their situation, but they lose their intent or desire in compensatory satiation through entertainment. Popular culture, movies, sports—all these substitutes for useful social action—divert people from critical thinking that otherwise would allow them to see through these illusions.

As a consequence of the 1933 Nazi assumption of control of the government, Horkheimer, Adorno, Lowenthal, Marcuse, and others left Germany. Arriving in the United States in May 1934, Horkheimer was welcomed by prominent sociologists at Columbia University, including scholars such as Robert Lynd but also Charles Beard, Robert MacIver, and Reinhold Niebuhr. Columbia provided the institute physical space, and soon other members of the group and their acquaintances moved, including Paul Lazarsfeld. Adorno arrived later, in June 1937, and took up an offer in February 1938 to work at Lazarsfeld's Princeton Office of Radio Research as head of its music study.

Within that year, Adorno published "On the Fetish-Character in Music and the Regression of Listening." This essay demonstrates a Frankfurt analysis of popular culture as well as it illustrates major methodological differences between some of the arriving Germans and the local sociologists. Adorno argues that most music reduces individuals to hearing without listening. Citing a comment from an American advertiser, he writes that "people have learned to deny their attention to what they are hearing even while listening to it" (Adorno, 1938:271). Worse than that, though, is the false sense of the amateurs or fans who think they are involved: "Whenever [individuals] attempt to break away from the passive status of compulsory consumers and 'activate' themselves, they succumb to pseudoactivity. . . . Their ecstasy is without content" (292). This radical pessimism derives from a proposition that the specific content source (here music) within its mode of production (here capitalism) so traps individuals that even their active engagement is false consciousness. They are merely "caught up in a standardized and routinized set of responses" as fans (Abercrombie and Longhurst, 1998:19). This is a very strong version of the power model of the relation between mass media and audiences.

Such a proposition about audiences leads logically to the criticism that Adorno had with the ongoing studies proposed by Lazarsfeld and other U.S. sociologists. If mass media necessarily produced a psychological regression for audiences, open-ended questionnaires and other sorts of empirical questioning of individuals made no sense: "The opinions of the listeners themselves were unreliable" (Jay, 1973:190; also see Rowland, 1983:59–76; Glander, 2000:105–29). As these writers increasingly published their views in English in the 1940s, their influence spread. Jay writes, "For the first time, popular culture was attacked from a radical rather than conservative direction" (1973:271). He writes that others such as Clement Greenberg, Dwight MacDonald, and David Riesman found these ideas powerful; these men would continue to affect the discussions of mass media in the 1940s and 1950s (see later in this chapter).

On the margins of the Frankfurt group was Walter Benjamin (Jay, 1973:197–212). In the 1930s, traditional media aesthetics focused on specificity issues, which, for technologically based media such as films, produced questions about whether form, style, and technological characteristics made any difference to the experience of the spectator. By no means was Benjamin a technological determinist; he was a historical materialist who considered the available means of production as part of the mode of production and thus pertinent for analysis, especially as it changed. Like the Frankfurt school thinkers, he assumed that media related to larger cultural formations as both reflection and producer of those formations, and that Freudian theory should be incorporated into that Marxist analysis. Unlike Adorno, Benjamin was willing to grant that certain stylistic and technological variables cut deeper into the problem of effects than just the obvious capitalist mode of production. Benjamin tried to see new technologies as dialectical, with opportunities for moving toward a communist utopia. In "The Work of Art in the Age of Mechanical Reproduction" (1935), Benjamin articulated one of the major texts of such theory, but a text that cautioned about effects based on form and style. In other words, Benjamin's theory is also a proposition about the power of a medium, even if an individual comes fully formed to the experience.

In "The Work of Art," Benjamin lays out the following historical analysis. Whereas reproduction was always possible, *mechanical* reproduction is new. The implications of these new technologies include that reproduction can be done so quickly that daily changes can be shown; that the reproductions can show information otherwise unavailable to the human eye (through close-ups, editing, slow motion); that these reproductions meet the masses halfway by coming into their homes (through records, home movies, lithograph prints); and that the "aura" of original art withers away, since reproductions are now in the contexts of the users rather than the sacred space of a single owner. Hence a use-value outruns exchange-value. Benjamin views all this as enabling for the masses, since it reduces authoritarian interpretations and the rule of tradition, which he considers political strategies useful to fascism.

This difference between old and new technologies can be placed into Benjamin's larger hypothesis that the reduction of aura works hand in hand with the creation of a distraction mode of perception. "The public is an examiner, but an absent-minded one" (Benjamin, 1935:241). In particular, film assails spectators, or has a "shock effect" (240), which prevents spectators from viewing in a concentration mode in which the work would absorb them through their identification with characters, making them ultimately passive before the work. For example, he claims, "Mechanical reproduction of art changes the reaction of the masses toward art. The reactionary attitude toward a Picasso painting changes into the progressive reaction toward a Chaplin movie" (235). Benjamin's theory of the features of a medium producing two perceptual modes (distraction or concentration) connects him to the ideas of Bertolt Brecht, whom Benjamin steadfastly supported through the 1930s.

In summary, like other Frankfurt school writers, Benjamin operates with a largely power theory version of the reception relation and concerns himself with the threat of passive viewers. However, he does see progressive potential for some cinematic techniques and for mechanical reproduction itself. This is unlike Adorno, who believes that the privileged techniques of Benjamin—the close-up, montage, slow or freeze motion—

have no progressive potential unless part of a "rigorous, advanced aesthetic totality" (Arato, 1978:217).

Leftist and liberal intellectuals in the United States in the 1930s were aware of not only their homegrown social scientific functional traditions but also these critical European Marxisms. Many activists took up Eisenstein's theories to produce social documentaries and criticism (Alexander, 1981; Campbell, 1982). Others took varying positions regarding Hollywood cinema. Anna Siomopoulos (1999) reviews the writings of Louis Mumford, Walter Lippmann, and John Dewey for this period. She writes that Mumford considered moving pictures to function as a "'shock absorber,'" which was "his term for any technology which acts to relieve the strain of modern life by establishing new norms of conduct, norms that work to make social relations more routine and mechanical." The effects were passivity and "'a decrease of . . . *substantial rationality*'" (Siomopoulos, 1999:48, quoting Mumford, 1938:475). Like Mumford, Lippmann had serious concerns about whether Hollywood would be the source for Americans' representations of the past. And Dewey "suspected that the universalizing function of mass culture enforced consensus, standardized habits and weakened civic virtues like fraternity" (50). Thus, even if these men did not reject capitalism as Marxists might, tendencies within an economic and political system geared to profit making through mass-manufacturing representations required their vigilance.

The 1930s worldwide depression, the rise of fascisms and Stalinism, and the spread of mass media through not only cinema but also radio need to be recalled as part of the context for this group of theories, as well as for what will happen in theorizing media effects after World War II. Concern existed that mass media's relation to its audience was one of power. For critical theorists of society, often supported by a Freudian psychology, cinema's technology—perhaps reinforced by specific form and style—probably determined spectator response even if the audience members came from different class backgrounds (and the focus in these Marxist and liberal writings was primarily on class differentials).

Yet the analysis differed. "Shock" is a repetitive motif among the writers and may serve to point out at least some variables here. For all these writers, technology is thought to have some kind of material effect on a person. This effect can be a Pavlovian psychology of associational readjustments if the cinematic techniques jolt a viewer out of the theater chair. It can be the behavioralism of some of the Payne Fund researchers who hypothesized radio as overstimulating viewers and making them neurotic. It can be a Dada shock that prevents concentration and turns spectators into distracted but thoughtful viewers. Cinema can also be a shock absorber, protecting citizens from the cityscapes of modernity. Thus, mass media either provide the shocks or soften other shocks. Effects can be negative: neuroses or jitters or narcotic defenses. Or effects can be positive: experiencing art has a critical and public use-value.

Post–World War II Theory: Academic Mass Communication Theory

As the global conditions mattered in thinking about the effects of mass media during the 1930s, World War II increased the social significance of figuring out causal relations between media messages and individuals. In particular, concern about propaganda—from the right in fascism or from the left in Soviet Communism—drove research agendas in Europe and the United States (Rowland, 1983:52–86; Glander, 2000:xi). As well, audience research could help capitalist profit making, and juvenile delinquency might be related to media consumption.

In looking back from the late 1950s over the apparent beginnings of American communication research, Wilbur Schramm described four men as its "founding fathers" (1963a:2–4; also see Rogers, 1994, for a revision of Schramm's history, and Glander, 2000). These were Lazarsfeld, Kurt Lewin, Harold Lasswell, and Carl Hovland. As already noted, Lazarsfeld had moved from Vienna to the United States via the support of Horkheimer and the Institute of Social Research. He arrived in the United States in 1933 as a Rockefeller Foundation Fellow and eventually received funding in 1937 from that organization to study effects of radio on American society. Opening the Office of Radio Research at Princeton, Lazarsfeld and his team (and later students such as Elihu Katz and Joseph Klapper at Columbia University) engaged in significant empirical research on audiences, voting, and social influences on beliefs and behaviors. Lewin also came from Vienna, educated in Gestalt psychology. His focus was group dynamics and design of experiments. Lasswell trained as a political scientist at the University of Chicago and studied large systems of communication across nations and social groups; he also pioneered in content analysis from about 1938 (Handel, 1950:165). The fourth person was Hovland, who chose inductive experimental methods to look at attitude change.

The common thread among these communication scholars is, according to Schramm, that "they are behavioral researchers" (1963a:5). Indeed, their investigations explored the social and psychological dynamics involved in communication behavior, but each scholar held particular social and psychological theories, and these theories changed over the years as research directed them to revise prior hypotheses and as research tools proved inadequate. For example, while not bowing in full to criticisms by Adorno that surveying people was a useless method, Lazarsfeld did step away from "preference" questionnaires of audiences because they seemed at odds with actual behavior (Jowett, 1985:31).

Moreover, new theories seemed to offer much to these empirically minded scholars, as did a reigning analogy in which social sciences ought to mimic natural sciences as much as possible. Hence, quantification appeared "objective," whereas qualitative research increasingly was dismissed as "subjective." In 1949, Claude Shannon and Warren Weaver's *Mathematical Theory of Communication* theorized communication as capable of being digitalized: split into bits for binary (and statistical) analysis (Rogers, 1994:411–42). The use of this theory for computing and machine application has been revolutionary. It also produced a favoring of the textual method of content analysis in communication research, since this analytical tool relies on counting and numerical manipulation of the data to reach conclusions. As Handel, a major Hollywood audience researcher, explained in 1950, content analysis "may constitute the basis of a sociological study to determine what cultural patterns and stereotypes are reinforced in a given medium . . . or it may be used as the first steps in an 'effects' study" (165). Handel provides as examples of the use of content analysis studies by Dorothy Jones, Edgar Dale, and C. C. Peters within the Payne Fund studies, the 1942 study *Propaganda and the Nazi War Film* by Siegfried Kracauer, which became the research basis for his *From Caligari to Hitler* (1947); and the 1947 study by Martha Wolfenstein and Nathan Leites of "the good-bad girl" in Hollywood films published in *Movies: A Psychological Study* (1950). Yet these three publications hold different theories of human behavior. For instance, Kracauer argues from a Frankfurt school position that combines Marxism and Freudian theory, whereas Wolfenstein and Leites credit Margaret Mead, Gregory Bateson, and David Riesman as their intellectual mentors (Wolfenstein and Leites, 1950:7).

The "bit" motif of Shannon and Weaver additionally functioned well within physiological experiments and recent radical (basic) behaviorist psychology dominated by B. F. Skinner who argued that operant stimulus-response conditioning explained learning. By the mid-1940s, communications researchers were devising mechanical devices to study real-time reactions of radio audiences—thus trying to respond to criticisms such as Adorno's that post facto audience reports were unreliable evidence (Handel, 1950:46–52). Lazarsfeld and Frank Stanton of CBS radio built the Lazarsfeld-Stanton program analyzer, which allowed people to press buttons indicating "like" (green), "dislike" (red), or "indifferent" (no pressing) during a program. Charts graphed responses, and questionnaires and group interviews followed the in-time testing. Bernard D. Cirlin developed the Cirlin Reactograph, which accomplished fairly much the same thing. George Gallup's Audience Research, Inc. (ARI) used the Hopkins Electric Televoting Machine, which had five choices, and the Schwerin System allowed viewers variable choices for "voting" during a film screening. Thus, during the 1940s and 1950s, American mass communication theory acquired reliable tools that appeared to promise objective results, and those tools worked fairly well with several dominant psychological and sociological paradigms for explaining the specific data.

To what ends were these methods and theories applied? Three research problems were important: continuing media research about audiences of film and broadcasting; public opinions and political policy; and juvenile delinquency and social well-being. As I have noted, social science research out of the Chicago school and research informed by behavioral psychology began in the teens. While some of this research remained within an academic sphere, businesses that hired the scholars doing the research adapted much of it to commercial ends. Daniel Pope (1983:141) points out that industrial market research began around 1880 but was not a common part of a business strategy until the 1910s. At that time it would be called "trade investigation." For example, in 1917 the film company Essanay announced the formation of a new "investigation department" to determine what distributors, exhibitors, and film critics thought of its movies and to "secure all available information from the public direct" ("New Department Installed," 1917:98). By the end of the 1920s, movie companies had internal departments and external contracts for audience research, with methods including reader responses to advertisements, surveys, and an in-house psychologist to analyze audience preferences (H. Lewis, 1933:87; also see Staiger, 1990). This, however, was well within the norm of broader up-to-date advertising and marketing routines. Stanley B. Resor at J. W. Thompson decided by the early teens that his advertising firm would make advertising a science; he hired a marketing professor from the Harvard Business School and the behavioral psychologist Watson in the 1920s (Fox, 1984:84–86; Pope, 1983:141).

This increasing conversation between scholars and firms in advertising and entertainment media continued. In the 1920s Gallup was teaching journalism and advertising at Northwestern University. His research regarding audience attention to print media produced some surprising results, and in 1932 the advertising firm Young and Rubicam hired him (Fox, 1984:138–39). Audience Research, Inc. functioned as its main business unit doing audience research work. Headed earlier by David Ogilvy, ARI was turned over to Gallup, who tried to sell its strategies to movie firms and producers such as RKO and David Selznick (Jowett, 1985:30). One of Gallup's important innovations that made his research turn out better results than earlier studies was that he distinguished between stated preferences and actual behavior. In responding to pollsters, Gallup "argued, people would elevate their interests, exaggerating their concern with news and minimizing the attraction of entertainment features" (Ohmer, 1991:5). To counter this, Gallup used alternative means to find out what people actually read. Additionally, he did "cross-section sampling," which allowed him to poll fewer people but to poll for those characteristics that mattered for determining what he was seeking to know. Gallup's adjustment to traditional surveying derives not from a psychological theory but from a sociological presumption about individuals' views of cultural norms and prestige: from the 1910s, the terms *lowbrow* and *highbrow* (with lots of middlebrows in between) were discourses structuring perceptions of the U.S. culture, and status mattered to individuals responding to questionnaires. Thus, he reasoned, this feature in social behavior affected the responses and needed to be accounted for to produce better results.

Indeed, commercially funded research about audiences mattered for advertisers on radio and for theater owners. However, the research also reproduced stereotypes and jokes. As Butsch (2000:201) discusses, radio studies of the 1940s such as those conducted by Lazarsfeld and others indicated that women listened habitually to soap operas, and the reasons for this sound exceptionally familiar: listening helped pass the time while doing housework, provided "parasocial" relationships with the characters, taught lessons, offered emotional release, and furnished role models.

By 1950, broadcasting analyses and Gallup's occasional work for Hollywood resulted in an array of standard methods for movie audience research. Handel (1950:6–90) surveyed these methods, along with their individual problems. Box office numbers told executives something about quantity of attendance but little about who came and why. Sneak previews began to be viewed as inadequate because of deficient sampling, a tendency for those who liked the film to answer the questionnaires, and answers that were not easily quantifiable (see here the strong influence of Gallup and the science analogy on perceived deficits). Fan mail and exhibitor opinions were available but, again, were unsystematic and biased. Controlled research on stars, "want-to-see" surveys, and pretests of stories provided some information. Handel indicated that the reason for desiring improved research was twofold: (1) filmmakers could do a better job giving audiences what they wanted; and (2) moviemakers with social issues to present might be able to determine how to present that material "without losing a sizable portion of the audience as a consequence" (60).

These sorts of target marketing studies using social science audience studies continued not only in the commercial realm but also in the scholarly one during the 1950s. Examples are the reports of Smythe, Lusk, and Lewis (1953) and Smythe et al. (1955) of two types of audiences: those at the art theater and the first-run theater. In both studies, Smythe and his teams constructed elaborate procedures to question individuals in the most approved methods to avoid distorting the results. The respondents and their views were placed into categories, with statistical analysis determining when answers were significantly varied within the groupings. Finally, Smythe applied social and psychological theory: citing Riesman's *Lonely Crowd* (1950) as providing a "motivation profile" (Smythe et al., 1955:397), the studies concluded whether the moviegoers were "inner-directed" or "outer-directed."

Advertising historians Daniel Pope and Stephen Fox note that by the end of the 1950s, research procedures and statistical manipulation of data had become increasingly accurate in predicting some consumer behavior. Polling and counting were favored less, however, as "motivational research" increased (Fox, 1984:181–87). This inquiry method relied on depth psychology and psychoanalysis to figure out how to influence consumers. While advertising researchers debated its merits in creating any purchasing effects, Vance Packard published *The Hidden Persuaders* (1957), which seemed "bleakly Orwellian" (Fox, 1984:185) about the dangers of such manipulations of innocent purchasers of products. Additionally, publicity spread that "subliminal messages" were being projected into films and broadcast shows. In 1958, the U.S. National Association of Broadcasters banned such "flash" messages. As a result of fear of such incursions into the minds of American audiences, Pope (1983:282–83) argues that researchers began to emphasize how difficult it was to persuade an "obstinate" audience; some advertisers went so far as to claim no persuasion through advertising even occurred.

Whether or not advertisers were forestalling a potential backlash, communication research theory was also backing off from claims that *individual* messages could affect people as it devoted attention to propaganda, opinion making, and voting patterns. While research agendas during the Great Depression era derived in part from concerns about modeling violence or sexual deviancy (although research also considered the possible development of beliefs and attitudes such as racism due to media exposure), after the war political opinions consumed attention. According to Karsten Renckstorf and Denis McQuail (1996:7), Lazarsfeld and Robert Merton in 1948 declared: "The power of radio can be compared only with the power of the atomic bomb."

But it was not power per se that mattered, but in whose hands that power might reside. Lazarsfeld wrote the foreword to Handel's 1950 book on motion picture research (discussed earlier). There Lazarsfeld directly connected the capacity of messages to affect contemporary political affairs to messages from the iron curtain and Communist influences in Europe and internal to the United States. Lazarsfeld writes that coercion of American opinion was not possible, but popular opinion could be influenced. Yet, what if American messages "boomeranged" (Lazarsfeld in Handel, 1950:xi)? Turning to the past, he noted that "functionalist" anthropology as a social science developed during the nineteenth century when the British colonial administration needed to control populations. Missing the irony, Lazarsfeld called for a new social science for the present political concerns: "The anxiety of the administration is matched by the anxiety of the communications research man" (xii).

A major monograph in this sort of inquiry is Merton's *Mass Persuasion*. In his preface, Merton discusses propaganda as capable of "good or evil" use. An example of good propaganda was the highly successful Kate Smith marathon program of September 21, 1943, in which Smith "succeeded in selling some $39,000,000 of war bonds in the course of one day's broadcast" (Merton, 1946:xi). Merton considered his study original, however, because it focused on the process of the event, not its content. Among the features he emphasized as significant for his research design were that what was studied was a real event (not concocted in the laboratory), those people studied were from the population as a whole (not college students required to participate as part of a class assignment), and the context was clearly defined. In describing the event, Merton wrote, "The process of persuasion did not consist of atomistic responses to a limited number of readily detectable stimuli. Listeners responded differently in terms of the constructions of 'what Kate Smith was really like.' Other responses clearly involved reference to the 'kind of world in which we live'" (10).

Merton promoted a *"differential analysis* of content and response" (12), by which he meant that content and response needed to be related throughout the experience rather than lumped together into a statistical summary. His research produced several conclusions, among which was that giving to the fund was partially due to guilt or anxiety about loved ones in the war, and partially due to Smith's star image as maternal, asexual, sincere, patriotic, and honest, which fit well with the event as a marathon. Merton's theory rejected some social science practices (laboratory experiments, for one) while it drew on a variety of social and psychological theories, including Freudian psychoanalysis (149). In fact, as this postwar group of mass communication theorists attempted to understand audience effects and behaviors, they, like the Frankfurt school, sought combinations of social and psychological theory. Talcott Parsons, who provided sociology with its dominant contemporaneous theory of structural-functionalism, also incorporated psychological assumptions into his model of how society worked.

As Merton tried to establish methods that were capable of determining what precisely in a message was producing potential persuasion, and as he combined social and psychological theory, so did other mass communication researchers. Lasswell's psychology, however, was behavioral. In a major essay, "The Structure and Function of Communication in Society," published in 1948 but formed in essence by 1940 (Rogers, 1994:221–23), Lasswell outlined what had become the prototypical description of the communication process for these scholars: (1) who (2) says what (3) in which channel (4) to whom (5) with what effect, producing the five types of corresponding analyses: (1) control, (2) content, (3) media, (4) audience, and (5) effect. To comprehend the whole social process, it was necessary to locate both the structure and the function of individuals who were involved in surveillance of the environment (e.g., diplomats, foreign correspondents), correlating parts of that social process (e.g., editors, journalists, commentators), and transmitting its social heritage (e.g., educators). All these individuals were like a single-cell organism that sought equilibrium. Lasswell wrote:

> At the risk of calling up false analogies, . . . [a] vital entity . . . has specialized ways of receiving stimuli from the environment. The single-celled organism or the many-membered group tends to maintain an internal equilibrium and to respond to changes in the environment in a way that maintains this equilibrium. The responding process calls for specialized ways of bringing the parts of the whole into harmonious action. (1948:118)

Hence, the specialized functions of individuals in their structural and functional roles each participated in a cohesive social arrangement with logic behind their duties and coherence to their tasks. Some roles might have more power structurally than others, based on the need of the whole for the sort of function those roles played.

This behavioral model coupled with its structural-functional sociology resulted in an education/mediation approach to the question of media effects. An individual arrived in a communication environment fairly free from preconstructed features. For any particular message to reach a level of stimulation so that it actually penetrated the attention of the individual who might carry it along, some need had to exist. Lasswell called this possibility for communication the "world attention process" and modeled it as a series of attention frames that moved a message from individual to individual. Moreover, "The lines leading from the outer environment of the state are functionally equivalent to the afferent channels that convey incoming nervous impulses to the central nervous system of a single animal" (121). Thus, he proposed as an example the events of a world moved from exterior regions toward the United States (although the flows could go toward the outer reaches of Brazilian jungles as well). Values that establish the social needs come from institutions that promote political doctrine (such as the proposition "individualism"), political formula (such as passages in the U.S. Constitution), and the miranda ("ceremonies and legends of public life" that articulate and reinforce that proposition) (123–24).

This theoretical model assumes the tendency toward efficiency within the organism. Indeed, Lasswell's concern at the end of the essay is the inefficiency or ineffectiveness of the process of moving information along. He notes that lack of skill and a resistant personality might hinder it. Or power may come into conflict with the needs of the whole: "Perhaps the most striking examples of power distortion occur when the content of communication is deliberately adjusted to fit an ideology or counter ideology. Distortions related to wealth not only arise from attempts to influence the market, for instance, but from rigid conceptions of economic interest" (126–27). Thus, Lasswell notes that it is important to look at relays—people in positions to forward (or not forward) a message. This classic "transmission" model of communication is already articulating glitches in the process. People may not function as pure automatons within a mechanical flow of data; personal interests and quirks may intervene so that a transparent stimulus-response model is inadequate for understanding potential messages available to effect relays, those people who themselves may not care to turn their attention to those messages. Effects cannot happen without sufficient impact and circulation of meanings. A mediation model had greater correspondence to this representation of how communication worked, but Lasswell's 1948 theory assumed efficiency as the primary value for communicators and did not consider the multitude of other personal values that might affect reception (see chapter 3).

Indeed, while Lasswell's transmission model offered an elegant picture of society generally working well, it also established grounds for further complications. A second major essay of the period is Lazarsfeld and Merton's "Mass Communication, Popular Taste, and Organized Social Action" (1948). In this work, Lazarsfeld and Merton state that the chief social function of mass media is to reinforce norms and values. This occurs through conferring status by legitimating particular people or institutions, enforcing social norms through publicly chastising deviance, and "narcotizing" the masses to be "politically apathetic and inert" (565). This last process sounds as bleak as Adorno's views about the media, although the bases for the proposition come from different theory. Rather than critical or Marxist propositions, Lazarsfeld and Merton speak in standard sociological terms about the need for education of the masses and the necessity to prevent monopolies of information sources.

Indeed, Lazarsfeld and Merton articulate the common fear circulating after the war in order then to dispel it as a credible concern: that some organized group may adopt communication techniques to manipulate the masses into believing some ideas, abdicating critical thinking, or lowering aesthetic tastes. They refute the validity of this fear by reviewing what research was showing about the possible effects of mass media propaganda. To change attitudes, one or more of three conditions must be met:

"(1) monopolization, (2) canalization rather than change of basic values, and (3) supplementary face-to-face contact" (573). Monopolization would occur if the entity seeking to persuade the populace were able to control most, if not all, of any oppositional information (hence, the interest by these scholars in the industrial structures of ownership of media and the social norms of what counts as news or aesthetically valid art). While monopolization was a standard strategy in an authoritarian government, the democratic structure of the United States permitted sufficient counterpropaganda from the various contending parties to eliminate any chance for powerful effects of specific messages. In part this is also because of the canalization thesis. Lazarsfeld and Merton point out that advertising works primarily in situations in which a general behavior already exists, so that all advertising does is to alter specific preferences related to that behavior. Their example is brushing teeth. The socialized behavior is established outside of the advertising realm; ads merely reinforce the value of that behavior and try to direct the consumer toward one or another brand of toothpaste. Reshaping can occur, but "abolishing deep-seated ethnic and racial prejudices, for example, seems to have had little effectiveness" (575).

Even if some message seems possibly to reach the potential for an effect on an individual, research suggests that the best chance for it to work is if the individual has direct contact with someone else who holds the view being considered and if the contact is positive. Such a personal supplementation enhances any mass communication. The personal contact might also be via the mass media, which Lazarsfeld and Merton note are powerful status-conferring institutions. Indeed, Handel discusses the significance of opinion leaders in influencing people's decisions to go to movies (1950:88–90). However, countervailing factors in a democracy reduce the likelihood of a significant outcome for much more serious issues of social and political beliefs. The writers conclude: "The present role of the media is largely confined to peripheral social concerns and the media do not exhibit the degree of social power commonly attributed to them" (Lazarsfeld and Merton, 1948:577). They do caution that our liberal democracy may also make us unduly comfortable about this situation. Thus, as the mainstream mass communication theorists worked through research on propaganda and political preferences, they retreated from any radical claims about media effects. Their hypotheses about effects are within the reinforcement or mediation theories. Individuals come to the media with a set of characteristics and attitudes; media might reproduce or facilitate what the individuals already are. Willard D. Rowland (1983) cautions that capitalist companies eager to fend off state regulation supported the research that produced these findings. With this criticism, he does not question the research as much as note that the groups found each other's goals beneficial; that produced a symbiotic relationship, potentially leading researchers to avoid moving in directions that might eventually prove less comfortable for the partnership. This compatibility would reoccur for mass communication researchers responding to U.S. governmental inquiries in the 1950s and 1960s (see later discussion and Glander, 2000).

While audience research about media effects for consumption and politics was a major line of social scientific study, a third was the postwar concern about teenagers. James Gilbert (1986) describes the moral panic that ensued around media and juvenile crime. Although the peak for this occurred between 1953 and 1956, federal government interventions began as early as 1946. In that year, Attorney General Tom Clark established two committees: the Continuing Committee on the Prevention and Control of Delinquency, with staff members Eunice Kennedy and Sargent Shriver, and the Children's Bureau. These committees did not assume media caused delinquency; in fact, Kennedy sought help from the motion picture industry to fight juvenile crime. What concerned these people was evidence that delinquency was occurring within the middle class, belying older social theories that proposed poverty caused crime. New theories looked to family structure, psychology, and social theories, including Merton's extension of Émile Durkheim's conceptualization of anomie (Gilbert, 1986:134) to explain this.

Still, an easier way to think about the problem was that some external source—such as mass media—was "infecting" or "contaminating" the middle-class child (Gilbert, 1986:75). This theory gained substance when Fredric Wertham drew on behavioral psychology and physiological theory to propose direct causal effects from reading crime comics and watching television shows (Barker, 1984). Applying behaviorist psychology's conditioning theory (and an education theory of effects), Wertham used case studies (rather than experimental studies) to conclude that racism could be taught. He testified for the National Association for the Advancement of Colored People in court battles that eventually ended in the *Brown* v. *Board of Education* school desegregation decision.

Despite Wertham's liberal leanings, sociologists disagreed strongly with his reasoning and conclusions, considering them too linear and monocausal. As early as 1949, Frederic M. Thrasher refuted Wertham in a Payne Foundation–funded publication with an article entitled "The Comics and Delinquency: Cause or Scapegoat" (Thrasher, 1949; Gilbert, 1986:91–108; West, 1988:47–48). Thus, Wertham's education hypothesis about media effects met heavy resistance in part because by the early 1950s even structural-functionalist sociologists turned to psychoanalysis (rather than behaviorism) as a preferred theory of the development of the individual. Indeed, they envisioned the child as naturally "aggressive and sexual" (West, 1988:53). Wertham published his arguments in *Seduction of the Innocent* in 1954, fueling much public interest in the question about media effects.

By the end of the 1950s, social scientific approaches to media effects privileged reinforcement and mediation hypotheses rather than education models. Moreover, increasingly sophisticated quantitative studies backed away further and further from any direct-effects thesis. In 1955, Elihu Katz and Lazarsfeld published *Personal Influence,* in which a "two-step flow" was theorized. Peer groups and opinion leaders intervene strongly in the reception of any specific media message (Couldry, 2000b:3). By 1959, Herbert Blumer criticized the behaviorist "effects" model of a vacant individual conditioned by individual media messages because "it ignored three factors: the variability of media contents, the variability of people's responsiveness to media contents, and 'the independent connection of all forms of communication'" (i.e., repeat messages come from many sources; Couldry, 2000b:4–5, quoting Blumer in *Symbolic Interactionism,* 184). Likewise, in 1963 Schramm detailed a whole array of reasons why the receiver in the classic transmission communications model might interpret a message differently than the sender intended: a receiver interprets from a "frame of reference"; messages have not only denotative but also connotative meanings; messages come with additional communications (e.g., facial gestures accompany a voice message); and messages may have to hurtle barriers, including the massive number of messages in the communication environment, gatekeepers, "beliefs and values" already held by the individual, ego distortions (note the application of psychoanalytical vocabulary), and "group norms" (Schramm, 1963a:2–13). Thus, rather than finding that mass media directly affected audiences, the academic mass communications theory found more and more interventions and complications.

Post–World War II Theory: Critical Theory and Its Influences

Individuals holding critical rather than functional views of society also came out of World War II concerned about propaganda and authoritarian political systems. Those with allegiances to Marxism did face the problem of Stalinism in the Soviet Union. Still, many intellectuals retained the broader tenets of Marxism: powerful inequities resulted in an inability of a social system to right itself without major interventions by those in subordinated roles; this was no instance of a social organism finding its equilibrium. Members of the Frankfurt school were still prominent in U.S. intellectual life and had influenced others' thinking about society and aesthetics, although in 1949 the Institute of Social Research returned to Frankfurt, where it trained Jürgen Habermas and Oskar Negt.

Before leaving, Adorno and Horkheimer wrote "The Culture Industry: Enlightenment as Mass Deception" (1944). A major essay that is full of pithy observations, it articulates a growing pessimism about the triumph of capitalism and mass culture. As Paul Piccone describes their view, by the end of the 1950s, "the subject disappears, society becomes all-powerful," and that society is "the 'totally administered society'" (1978:xix). Still masterful, the essay is difficult to summarize. Adorno and Horkheimer view the primary problem with contemporary social organization to be its capacity to be transparent and yet to hold the consumer enthralled through satisfaction of artificially created needs. For instance, their closing sentence states, "The triumph of advertising in the culture industry is that consumers feel compelled to buy and use its products even when they see through them" (Adorno and Horkheimer, 1944:167).

How could this happen? In short, Adorno and Horkheimer propose a power model of communication in which audiences have become consumers who are helpless in the face of mass media. Whereas once people may have had the potential for critical thinking and even for action, mass media have drained them of any capability for action. Thus, along with their Frankfurt colleagues, Adorno and Horkheimer are participating in rewriting the concept of ideology as due to a false consciousness to being due to a social illusion, occasionally capable of being seen through but so enmeshed in the pleasures of consumer capitalism that the masses prefer ideology over the real, or at least are unable to resist it.

Within the essay are multiple propositions based on analysis of films and other cultural productions. These media texts are analyzed through Aristotelian, rhetorical, and formalist textual methods. Examples of problems they locate in Hollywood cinema are the failures to develop character in relation to the plot, tendencies to reduce potentially valuable nonsense to "sexual symbolism," and an organized cruelty (Adorno and Horkheimer, 1944:137–38). Adorno and Horkheimer admit that movies require of the spectator "quickness, powers of observation, and experience . . . to apprehend them at all; yet sustained thought is out of the question if the spectator is not to miss the relentless rush of facts" (126–27).

Thus, although Adorno and Horkheimer do not conceive of spectators as "empty" or able to be affected directly by a specific movie, they do conceptualize the spectators as so overwhelmed by the form, style, and content of movies produced within the culture industry that they have no power to resist the experience through critical thinking. "The sound film . . . leaves no room for imagination or reflection on the part of the audience. . . . The stunting of the mass-media consumer's powers of imagination and spontaneity does not have to be traced back to any psychological mechanisms; he must ascribe the loss of those attributes to the objective nature of the products themselves" (ibid.:126). Texts with other features than those of Hollywood produce a different experience for the individual. In a conceptual system that is more of a triad, Adorno and Horkheimer posit three modes of aesthetics: *sense* (such as exists in "art"), which would produce intellectual thought; *amusement,* which is what the culture industry offers; and *nonsense* (such as the circus, farce, and clowning), which might provide "pure amusement" and exists in popular culture. Moments of nonsense in movies do occur: Chaplin, the Marx Brothers, early cartoons before the Hays Office restricted plots to morally justified endings (137–38). In terms of dialectics, Adorno and Horkheimer consider nonsense the antithesis of art and as equally functional as art for potential critical thinking.

The really dangerous mode is the "surrogate," the "amusement on the market" (ibid.:142–43). The effect of culture produced in this middle mode is not that people find escape in its content but that the content makes them helpless to resist the culture industry. Aware as people may be of its illusion, "in this age of statistics the masses are too sharp to identify themselves with the millionaire on the screen, and too slow-witted to ignore the law of the largest number" (145). Chance begins to appear to order reality. Likewise, expert knowledge becomes the disciplinarian for social order, replacing the church, club, or social organization. Thus visits to museums are not about developing aesthetic or rational thinking but accumulating facts for social prestige.

What might be called use value in the reception of cultural commodities is replaced by exchange value. . . . [Everything] can be used for something else. . . . No object has an inherent value; it is valuable only to the extent that it can be exchanged. The use value of art, its mode of being, is treated as a fetish; and the fetish, the work's social rating (misinterpreted as its artistic status) becomes its use value—the only quality which is enjoyed. (158)

This last passage not only illustrates Adorno and Horkheimer's analysis of the circularity of the logic of culture within capitalism; it also displays the Frankfurt school's synthesis of Freudian theory and Marxism. Adorno would go on to reassert this position in his essay "Culture Industry Reconsidered" (1967). Repeating the general propositions, he particularly attacks social science equilibrium models of culture that often are coupled with supply-and-demand economic theory. Moreover, he sarcastically refers to "uses-and-gratifications" theory that will be a major post-1960 attempt to resolve the growing problems in mass communications theory to explain audience relations to media texts. Adorno writes, "Among those intellectuals anxious to reconcile themselves with the phenomenon . . . a tone of ironic toleration prevails. . . . All of [mass culture], however, is harmless and . . . even democratic since it responds to a demand, albeit a stimulated one. It also bestows all kinds of blessings . . . through the assimilation of information, advice, and stress reducing patterns of behavior" (Adorno, 1967:15–16).

This listing of personal functions of mass media is typical of the lists social science theory develops in considering media-effect patterns. Adorno assails this thinking by using structural-functional social theory against itself: "As every sociological study measuring something as elementary as how politically informed the public is has proven, the formation is meager or indifferent. Moreover, the advice to be gained from manifestations of the culture industry is vacuous, banal or worse, and the behavior patterns are shamefully conformist" (16). Yes, people may seek out media for specific gratifications, but these are hollow and bereft of true social and personal satisfaction.

This sort of fatalistic perspective on mass media had its supporters beyond the Frankfurt school. The research and writing of Adorno, Horkheimer, Lowenthal, Marcuse, and others directly influenced intellectuals such as Dwight MacDonald and David Riesman (Gilbert, 1986:109–21). In his *No Respect: Intellectuals & Popular Culture*, Andrew Ross (1989:42–64) argues that the term *mass* had "un-American" connotations in the early 1950s as the United States attempted to secure its national culture against foreign contamination from ideologies such as fascism or communism that appealed for their legitimacy on the basis of the mass. Thus, mass had to be redefined: what appeared to be mass in the United States was a rational, independent preference by individual Americans to operate in a group consensus—the evidence of liberal democracy. Ross views this redefinition as a process of containment of Marxist theory, shifting the criticisms of "mass" in foreign contexts to praise of it domestically as indicative of the freedoms of choice offered within capitalism and its plenitude of products desired by U.S. consumers. Supply and demand proved the superiority of the American system because mass was built on individual choice rather than imposed by an authoritarian system. Thus, it is significant to consider how those influenced by the Frankfurt school could hold a skeptical view of mass media while simultaneously attempting to approach it as typically American and thus good in contrast with other nations' media.

Ross turns back to Clement Greenberg's essay "Avant-Garde and Kitsch" (1939) for part of the answer. Greenberg was responding to earlier essays from 1938 and 1939 by MacDonald about the unenthusiastic responses of the Soviet people to avant-garde cinema as due initially to a lack of education but later to "conditioning" by Soviet propaganda for socialist realist aesthetics (D. MacDonald, 1939:88). For Greenberg, the cause of the dissatisfaction was not simply "conditioning," for it did "not explain the potency of kitsch" (1939:42). Instead, kitsch is irresistible in its simpler reiteration of more difficult artworks: kitsch "predigests art for the spectator and spares him effort, provides him with a short cut to the pleasure of art that detours what is necessarily difficult in genuine art" (44). MacDonald rephrased this, according to Ross, to the position that "kitsch already *contains* our response to it" (Ross, 1989:44). Masses could learn to respond to serious art because they had initial, reduced experiences with it.

Thus, in the early 1950s, the task for MacDonald and others holding his view was for intellectuals, operating as leaders in American society, to realign popular or mass culture tastes toward high art. Hope in the people to prefer more complicated art when given the option lay beneath strategies of promoting diversity in consumer offerings. In particular, MacDonald decried "masscult" and "midcult" as homogenized and degraded high art (Gilbert, 1986:119–21) and argued for improved movies.

By the middle of the 1960s, however, MacDonald invoked a sort of distance from the entire problem. In recounting for *Esquire* in 1966 his experience with watching *The Sound of Music*, MacDonald wrote,

> There is something interesting about any man-made product that approaches perfection of its kind, also about any exercise of supreme professional skill, and [*The Sound of Music*] was both: pure, unadulterated kitsch, not a false note, not a whiff of reality. . . .
>
> There's one little puzzle, however: how can both *Psycho* and *The Sound of Music* make box-office records? Is it possibie to enjoy both the Marquis de Sade and *Rebecca of Sunnybrook Farm*? Perhaps we have two mass audiences, like the offensive and the defensive teams football coaches alternate, each of them patronizing only its own kind of movie.
>
> Or perhaps the American public is even more schizoid than I had thought. (1966:65–66)

Concurrently, Riesman also depicted cultural consumption occurring with a " 'series of audiences, stratified by taste and class' " (A. Ross, 1989:53, quoting Riesman in 1952). However, unlike the Frankfurt school or MacDonald, Riesman believed that audience response was not necessarily a consequence of the text: " 'The same or virtually the same popular culture materials are used by audiences in radically different ways and for radically different purposes' " (53, quoting Riesman in 1954). Thus, Riesman's solution to the threat of mass media and its potential effect on audiences was to fragment both of them into segments and to conceptualize a capacity for movement between tastes and audience groups. Upwardly mobile, potentially educable, and individualistic within liberal-pluralistic society were the characteristics of the mass, now often popular, culture audiences.

This sort of thinking would produce a position such as Newton Minow's in 1961 that America's television programming was "a great wasteland," but that diversity in television content was the solution (Staiger, 2000a:54–80). Given better content, audiences would "naturally" move from the current focus on violence and lowbrow comedy. This liberal thinking also explains Riesman's interest in how social groups and psychology produced both the inner-directed and the outer-directed person—but with the latter person less likely "naturally" to pick the better culture. Greenberg, MacDonald, and Riesman may have agreed somewhat about the problems of mass or middlebrow culture as lower in aesthetic stature and less demanding for the spectator, but Greenberg and MacDonald tend toward power theses about the relation between art and individuals. The work determines the reception. Riesman's position is an instance of a mediation approach supported by sociological theory, since he conceptualizes different types of spectators with some agency before the art. Contemporary individuals following in these writers' wake include Neil Postman and Todd Gitlin.

Also taking a skeptical outlook on media's power over its audiences but turning to psychoanalytical theory in concert with social analysis were Wolfenstein and Leites and Kracauer. As mentioned, Wolfenstein and Leites turned to U.S. anthropology (Mead), sociology (Riesman), and psychology (Bateson) for the theory supporting their hypotheses about the relations between film content and audience effect. In *Movies*, they pointed out that while some social scientists were interested in audience opinions, they wanted to study the "recurrent day-dreams which enter into the consciousness of millions of movie-goers" (Wolfenstein and Leites, 1950:13). In a content and symptomatic analysis of all A films released in New York City between September 1, 1945, and August 31, 1946, they found numerous themes within various genres. To determine what might be specifically American about these (assumed) preferred daydreams, they produced a comparison with British and French films of the same quality and period. From these themes and in contrast with the other national cinemas, they made "guesses" (304) about what was going on psychologically in the American people and their lives that led them to prefer the sorts of themes that Hollywood films supplied. Although significant problems exist with Wolfenstein and Leites's method, *Movie* does provide a typical example of how social science was developing a "unified" mediation theory about movie reception. In this formulation, the features of the individuals were a sort of combination of group and personal needs related to the broader social complex of America.

More famous in film studies, Kracauer was also writing his major postwar books at this same time. Personally acquainted with members of the Frankfurt school while he was still in Germany in the 1920s, Kracauer thought then that mass culture had the potential to model anew human consciousness. But for Kracauer and many other European intellectuals, the rise of fascism in the 1930s produced grave concerns about the potential of art to create dangerous group unities. In particular, Kracauer differed from Benjamin in finding some avant-gardes especially susceptible to producing manipulation and control over their viewers. Expressionism and abstractionism were "empty and ornamental forms" that were easy to fill with conservative or right-wing content. Such forms could not reveal "the visible social world" (Petro, 1983:52). Kracauer produced a content analysis of Nazi propaganda films in 1942 and then proceeded in 1947 to publish *From Caligari to Hitler*. This seminal book displays Freudian psychoanalytical theory applied to a large social group —the Weimar bourgeoisie.

Kracauer's model is more complex than simply an assertion that German films display a German unconscious. Instead, he specifies that these films reveal hidden mental processes because their formulas and motifs (he calls them "visible hieroglyphs") continue through the decade toward the assumption to power by Hitler; it is the *repetition*—not merely the appearance—of the formulas and motifs that proves their attraction to the middle-class audiences watching them. For instance, "Like Homunculus, [the governor in *Vanina*] is a tyrant whose sadism appears to stem from a basic inferiority complex. If this explanation of tyranny had not touched something in the Germans, it would hardly have been resumed" (Kracauer, 1947:80). The dreams are wishes, but born out of very specific social circumstances—the trauma of losing World War I. A circularity occurs in this theory of repetition and compulsion. Effects (wishes) can become causes, and Kracauer argued that these films reproduced fantasy desires for a father figure of the sort that Hitler seemed to promise in his propaganda. Like Wolfenstein and Leites's work, Kracauer's *From Caligari to Hitler* uses both sociological and (here Freudian) psychological theory, and its methods are content and symptomatic textual analyses. His overall hypothesis is also a mediation approach: historical circumstances produce psychological disturbances and fantasies in audiences to whose needs media may cater.

By 1960, Kracauer's project has altered from an investigation of a negative outcome of expressionist cinema to a positive justification for the kind of art that cinema could provide—the photographing of visible worlds. He has in mind, however, a very specific visible world in which he is interested: physical reality as indeterminate, motion-filled, social, and relational (Kracauer, 1960:28). Moreover, he has dropped the psychoanalytical theory to a postulation that seems more behavioral, although remarks about spectators are rare. For instance, Kracauer claims, "the [traditional] concept of art does not, and cannot, cover truly 'cinematic' films—films, that is, which incorporate aspects of physical reality with a view to making us experience them" (40).

In the decades following World War II, the potential power of the culture industry mattered to critical thinkers, to individuals disturbed by the "mass-ness" of audiences. Assertions of the power of some media forms to overwhelm the consumers were prominent, but intellectuals holding mediation theories hypothesized media within specific historical circumstances supplying something—perhaps good, perhaps dangerous—to audiences. While the Frankfurt school put forth an important critical theory of mass media effects, liberal thinkers sought social and psychological differences among people that might be altered and channeled to positive outcomes. Yet all these writers, including the academic mass communication scholars, drew on contemporary models of society and individual development.

Continuations of Mass Communication Theory

Academic mass communication theory has continued from the 1960s to make use of developments in sociological and psychological theory. Accounts of its history describe various approaches to the hypotheses of possible effects (Durkin, 1985:15–18; McQuail, 1987:252–54; Cumberbatch and Howitt, 1989:3–30; Renckstorf and McQuail, 1996:9–11; Linné and Wartella, 1998:105–14; Butsch, 2000:255–94). I will discuss these developments as occurring within four groups: "uses and gratifications" theory; behavioral theory (also commonly known as "effects" theory); cultivation theory; and "script" theory.

The increasing complexity of the mass communications model in the late 1950s—with all sorts of factors to be considered in hypothesizing media causing attitudinal or behavior change—turned researchers to studying directly the receiver of the text rather than the text itself. Already, in any actual case of communication, proposals about the preestablished features of the individual required researchers to consider the beliefs and values of an audience member or the influence of other media texts and other people. Thus, what would become known as the "uses and gratifications" model developed. An early statement of it occurs in Katz's "Mass Communications Research and the Study of Popular Culture," where he suggests that mass communication researchers ought not to study "what media do to people" but "what people do with the media" (1959:2).

Karsten Renckstorf and Denis McQuail (1996:9) state that this is the beginning of the "active" audience proposition. As I have suggested, however, throughout the first half century of mass media theory, various authors have considered individuals as coming to texts with characteristics that determined or at least influenced their relation to those texts. It is the case, though, that thinking of audiences as empowered to select their access to specific media and to use that media within the ranges of possibility is a twist not seen since the work of scholars such as Cressey in the 1930s.

By the early 1960s, a functionalist model existed. For example, Joseph T. Klapper described this sort of research as typified by lists of "uses" of media, which he argued were much better than the "dichotomous" questions about criminal behavior or tastes that forced "one-to-one cause and effect models" (1963:517). It broadened inquiries from negative effects (such as violent behavior) to possible positive outcomes and contravening consequences.

Moreover, uses-and-gratifications theory was already tacitly engaging with what would be its main competitor: behavioral theory. Scholars such as Russell Middleton revisited experimental research of the sort employed in the Payne Fund studies through the 1950s to consider possibilities of single viewings of films altering attitudes. In an analysis of audiences of the "anti-ethnic" film *Gentleman's Agreement*, Middleton incorporated "social factors and attitude constellations," as well as "susceptibility to persuasion in the area of ethnic prejudice" (Middleton, 1960:680). He determined that individuals who already were less anti-Semitic understood the film and reduced their prejudices much more than those who only vaguely comprehended the theme of the movie. Middleton postulated that no single film against all other media experiences would have any lasting effect; people could evade messages in fictional movies by trivializing them as entertainment; and people could actually reject the message, creating a "boomerang" effect (679–80). Although not the "resisting" reader of cultural studies that I will discuss in chapter 3, Middleton's "rejecting" moviegoer is able to ignore stimuli.

Other studies confirmed the view that preestablished beliefs affected attitudes. A similar study of attitudinal change after seeing *All the President's Men* indicated that Democrats rejected the idea of controls on the press while Republicans sought them (Elliott and Schenck-Hamlin, 1979). Preestablished beliefs, however, also required the right approach.

Interviews with audiences predisposed to be against the Vietnam War who watched an antiwar documentary ended up disliking the film because it took an "'overly emotional' approach" and had a "lack of rational argument and objectivity" (Paletz et al., 1972:52). Also, media might direct attention. In studying whether news media had any effect, the prevailing wisdom became, quoting Bernard C. Cohen in 1963, "The press 'may not be successful much of the time in telling people what to think, but it is stunningly successful in telling its readers what to think *about*'" (McCombs and Shaw, 1972:177, emphasis in original).

Uses-and-gratifications theorists also questioned the laboratory experimental methods favored (and perhaps even required) by behavioral theorists. Charles Winick pointed out that C. I. Hovland in 1959 had shown that attitude changes occurred more in an experimental setting than in a natural one (1963:289). Given that, Winick constructed an in situ study of New York City teens viewing *The Man with the Golden Arm*. Among his hypotheses were ones typically associated with racist and sexist biases: that "less-adjusted," "lower-class, male, and Negro viewers would show greater change after seeing the film than ["relatively adjusted,"] middle-class, female, and white viewers" (290–91). In fact, he found no differences between the groups in attitude change. What he did discover was that the descriptions of what the film was about varied between the groups. "By and large, the relatively less adjusted viewers emphasized the positive and admirable qualities of the hero and heroine, and perceived the 'magic helper' theme in which the hero's passivity and circumstances beyond his control lead him to addiction. . . . The relatively adjusted viewers generally saw the hero as a weak person." Thus, the "viewer's personality was related to how he perceived the theme" (299).

Uses-and-gratifications studies have been summarized as being "concerned with (1) the social and psychological origins of (2) needs, which generate (3) expectations of (4) the mass media or other sources, which lead to (5) differential patterns of media exposure (or engagement in other activities), resulting in (6) need gratifications and (7) other consequences, perhaps mostly unintended ones" (Renckstorf and McQuail, 1996:2). As the theory has been expanded, a study considers not only psychological needs (stressed more in the 1960s) but also social uses (incorporated in the 1970s; Reeves, 1996:267–68). For example, in his essay "The Needs of Motion Picture Audiences," Lee Garrison claimed that limited information existed on the psychological needs of audiences beyond some speculation about film viewing for escape and education, but social needs were obvious: "Most people attend motion pictures in the company of others," and half of attendees simply went to the movies rather than to a specific film (1972:149). Social uses (such as for an "atmosphere generator" or education for children) seem exceptionally significant in cases of viewing television in homes (K. Jensen, 1987:25). Without a directed goal, retention of information seems weak (Gunter, 1991:229–35). Denis McQuail's (1987:73) long list of uses was heavily social and functional: for information, personal identity, integration and social interaction, and entertainment as well as escape.

Still, as McQuail points out, even though uses-and-gratifications theory took a mediation approach to the question of media effects and gave much more agency to individuals than behavioral theory did, critical theorists viewed it as "positivism, scientism, determinism" (1984:154). Indeed, McQuail criticized the theory on three grounds: (1) the lists of uses were just lists, with no hierarchy or weight (and thus the theory was not genuinely scientific); (2) the theory's underpinning was a "conservative model of a social system," since it assumed people used media to adjust to whatever system was in place; and (3) the theory still inadequately addressed important social functions such as ritual uses of media and aesthetic pleasures (a point being made by cultural studies scholars by this time) (155).

A major competitor to uses-and-gratifications theory has been behavioral theory. Influenced by radical psychology theory and the seemingly objective method of experimentation, behavioral psychology gained significant favor in U.S. laboratory research during the post–World War II era. This theory is best called "effects" theory or the "hypodermic needle" model (Gauntlett, 1996:40–41) and assumes an education model of the individual in which the individual is vaguely "open" or "empty" to stimulus-response training. As I have suggested, the Payne Fund and mainstream mass communication theory did not adopt this psychological theory and often turned to psychoanalytical models of individuals. However, behavioral theory also limited its claims to fairly fundamental psychological processes involving perception and lower-level physiological and emotional development.

It is this theory that, when applied to questions of effect of violent or sexually explicit materials, suggested the threats of significant harmful outcomes, especially to "weak" or unformed minds. Willard D. Rowland (1983:101–96), Guy Cumberbatch and Dennis Howitt (1989), and

William Boddy (1996) describe the political history of the application of this theory to television violence during the 1950s and 1960s. For instance, the television series *The Untouchables* (1959–63) resulted in a public outcry, in part, certainly, because representations of violence selected by viewers in theatrical settings were far different from free access in homes. In 1961, Thomas Dodd began a U.S. Senate subcommittee investigation of juvenile delinquency to consider television sex and violence, not far on the heels of the mid-1950s hearings on comic books discussed earlier. In fact, once again congressional advocates for regulating television content (including Dodd) turned to Wertham and behavioral theory to claim a causal relation between TV images and criminal behavior. The National Association for Better Radio and Television and Wertham used "social ego" theory, long-term studies of content (content analysis), and anecdotal stories to claim fairly direct media influence. Dodd and his team also drew on clinical psychologists and experimental work, especially studies of children exposed to filmed violence. They liked Albert Bandura's study of a girl hitting a Bobo doll after watching similar imagery and eventually concluded that extensive research into media effects was needed.

By 1968, urban riots motivated the creation of the National Commission on the Causes and Prevention of Violence, which reported that the representation of violence on television encouraged violent behavior and attitudes. Many mass communication researchers questioned these claims in terms of evidence and reasoning. Eventually funds from the federal Department of Health, Education, and Welfare poured into the academy to study TV violence, with more than sixty projects funded. The surgeon general's Advisory Committee on Television and Behavior concluded in 1971 that a causal relation existed between viewing violence and aggressive behavior, but only for some children who were predisposed to be aggressive and, then, only in some environments. Researchers who believed these results were too cautionary produced new Senate hearings in 1982, with an updated surgeon general's report that was no stronger than the 1971 summary. Rowland points out that if the U.S. Congress had accepted a violent-images-produces-bad-effects finding, it would have had to rethink its fairly hands-off approach to regulating broadcasting, intervening in "the entire system of private free enterprise communications" (1983:225) in the United States. Still, not even behaviorists who were inclined to be protectionists were willing to make strong causal claims between individual images and behavior.

Similarly, behavioral studies of physiological or sexual arousal while viewing images of nudity or sexual acts received attention. An example is the—admittedly cautious—1970 review of the research by Robert B. Cairns, J. C. N. Paul, and J. Wishner as part of the *Technical Report of the Commission on Obscenity and Pornography*. Cairns and colleagues concluded fairly negative substantiation of a relation. In particular, no evidence existed of a correlation between images and self-reports of arousal, and the causes for arousals detected by physiological change were not obviously a feature of sexual imagination, since the arousal might as well be due to guilt, shame, or fear. However, the researchers did support further research!

Concerns about violence and sexually explicit images (and both together) continued to be major concerns (see further discussion in chapter 7), and uses-and-gratification theorists simultaneously disagreed with behavioral theory. For example, an excellent response to the violent-images-and-crime hypothesis is Richard Dembo's 1973 study of British teen boys and aggressive behavior. Dembo redefined structural-functional theories for behavior away from generalized group norms and values, which tended to be deterministic, and toward specific contexts for an "individual actor" who had "self-designated sets of values" (517–19). Moreover, Dembo argued that understanding teenage boys, for example, required ethnographic study of them in their environment. This social context was voluntaristic. When he then considered the uses of violent images for aggressive and nonaggressive boys, major reasons for viewing them were excitement and escape from worries or routine rather than learning crime per se.

Winick (1970) asked viewers about the functions of sexually explicit materials. Surveying one hundred actual consumers of heterosexual adult films in several large cities, Winick's team was meticulous in its survey, interview, and content analysis methods to avoid biasing results. The functions indicated as significant for consumers included enjoyment of the group experience; information about sex practices and women's bodies; self-arousal or foreplay for later coupled sex; fantasy and humor rewards; and a development of their connoisseurship of the genre. A contemporaneous study (Cairns, Paul, and Wishner, 1970:9) reported that no difference existed in the use of sexually explicit materials or self-reports of arousal among criminals (but not sex offenders), noncriminals, and sexual offenders. Additionally, women more than men reported more sexual arousal to hard-core obscene stories (8).

Mass communication and critical theorists continued to criticize behavioral theory on many points. Strong opponents such as Guy Cumberbatch (1989), David Gauntlett (1995, 1996), Ian Vine (1997), Martin Barker (1997a), David Buckingham (1997), and Willard Rowland (1997) have gone so far as to argue that if the theory is not defunct, it should be (Gauntlett, 1995:1–2). Problems with behaviorism are often conceptual.

- Definitions of "violence" are vague to inadequate (Morrison et al., 1999).
- If watching violent films made people violent, the censors should be very dangerous (Gauntlett, 1995:10–12).
- Television viewing occurs in context with distractions (Cumberbatch and Howitt, 1989:5–12; Gauntlett, 1995:10–12).
- The model assumes that viewers will imitate rather than be repelled by the images (Gauntlett, 1995:10–12; Barker, 1997:23).
- Effects tend to be presumed to be negative although, if they exist, they may also be positive in that viewers might learn a lesson from the representations (Buckingham, 1997:39–41).

Sometimes the problems are methodological.

- Effects studies that do not work are not likely to be published (Gauntlett, 1995:10–12).
- Laboratory, field, and correlation studies are filled with procedural concerns such as suggesting to a subject what the researcher seeks to know or reducing the experience from a real-life one to control variables (Cumberbatch, 1989; Gauntlett, 1995:17–21; Rowland, 1997:105–24).

Behavioral theory does continue through to the present-day, with much more sophistication in modeling and experimentation than earlier. A major researcher in the field, Dolf Zillmann (1991a, 1991b; Zillmann and Bryant, 1991), has been extending detection of physiological responses to stimuli into the field of emotional response such as empathy, suspense, and laughter. Zillmann postulates that responses may be "reflexive," "learned," or "deliberate" (Zillmann, 1991a:146) and is willing to conceptualize personal choice or mood (or place in a menstrual cycle) as determining responses (Zillmann and Bryant, 1991:273). Other researchers such as David M. Sanbonmatsu and Russell H. Fazio (1991) are applying this theory to attention and memory, arguing that repeated activation of specific mental constructs increases the likelihood of their association with the stimuli. This sort of research at times flows into cognitive psychology theory.

If the behavioral theory that involved an education approach to causality seemed weak in demonstrating linear effects from stimuli, one solution was to argue that the stimuli should not be thought of as discrete, single-event happenings. Thus, cultivation theory (which is something of a hybrid of behavioral effects theory and critical theory) argued that it is the accumulation of media experiences that explains media influence. As Nick Couldry describes it, cultivation analysis tries to find correlations among "(a) television content (that is, the most recurrent and stable patterns of television content), (b) viewers' 'conceptions of social reality' and (c) the amount of television watched" (2000b:6, quoting Robert Morgan and Nancy Signorielli).

Developed most notably by George Gerbner in the 1970s, cultivation theory is remarkable as a long-term content analysis of television's programming. For instance, Gerbner and his colleagues report that in the 1984–85 season violence occurred eight times per hour in prime-time programs and twenty-one times per hour in children's television programs (Signorielli and Gerbner, 1988:xii–xiv). Thus, the hypothesis goes, it is the overwhelming aggregation of violence that desensitizes viewers to it and, consequently, to real-life violence. Or, the effect is "mainstreaming": "'heavy viewing may absorb or override differences in perspectives and behavior that ordinarily stem from other factors and influences'" (Abercrombie and Longhurst, 1998:7, quoting Michael Morgan and Nancy Signorielli).

Such claims have been criticized. Gauntlett (1995:41–45, 95–100) replies that (1) effects presumably from heavy television viewing are difficult to distinguish from other possible social sources; (2) "correlations found between amount of viewing and fear of crime tend to be very small," and causes for these correlations may not be the amount of viewing, but the preestablished fear may be the cause for the viewing; (3) heavy TV viewers tend to live in higher crime areas; (4) no proof exists that the effect of watching will be a sense of powerlessness rather than a raising of political consciousness; and (5) the presumption is that television is monovocal and the only source of information for the viewer.

The fourth ongoing mass communication theory is script theory. An outgrowth of the rise of cognitive psychology and ritual theory in anthropology and cultural studies, script theory tries to place media experiences within individuals' understandings of fictional narratives and real-life contexts and the individuals' goal orientations. Presumptions include that people learn rules, scripts, or schemata within the social sphere; people are meaning-making with purposeful actions; and people both interpret and use media within the scripts pertinent to them (Durkin, 1985:18–19; Tulloch and Tulloch, 1992; Renckstorf and McQuail, 1996). This view applied to the problem of violence would describe the linkages thusly: "Media portrayals of violence stimulate association networks or cognitive scripts or thoughts. When primed by a real world situation, a media-related script sparks an acting out of an aggressive behavior" (Linné and Wartella, 1998:114). Script theory assumes learned agency by individuals and is another mediation approach to the relations between media and individuals. I will discuss this sort of approach further in chapter 3.

The history of social science theories applied to media reception has been a steady application of new social and psychological theories to the questions of relations between media and its viewers. Both liberal and critical views have produced hypotheses running from education and reinforcement to mediation and power. The liberals of the Chicago school, the Payne Fund studies, and the postwar mass communication theorists argued that context produced complex individuals who had complex relations with the media. Others, such as the Marxists Eisenstein and the Frankfurt school, feared powerful, overwhelming effects of mass media. So have behaviorists and cultivation theorists, who intuit some sort of causal relation from the text to the individual. Social science theories, however, experience a major intervention with the introduction of new theories of language. Obviously language would matter in answering questions about how people interpret or experience media texts and what effects might occur from those encounters. That intervention is studied in chapter 3.

3

Linguistic and
Cultural Studies Theories

This chapter continues the history of theories influencing propositions about media reception and effects. As with the social science approaches, the theories described here employ various versions of the four causal hypotheses of education (rarely), reinforcement, mediation, and power. However, the introduction of theories of language and comprehension of visual material raises important issues for this question, since obviously these fundamental mental processes underpin psychological and social processes.

Linguistic and Semiotic Theory

Although film theorists such as Sergei Eisenstein and Alexandre Astruc had made equations between films and written texts, most of the discussions of media effects up to the 1960s drew on psychological and social theory to hypothesize the relations between images and viewers. Textual methods were not specific to visual material, using neo-Aristotelian, rhetorical, phenomenological, and content analysis as the usual ways to describe what was in the film. For example, the French cinephiles of the 1920s and André Bazin in the 1940s use variants of hermeneutics and phenomenology. Rudolf Arnheim (1933) employs Gestalt psychology, Kantian aesthetics, and content analysis.

With the republication of Ferdinand de Saussure's 1916 lectures in France in 1949 and their subsequent influence on Claude Lévi-Strauss, structuralism and semiotics burst onto the literary and anthropology scene, giving further support to the sort of narrative analyses promoted by American New Criticism and neoformalism. Depending on the scholar, these methods might incorporate social variations. For example, in discussing how language systems build semantic categories, Pierre Maranda writes, "Semantic charters condition our thoughts and emotions. They are culture-specific networks that we internalize as we undergo the process of socialization" (1980:185). Other writers remained at universal levels, hypothesizing semantic features that were uniform across all languages.

This flurry of new ways to describe what was in a film or TV program quickly excited media scholars, and by the early 1970s a massive application industry had developed. Using semiotics and structuralism for literary texts, while hampered by various difficulties (How did a scholar move from individual signs to complex sentences? How did a scholar know which binary oppositions structured a text? What were signs to cue third-person narrators or nonfiction texts?), was additionally an uneasy transfer to visual materials. One of Saussure's innovations was to distinguish between signifiers (the materials of expression such as oral speech or graphic symbols) and signifieds (the concepts). This separation of signifier and signified calls attention to the arbitrariness of joining the two into a sign. Moreover, with visual materials, signifiers could actually look like what the signs referred to in the physical world—the referents. Such signs are described as "motivated" or "iconic" as opposed to "arbitrary." In every case, though, the oppositions create binaries that heave apart both means of expression and content. Yet, binaries are how meaning becomes possible.

Christian Metz—the primary film scholar to explore these questions— was also the primary individual to question how far the application could go for moving pictures. Metz took up Saussurian semiotics by the mid-1960s and began publishing a series of essays collected into two major anthologies by 1971 (Metz, 1971a, 1971b). Underpinning Metz's application is a fundamental phenomenological premise that in cinema "the impression of reality is also the reality of the impression, the real presence of motion" (Metz, 1971a:9). This premise raises two central and related problems for linguistic and semiotic applications to moving images: one is explaining nonverbal, visual experiences that seem like the external material world, or the problem of "illusions" in perception of texts; the other is considering what is natural versus cultural in the processes of vision. Furthermore, Metz argues that this visual experience explains identification by the spectator with the fictional world, and it explains how spectators understand filmic narratives. He states boldly that narrative is one of the "great anthropological forms of *perception*" (28, emphasis in original). From these propositions, he then moves to three questions of application: (1) What is the nature of the photographic image? (2) Does cinema have a langue (language system)? And (3) if film does not have a langue, how do spectators know cinema's meanings? Each of these questions both reinforces the application of semiotics to cinema and eventually troubles it.

Regarding the question of the nature of the photographic image, Metz argues that the codes spectators use to perceive referents are related to the codes used to read visual images. Thus, the spectator reads moving images the same way as he or she perceives the physical world (Metz, 1971a:78n, 80n). Metz concludes that cinema does not have a langue because it has no double articulation (unlike oral language, which has phonemes and morphemes). Moreover, it has no signs as such. Each image is much more than a sign; it is a sentence. (The image of a revolver says not "revolver" but "here is a revolver.") Finally, cinema has no paradigmatic limits because any shot could replace any other shot. Thus, the notion of an ungrammatical statement does not make sense, and cinema has no syntactical rules.

Having eliminated many of the analogies between aural or written language systems and moving images, Metz does want to account for how people "read" film. Given his phenomenological premises, he asserts that filmgoers know what cinematic images mean because of prior experiences with understanding what is occurring in the real world. Five codes—all learned—aid this understanding: perceptual codes that structure space and figures within a space; iconology codes that recognize and identify objects; iconography codes that relate cultural or textual connotations to objects; the narrative *disposition* (or *grande syntagmatique*), which is a set of optional temporal and spatial possibilities for shots that is underpinned by the anthropological ability to structure this material into a narrative; and specifically filmic codes (such as fades or dissolves).

Metz's theory of cinema as a semiotic system fits within the reinforcement model of effects. People interpret films as they do because they already have learned cultural codes to understand what is presented to them. Faced with a filmic text, an individual will automatically convert the information. As a self-declared Marxist, Metz does not usually discuss the variable ideologies of texts because he assumes most mainstream films duplicate dominant ideologies.

Metz's theory, along with other semiotics of moving images, produced a rich proposition because the language model goes to the heart of the question of the relation between people and any text. Even if social or psychological theories are also involved in interpretation, answering the fundamental problem of how visual material is processed mentally has to be addressed. As I shall discuss later regarding cognitive psychology, however, a language model is not the only available thesis. Yet, as of today, the language-model is one of the two major contenders to solve this basic question of processing images.

My account of Metz's theory indicates some of the problems with applying Saussurian semiotics to cinema, although many scholars continue to use his work to describe the narratives of visual texts. Other scholars have applied different semiotic or linguistic theories. Peter Wollen (1972:116–74) borrowed from Charles Sanders Peirce's semiotics and sketched out a tripartite arrangement of motivated and arbitrary signs (icon, index, and symbol) but also argued that most filmic shots contained all three types. Jurij Lotman (1970, 1973) used semiotics and Russian formalism to create a thesis that cinematic meaning occurs through a binary system of normative versus disruptive perceptual experiences. Noam Chomksy's transformational generative grammar influenced Michel Colin, Dominique Chateau, and Warren Buckland (Buckland, 1995:27–110). Among the applications is Colin's attempt to rewrite Metz's *grande syntagmatique* into preference rules (Colin, 1992:87–110). In his early work, Edward Branigan (1984) also was invested in a linguistic-based project to explain how spectators use a limited number of transposition rules to comprehend syntactical features of film such as point-of-view shots.

Literary and semiotic theory has advanced into narratology and pragmatics. Narratology is the exploration of analogies between sentences and extensive texts: What are the equivalencies of syntactical rules for sentence construction, voice, and tense? Seymour Chatman (1990:38–55) has been aggressive in this area, not only describing orders to narratives but also equating mise-en-scène to written description, camerawork to exposition, and other visual material to argumentation. Pragmatics is a linguistic proposition that most utterances rely on context to fill out the connotations of a statement. Roger Odin and Elena Dagrada are working in this area to explain how spectators interpret visual materials (Buckland, 1995:209–49). While these linguistic and semiotic approaches are usually applied to broad types of text (such as classical Hollywood cinema or art cinema), Rick Altman (1999) has a long career of describing genres in terms of their semantics, syntactics, and, recently, pragmatics.

As I indicated earlier, some of these writers give spectators features that might account for some individuality in interpreting films. For one thing, Saussure made a sharp distinction between langue and parole. *Langue* is the abstract structure of a language at any particular moment; *parole* is an individual event of speaking a langue. Saussure devoted great attention to the problem of historical change in language, and as semiotics and structuralism shifted to poststructuralism, that every event of speaking is in a new context raised awareness of the arbitrariness of trying to freeze a language into an ideal state. Moreover, different groups within a culture might produce different codes for the same apparent words (i.e., the variable meanings of "bad"), yielding polysemy as a fundamental condition of actual discourse. Further, to express ideas unavailable in the langue, individuals expressed some agency through ad hoc combinations of signs. This practice is *bricolage*.

Still, within general semiotic studies, most of the scholars are embarked on a project to explain large-scale, general practices of reading films and visual material. Even if culture enters, the presumption is that everyone has fairly similar cultural experiences, or that the differences do not matter in the event of watching a movie for what these scholars want to explain. Consequently, not necessarily by requirement but generally by practice, these theories all sound like reinforcement propositions, although most of the writers do not even raise the question of any effects other than comprehending the film.

Revised Social-Psychoanalytical Theory

The site for a much more explicit articulation of a reinforcement thesis is within a second wave of scholarship using linguistic and semiotic theory in combination with sociological and psychological theory. Crucial in this supplementation are Jacques Lacan's revision of Freudian psychology through Saussurean structuralism and the intervention of Louis Althusser and structural Marxism (see Coward and Ellis, 1977, for an extensive version of this). Lacan rereads Freud's story of the development of the child into a sexed and gendered subject through experiences of viewing one's self in a reflective surface (the "mirror" stage) and seeing the social differences between males and females articulated through the signifier of the phallus (the "symbolic" stage). The mirror stage develops an individual's ability to identify with others (a misrecognition that self and other are the same, but crucial in civilization's maintenance). The symbolic stage generates meaning-making, since (binary) difference is now seen and understood as consequential. Thus, all individuals are socially constructed into subjects to "fit" into the social world. This proposition assumes power differentials, and the theory falls within a conflict sociological perspective.

In his essay "Ideology and Ideological State Apparatuses" (1970) and other writings, Althusser proposes to explain how social institutions such as churches, schools, and families participate in reproducing the exploitive relations of production in which workers become workers within capitalism—also an example of conflict theory. While some of this reproduction occurs through overt violence via repressive state apparatuses such as the government, police, prisons, and courts, much of it happens in more subtle ways through ideological state apparatuses. Althusser postulates that social groups—both those complicit with the ruling class and those in apparent opposition to capitalism—function by representations "hailing" (interpellating) individuals to take up roles as "subjects." Drawing on Lacan's description of how an individual is made into a subject, Althusser produces a theory combining semiotics, psychology, and sociology.

Like so many other theories, structural Marxism had a specific purpose: to account for the typical. While Althusser opens a space for individuals' opposition to the dominant, referring to Antonio Gramsci's remarks about the artificial construction of private and public institutions and noting that class struggle can occur within the ideological state apparatuses (Althusser, 1970:144, 147), within structural Marxism the individual is conceived of as having no agency. Indeed, one of the significant moves of the last decade has been to review this theory in order to return agency to people as a power to effect events, while still acknowledging that people are socially constructed.

Certainly, the end result of linguistic and semiotic theory combined with structural psychology and conflict social theory is to understand that individuals are produced within a representational system that far exceeds our ability to grasp it. We may be competent performers of that system, but we perform in a system of which we have no full knowledge. This view of the subject in relation to a media text implies either a reinforcement model or a power model in terms of media effects.

Such an overwhelming prospect fed much film theory of the 1970s. The major lines of argumentation follow through from Metz's observations about the illusion of cinema and from the recurring emphasis of the functions of vision in Lacan's story of the socialization of a child. If representations interpellate individuals into subjects compliant with capitalism, how does mainstream cinema cooperate in this? One thesis suggested that by reproducing through the choice of lens-making the visible world (grinding lenses to reproduce preferred human vision), cinematic technology produced an ideology that what was visible was what was real (Baudry, 1970; Comolli, 1971–72). Marxist theory criticized this "realism" thesis as a false consciousness, for what is real is the social dialectics of exploitation. Thus, these scholars often refer disparagingly to mainstream cinema as "classical realist cinema."

Further investigations of the vision theses theorize other aspects of the cinematic technology (quick editing, seemingly omniscient camerawork, and multiple point-of-view positions) cooperating with a general drive in modernity toward stimulation. Jonathan Crary argues that the urban stimuli available in the late 1800s required a disciplining of the gaze: "pushing attention and distraction to new limits and thresholds . . . and then responding with new methods of managing and regulating perception" (1995:47). This recent argument implicates cinema in twentieth-century sensual dynamics and the development of modernity. Whether the result of this is positive or negative in terms of the effect on the spectator depends on the critic.

For Tom Gunning, cinematic strategies of engrossing a viewer into the plot of narrative film create a passive voyeurist spectator, complicit with "absorption in 'illusory imitativeness'"; however, cinemas of spectacle and avant-gardism generate in the spectator an "exhibitionist confrontation" and critical viewing of the sort praised by Bertolt Brecht (Gunning, 1986:66). Thus, Gunning's position, which is highly dependent on cinematic style and content, is a reinforcement theory of effects and seems, here at least, to prefer modernism to nineteenth-century illusionism. But later, following Crary and others, Gunning claims that the cinematic technology produces "a consequent transformation of the body through new thresholds of demand and danger, creating new regimes of bodily discipline and regulation based upon a new observation of (and knowledge about) the body" (1995:16). Or, as Mary Ann Doane expresses it, "The body as the support of both identity and subjective perception is assaulted by a modernity understood as disruption, speed, and anonymity" (1993:9).

Both Gunning and Doane describe vision, modernity, and gazes within the confines of theorizing cinema. Anne Friedberg (1993) sees things differently, invoking a media specificity difference. For her, twentieth-century culture and consumerism disrupt the "panoptic gaze" with its "structured visuality"—all associated with cinema as a holdover of nineteenth-century visual culture and early modernity. However, certain recent forms of spectatorship such as the "mobile and virtual gaze" associated with the "female urban subject," the "flâneuse" (borrowed from Walter Benjamin), create a postmodern subjectivity. Television and VCRs are symptoms and causes of this new spectatorship. Associated with this postmodern culture is TV's "flow," the constant onslaught of images that produces a banality to all information. Thus, depending on the imagery of the writer, this experience of (post)modernity produces a critical, invaded, distracted, or mobile spectator; at any rate, the reinforcement model continues, since all these scholars indicate that media specificity produces the range of spectatorship possibilities and works to reproduce the status quo (the broad social and cultural world of contemporary Anglo-America).

Another way to use the visual model provided by Lacan and Althusser is to connect it to the gendering of the subject. In a revision of his earlier work, Metz argues in "The Imaginary Signifier" that the medium of cinema facilitates a viewer's identification with characters, with humans in nonfiction films, with the camera as provider of the narrative, and, finally and most significantly, with the self as the perceiving and meaning-making subject (Metz, 1975b). In an elegant passage, he writes, "I am at the cinema, attending a film show. *Attending.* Like a midwife who attends at a birth, and thereby also helps the woman, I am present to the film in two (inseparable) ways: witness and helper. . . . I help it to live, since it is in me that it will live and it was made for that: to be seen, i.e., to come into existence only when it is seen" (Metz, 1975a:22). This rhapsodic account of watching cinema does not end in naïveté, for Metz considers this an ideological trap. "I have loved the cinema, I no longer love it. I still love it" (Metz, 1975b:79).

Metz's account, however, assumes that everyone is the same. Yet his discussion of the processes producing this construction of the self is written from the perspective of a male subject experiencing the mirror and symbolic stages—especially the disavowal of the female's lack of the phallus and general anxieties of the threat of castration. Additionally, only minor attention is paid to how sound, dialogue, and viewing context might matter in the experience.

Metz was writing just as second-wave feminism was expanding. Nearly simultaneous with the appearance of "The Imaginary Signifier" was the publication of another major theoretical essay, Laura Mulvey's "Visual Pleasure and Narrative Cinema" (1975), which introduced sexual difference into the discussions of subject effect. Mulvey also uses the psychoanalytical and structural Marxist presumptions generally operating at this time but turns the theory into a different, feminist criticism: "demonstrating the way the unconscious of patriarchal society has structured film form" (6). Whereas the focus in the earlier work has been on how some cinematic style reinforces capitalism or modernity, this intervention raises sexism as the potential negative effect. Mulvey points out that mainstream narrative cinema has two ways to deal with the anxiety of the connotations of woman and her lack of the phallus: the film can investigate the woman and punish her (voyeuristic sadism), or it can disavow the original belief that she had a penis and reconstruct her as having one (fetishistic scopophilia). Cinematic technology and style facilitate these options through three "looks." The camera records the events but as if from a perfect position; the audience can see the events but in a safe position; and characters look at each other through eyeline matches and point-of-view shots that favor the male's ego.

As scholarship has continued, theorists have grappled with more specific applications of the broader theory (Heath, 1978). What are the potential implications of various types of narrative plots? For example, do some mainstream genres such as the women's film provide implicit fracturing of these favored looks? What about identification? Is it necessary that a male identify with male characters, or can cross-sex identification occur? What about sound and viewing context? Where is the place of the woman's ego? Do female spectators identify with male points of view, accept their position as masochistic objects of desire in these narratives, or masquerade as female spectators to create for themselves a distance from the plot (Doane, 1982)? If a film produces a contradictory situation for a spectator, what does the spectator do? In her summary of debates over *Stella Dallas*, Judith Mayne points out that Linda Williams concludes that "'the female spectator tends to identify with contradiction itself,'" Ann Kaplan believes that females suppress the contradiction, and Mary

Ann Doane points out that a narrative "contradiction is less than eman-cipatory" anyway (Mayne, 1993:71–72).

Feminism has been combined with theorizing about capitalism, poli-tics, and modernity. Miriam Hansen's scholarship is a good example of this conjunction. Using German public-sphere theory (Jürgen Habermas, Oskar Negt, and Alexander Kluge), Hansen posits that cinematic styles determine spectators' ability to think critically while watching movies, with mainstream techniques creating the managed spectator engrossed in the filmic image rather than someone able to engage as a "member of an anticipated social audience and a public" to produce a "critique of bour-geois culture" (1991:34, 29). She adds to this a gendered opposition in which the voyeurist opportunities of the classical narrative cinema offer the subject a "structurally masculinized" position and a "patriarchal economy of vision" (5, 40).

This revised social-psychoanalytical theory has a strong tradition in contemporary media studies. It is a very powerful example of the rein-forcement model of effects, since it posits that culture has features (capi-talism, modernity, patriarchy) and that media can reinforce those fea-tures, maintaining order. This theory does consider the potential radical effect of nontraditional media, but in that instance it is still the different media style or content that produces the subject as potentially active or critical during a viewing experience. At times an application of the theory can tend toward the power model, in which a person may have features (proletariat, embodied, sexed, raced, political citizen) and is then pres-sured or fascinated into conforming to the ideological thrust of the text being viewed (the commodity fetish extension of this position). In its nor-mal articulation, however, the differences of the spectator are subsumed to the medium, and the medium controls the effects on the spectator.

Cognitive Psychology Theory

Linguistic and semiotic theory as negotiated by Lacanian psychoanalysis and structural Marxism employed an extensive reliance on a theory in-volving vision and signs in multiple forms: aural, written, and pictorial. Cognitive psychology and psycholinguistics participate in these debates by offering alternative theories of how the mind processes perceptual matter. For example, one way to split arguments about how we know the world is the distinction between the descriptionalists and the pictorialists.

The former group believes that knowing is the result of proposition-based, nonvisual representations. The latter group thinks that images have a fundamental function within cognition and are not necessarily translated into discourse. The outcome of this debate matters greatly to visual media scholars, since the linguistic model falls into a descriptionalist category, whereas some film scholars (see later discussion) dispute such a linguistic premise to knowledge of the perceptual world. As recently as 1997, the judgment was still out as to whether mental images are "pictorial, or linguistic, or both" (Reeves, 1996:273). Obviously, however, cognitive psychology presents a potentially different explanation of primary engagements with visual information and then moving images. How are images perceived? Are they translated into signs (in the linguistic sense)? Are the signs ordered into equivalencies of sentences, or is another ordering process (such as a network of associations) going on?

In a survey of the approaches to understanding the ordering process, Kathryn T. Spoehr and Stephen W. Lehmkuhle (1982) indicate that scholars have proposed at least three models to explain one of these problems: the categorization of visual information. None of these models assume linguistic knowledge is required to understand images. The *template* model hypothesizes the human visual system synthesizes perceptual data into a composite and matches it to images stored in memory. Problems with this model include the large number of images that must be stored to find matches for all visual experiences. The *prototype* model conceptualizes visual images as being compared to an "average" of the class. This comparison occurs in part through schemata, which are "rules that describe the essential characteristics of a prototype of a class" (Spoehr and Lehmkuhle, 1982:41–47). Still, the questions of how the schemata are stored, how or if new ones are developed, and what happens when differences are so extensive that no schema can reconcile the information are left unanswered. The *feature* model assumes that, rather than visual matching occurring, features in a list are coordinated. So far, in applications of cognitive psychology to media, most scholars have used the concepts of schemata, prototypes, templates, and scripts (general narrative outlines) to describe the mental activity of spectators.

Another significant part of cognitive psychology for media studies is one of its presumptions about the perceiving human. It is often noted that this theory starts with the premise that humans are goal- or task-oriented. We have objectives, and this human feature structures any encounter with our environment. Thus, Ulric Neisser cautions against an analogy of the human brain with the computer: humans are not neutral or "passive" to "bits" of incoming information. "Instead, they select some parts for attention at the expense of others, recoding and reformulating them in complex ways" (1967:7). Neisser argues that cognitive processing occurs in steps. An immediate one is a fast categorization, with further refinement occurring in later stages.

Cognitive psychology sometimes is at the basis of the script theory mentioned briefly in chapter 2, but it differs from social- psychology theories that also may underpin individual scholars' work. Social-psychology theories rely on behaviorist psychology that assumes human responses develop "exclusively by physical input"; cognitivists believe that "people make discretionary as well as involuntary responses to their environment" and that schemata are valuable mental processes to increase efficiency in processing information (Reeves, 1996:272–73). Indeed, script theory interconnects with narratology (described earlier) and may also use linguistic models. For instance, David Herman combines work on "knowledge structures," schemata, scripts, and frames (human expectations constructed at a special temporal moment) with a language analogy: "Semiotic features cue story recipients to activate certain kinds of world knowledge" (1997:n.p.). Manfred Jahn joins "[Marvin] Minsky's theory of frames [as "cognitive models"], [Ray] Jackendoff's concept of preference rules, [Menakhem] Perry's theory of literary dynamics, and [Meir] Sternberg's Proteus Principle . . . to conceptualize third-person narrative situations in terms of cognitive models" (1997:441). Nothing theoretically prohibits such bricolages, since cognitive theory has not yet reached any definitive conclusions on the descriptionalists-versus-pictorialists debate.

Indeed, cognitive psychology occasionally also finds collegial work in analytical philosophy or simple syllogistic reasoning propositions. The use of preference rules to explain human meaning-making has a strong recent tradition. An excellent example of an application to the interpretations of literary texts is Ellen Schauber and Ellen Spolsky's book *The Bounds of Interpretation*. They argue that in a situation in which a reader might want to try to categorize a text into a genre such as tragedy or romance, the decision would be pinned upon the text's meeting the conditions of "well-formedness" and "gradient-necessary" features as well as a sufficient number of "typicality and gradient typicality" conditions (1986:85). Other scholars are investigating the general function of schemata and language (especially metaphors) to construct our world.

Mark Johnson argues that imagination is "essential to the structure of rationality," and this imagination derives from our actual bodies in engagement with image schemata ("abstract structures of images"), as well as metaphors not as figures of speech but as "a structure of human understanding" (1987:ix–xx).

In applications to media, this sphere of scholarship runs the same sort of range of possibilities that has occurred in mass communication theory derived from other psychological and sociological work. Cynthia Freeland (1999) remarks that debates about the "illusions" of images split between conceptualizing the spectator as passive or at best a stimulus-response machine (the work of Joseph Anderson and Ed S. Tan) and conceiving of the spectator as imaginative (Noël Carroll). Eventually, individual writers may produce any one of the four causal hypotheses about moving image effects—education, reinforcement, mediation, and power—although most hypotheses are within mediation because of the presumption of the goal orientation of an individual.

Cognitive psychology developed from turn-of-the-century Gestalt psychology (see film theorist Hugo Münsterberg [1916], for instance), 1920s and 1930s Soviet psychology (particularly Lev Vgotsky), and postwar artificial intelligence (AI) research. As early as 1970, individuals were making nascent applications beyond interpretation and into media effects. In their study "The Prejudicial Film," Anne K. Nelsen and Hart M. Nelsen refer to Leon Festinger's 1964 "cognitive dissonance theory." Using this theory and some anecdotal information about audiences, they claim that for the film *Hurry Sundown,* when its audience is confronted by a representation at odds with its "version of a properly established one," the audience chooses either to reject "the proposed one" by ridicule or to "ignore the inflammatory part of the movie, detach itself from the actor, and find extreme amusement in some rather macabre scenes" (1970:145). Here Nelsen and Nelsen give the audience some agency to avoid information that fails to match their belief systems. In fact, this is a "resisting" audience. Of course, resistance also can be invoked against subject matter that tries to alter *or* reinforce racist stereotypes.

Another application is Peter Dahlgren's model of processing television news. Dahlgren combines linguistic theory (Roman Jakobson's [1960] model of six functions of communication) with theories of perception, cognitive association ("pre-existing knowledge and frames of reference"), and the unconscious ("subliminal" knowledge; 1985:242–46). This is a good example of a bricolage of contemporary theories.

The main advocate for cognitive psychology applications to moving images has been David Bordwell. Through about 1985, Bordwell turned to American New Criticism and then Russian formalism to produce critical analyses of films. However, Russian formalism requires artwork to disautomatize the perception of its viewer—if the work is to be called "art." While Russian formalism stressed the context in which an artwork is viewed as crucial to determining whether or not the artwork is successful in these terms, cognitive psychology provides a theory of spectatorship that matches well this critical method, given its notion of the behavior of individuals encountering visual (or other) information.

The first full-blown articulation of the application appears in Bordwell's *Narration in the Fiction Film* (1985). Here Bordwell sketches out his theory of the knowledgeable and cooperative spectator processing filmic information by appealing to prototype, template, and procedural schemata (34–36). The spectator is goal-oriented, working toward figuring out what is going to happen in the classical Hollywood film. Of course, other types of films produce different goals: the art film expects viewers to ask about what is real and why people behave as they do; the historical-materialist film solicits viewers to adhere to a rhetorical proposition; and the parametric movie requests viewers to discover patterns beyond the narrative plot. Bordwell insists upon a pictorialist thesis and refuses to use the term *reading* to describe viewer activities. While he might have included cultural differences within his discussion, Bordwell also chooses to focus on normative encounters with movies. Overall, his is a mediation theory of media-meaning making and effects in that viewers have schemata and goals and use these to access films for the kinds of cognitive experiences that will give them pleasure, such as solving plots or considering other intellectual benefits.

As I mentioned previously, not all individuals using cognitive psychology insist on the pictorialist proposition that images remain in nondiscursive form. Thus, Colin combines linguistic theory (knowledge is linked via "semantic networks") with AI cognitive theory ("frames," which are properties and values of an "object, concept, or a situation," help lump together ideas across a text; 1992:87–92). Additionally, Branigan's more recent work has used both linguistic and cognitive theory (although he subsumes the former to the latter) to propose a "narrative schema," specifically how individuals typically comprehend narrative information and order temporal events (1992:4–20).

Others such as Carroll agree with the pictorialist proposition and use analytical philosophy and syllogistic reasoning to make claims about how spectators interpret films. Carroll writes, "I do not think that film is a language, and hence I do not believe that films are read"; what he does is "explication," which is the analysis of "the presence of a feature or set of features in a film whether such explanation is (broadly semantic or) thematic, or functional or even causal (in terms, for example, of emotional effects)" (1998:1–6). Like Bordwell, Carroll assumes an ideal spectator, able to make inferences and knowledgeable about not only filmic conventions but also standard features of the everyday world. In summary, cognitive psychology has a great deal to offer scholars of media and a robust coterie of media scholars pursuing the questions of interpretation and effects through the theory.

Cultural Studies (Revised Social Theory)

Cultural studies is also a vigorous collection of researchers whose scholarly heritage derives from many of the same thinkers as the other groupings discussed in this chapter. Cultural studies distinguishes itself from the revised social-psychoanalytical and cognitive science theories through a focus on individuals' differences, usually premised as socially constructed through economic, cultural, or social positioning. At least two strands of cultural studies exist, now somewhat erroneously labeled to reflect their apparent source of development and weight of allegiance: American and British. Generally, I believe it is better to consider these strands under the rubrics of "structural-functional" and "critical" cultural studies. In both strands, however, cultural studies emphasizes microstudy of social arrangements and the roles of cultural products in the lives of individuals. It draws on methods such as participant observation, focus groups, and ethnography to gather data that are then subjected to textual analysis and social theorizing.

Structural-functional cultural studies, which comes out of the liberal functional sociology and anthropology described in chapter 1, assumes power equivalencies among the various members of a larger social organization. Power may derive from sheer numbers (the large working class may unionize, or pressure groups may use publicity to intensify their voices); often power springs from scarce resources (specialized skills or talents). Among the key figures for structural-functional cultural studies are John Dewey, Clifford Geertz, and Victor Turner.

In a major articulation of the position, James Carey uses Dewey to criticize the "transmission" theory of communication promulgated by mass communication researchers. Contrasting transmission (which Carey writes has a heritage with spreading the word of God) to "ritual," he argues that much communication is really about "the maintenance of society in time" and "the representation of shared beliefs." The ritual function of communication also has religious undercurrents, since it is "linked to terms such as sharing, participation, association, fellowship, and the possession of a common faith" (1975a:6). Indeed, his intervention is part of a hope to use communication for "reshaping our common culture" (21). Notice Carey's emphasis on what might bind a social group together —our common features.

In a related essay, Carey (1975b) finds much of value in Geertz's work. Indeed, Geertz (like Lévi-Strauss) builds on semiotics to alter the discipline of anthropology. Geertz states, for instance, that symbols are not expressions of "biological, psychological, and social existence; they are prerequisites of it" (Geertz, 1973:49). Meaning-making is fundamental to social groups, and scholars' tasks are to find how everyday events function in constituting a society that is able to negotiate its differences to remain a unit.

Likewise, Turner's combination of a semiotically informed sociology and psychology influenced another seminal argument in structural-functional cultural studies: how to understand the function of television within a social formation. Horace Newcomb and Paul Hirsch (1983) apply Turner's descriptions of ritual and liminoid events in a postindustrial, complex society to the social experience of watching television. Arguing that television series fiction is built on discussion of ideas in public circulation within a social context, Newcomb and Hirsch think that the expression of these variable positions through narrative conflicts among characters offers a "cultural forum." Even if a narrative resolves a socially contested problem with a conservative ending, the mere raising of and debate around the issue have potential for offering television viewers alternative outlooks. Like the liminoid space of Turner's model, television as a moment "outside" the routine of work contributes a safe space to explore different ideas.

Newcomb and Hirsch's faith in the middle of narratives contrasts with much other theorizing about narratives that focuses on conservative closure as shutting down the potential opened during the midportions of the text (see, for instance, the feminist debates over *Stella Dallas* described earlier, but also see Heath, 1975–76). Indeed, the question of whether parts of a text or the resolution affect the spectator more is a long-standing and major issue that has influenced censorship debates. Some claim textual effects to be "pointillist" (a scene of violence will harm a child); others hold a "total-picture" position (a morally compensatory ending ameliorates any midtext improprieties; Staiger, 1995:79).

Eventually, structural-functional cultural studies serves as the ground for drawing upon any contemporary liberal social scientific theories about how social groups work. "Deviance theory," which explores subcultural or countercultural groups such as youth as temporarily out of conformance with mainstream norms, fits in here (Marchetti, 1986). As I shall explore in chapter 4, much fan analysis is of this sort. One good example, however, is the discussion of audiences by Nicholas Abercrombie and Brian Longhurst. Using the work of Richard Schechner, Turner, and Erving Goffman, they describe how media may facilitate group interactions, emphasizing that "fans and enthusiasts [are] a form of skilled audience" that derive from individuals both presenting themselves as "spectacle" and taking narcissistic pleasure in that experience (1998:121, 77). As adherents of a structural-functional social theory, these scholars tend toward reinforcement and mediation models of how media produces any effects.

A contrasting approach is **critical cultural studies**, in which social groups are not assumed to have an ability to counterbalance each other; instead, power belongs for the most part to some groups and not to others. When it comes to media, those with control of the means of production run cultural life, although people may have some ability to refuse to be sucked fully into a dominant ideology. Thus, a "pure" power model of media effects is not theorized, although the existence of inequities and struggles permeates the discussions. In fact, one of the guiding research goals is to understand individual or group agency of those without significant power—economic, political, or cultural. This cultural studies draws its heritage from various Marxisms or adjacent social theories, including ideas by British midcentury writers such as Richard Hoggart, Raymond Williams, and E. P. Thompson, but also Althusser and Gramsci. Its institutional stronghold was the Birmingham Centre for Contemporary Cultural Studies (CCCS), founded in 1964 by Hoggart and then directed by Stuart Hall from 1969 (Turner, 1990:12–29) until its recent closing.

Most stories of the development of critical cultural studies caution against a simple teleology and canonical outline and then proceed to go with it anyway. Indeed, as with all the descriptions of these groups of opinion about media interpretation and effects, lines of influence and motivations for theories are more complex in longer and detailed discussions. Given this disclaimer, however, everyone turns to the importance of Hoggart's, Thompson's, and Williams's concerns about working-class culture. As in the other moments that I have discussed, critical social theorists have tried to understand what governs the events in successful and unsuccessful political change. Marx had predicted an insurgence of the proletariat as capitalism further suppressed the workers, but revolutions occurred in the "wrong" places (Russia, not Germany), and fascism sapped radical energies in major industrialized countries. One intellectual solution is to study the class that is charged with political agency but that folds in the moment of potential major social change.

Hoggart, Williams, and Thompson approached this problem in individual ways, but each at times focused on youth or social cultures within the working class. This move created heterogeneity within the unified economic classification typically informing Marxist theories. Eventually, youth or working class also came to mean boys, men, and masculinity— all features inflecting the pubs, sports, and other after-work lives. This attention has some similarity to the intellectual attention in the United States toward popular culture (described within the section on cold war critical theory in chapter 2). Indeed, both groups evince something of a "democratic-humanist interest" in these matters (Turner, 1990:46).

These writers, however, particularly focused on how cultural life played into the self-definitions of workers: for example, their association with "Britain" against other countries rather than, for instance, common international working-class identities. Williams emphasized the "constitutive" features of culture. Using semiotic language, he claims that cultural activities are not "simply derived from an otherwise constituted social order but are themselves major elements in its constitution" (1981:13). Elsewhere he notes that Marxism includes culture in the superstructure, whereas he insists it is a "constitutive social process" (R. Williams, 1977:19).

This emphasis on the place and nature of culture produces what for a while was a significant split in critical cultural studies: the **culturalists** versus the **structuralists**. Hall's description of this split has been influential in laying out the debate. In dividing the scholarship into these two camps (while acknowledging differences within the two groups as well as the on-going "political economy" view of some Marxists in which economics determine historical events), Hall (1980b) portrayed the culturalists as emphasizing the influence of culture and the validity of class "experience" or "structures of feeling." Structuralists (influenced by Althusserian Marxism) did consider culture as having effects but viewed experience with suspicion. Experience was not an authentic class attribute; rather, it was an effect of structures and relations and was caught up heavily within dominant ideology. This version of the differences surged through the scholarship on critical cultural studies (see Curran, Gurevitch, and Wollacott, 1982; S. Becker, 1984; K. Jensen, 1987) and produced two subsequent lines of inquiry: how to understand agency and pleasure. As Richard Johnson puts it (in a structuralist version), this is the problem of "'the education of desire'" (1979b:212).

Hall's outline of the debate concluded with his own assessment of both positions. While he appreciated culturalists for asserting a belief in consciousness in the political struggle, he tended to side with structuralists in their elaborations of ideology and questions about any authenticity to consciousness. Still, that Althusser had underpinned his portrayal of interpellation with Lacanian theory troubled Hall, who viewed Lacan's theory as a "trans-historical" and "universal" assertion. Moreover, making this move created the unconscious (and subsequently language) as the primary site of contradictions (hardly a very Marxist position). Hall and others involved with the CCCS granted that Althusser's theory might "constitute a necessary (but not sufficient) precondition for a materialist theory of ideology," but it needed to be fleshed out into historical and social contexts (Chambers et al., 1977/78:116). Along with agency and pleasure, this becomes a third agenda for critical cultural studies: historicizing culture.

All three matters still occupy the foreground of critical cultural studies. For the problem of agency and consciousness, the notion of hegemony helped mediate the original split (Turner, 1990:31–32). Turning to Gramsci's description of how ideologies can appeal to individuals, even against their own best interests, the concept of hegemony offered a sort of compromise position regarding why individuals would take up ideas that did not help their own subordinated class difficulties. The problem of pleasure will run through the scholarship, and I shall return to it later. And historicizing interpellation has reinforced how hegemony works. Specifically, Johnson writes, "One of our own recurrent arguments . . .

[with culturalists and the idea of a "whole way of life"] will be to stress the heterogeneity or complexity of 'working-class culture,' fragmented not only by geographical unevenness and parochialisms, but also by the social and sexual divisions of labor and by a whole series of divisions into spheres or sites of existence" (1979b:62).

Thus, the influence of identity politics—theorizing how the subject constructs a self with variable pertinent identities—produces an exceptionally complex social and political scene. In fact, class may seem to disappear when individuals align along other markers of difference. Identity politics also opens avenues to understanding groups and political alliances. (I return to this in chapter 6.)

These developments in thinking about the subject provided openings for a certain amount of self-consciousness within the structures of ideology; they could justify a limited agency in relation to texts and their potential effects. One of the most long-lasting notions in this research is Hall's encoding/decoding model of communication. Working from a structuralist angle but trying to avoid what he viewed as the errors of a rigid interpellation thesis, Hall criticized the empiricism of behavioral psychology and the transmission model of mass communication because they did not include social contexts of decoding, which he labeled "frameworks of knowledge" (1980c:128–30). Messages are polysemic but "not totally pluralistic" (Turner, 1990:91). "If there were no limits, audiences could simply read whatever they liked into any message" (Hall, 1980c:135).

Hall theorizes that people respond to messages in three general ways: (1) the "dominant-hegemonic" (often also called the preferred) way, in which individuals read and experience the text as the makers had hoped they would; (2) the negotiated way, in which individuals work around problems in the text in order to find their own meanings or pleasures; and (3) the "globally contrary" or oppositional way, in which individuals simply reject the meanings hoped for by the producers and put the message into "some alternative framework of reference" (e.g., a feminist reading "against the grain"; Hall, 1980c:136–38; Morley, 1980a:20–21, traces this ideological framework division to Parkin, 1971). Hall goes on to clarify that in the case of negotiated readings, "selective perception" might explain apparent failure to read the text as preferred, but " 'selective perception' is almost never as selective, random or privatized as the concept suggests. The patterns exhibit, across individual variants, significant clusters. Any new approach to audience studies will therefore have to begin with a critique of 'selective perception' theory" (Hall, 1980c:135).

This model of audience decoding as well as the call for explanations for patterns of alternative readings form a major paradigm of how to research audiences. What was clear was the rejection by both critical cultural studies groups of structural-functional sociology and mass communication research (Hall, 1980a). Findings from this research will appear in the following chapters. However, a couple of notable examples merit attention in this overview.

One is Tony Bennett's essay "Text and Social Process: The Case of James Bond" (1982). Whereas Hall employs poststructuralist language theory, Bennett furthers the application and links critical cultural studies with Jacques Derrida's deconstruction and the symptomatic textual analysis methods created by Pierre Macherey (1966), who applied structuralist Marxism to the production of literature. Bennett describes this textual method as understanding a text as "totally iterable; that, as a set of material notations, it may be inscribed within different contexts and that no context—including that in which it originated—can enclose it by specifying or fixing its meaning or effect for all time and in all contexts" (Bennett, 1982:5). This point provides the theoretical basis for the proposition that "*no* text [is] behind or beyond the diverse forms in which it is materially produced" (6, emphasis in original), which is to say that, in the abstract, any interpretation is possible. This is also to say, however, that contemporary circumstances may affect the range of possible readings. Thus, Bennett notes, "'Untutored' readings are just as real and material in their effects as 'tutored' ones and may, indeed, be considerably more influential" (9). This is a typical concern for a critical cultural studies scholar. What accounts for actual (as opposed to hypothetical) engagements, and what might this mean for social effects?

Using "James Bond" as a "portable signifier capable of being inscribed within an almost infinite variety of contexts" (Bennett, 1982:3), Bennett and Janet Woollacott (1987) attempt a historical treatment for this fictional figure within British politics. The study describes the preferred meanings within potential ideologically complicit processes in producing the nation and a conservative social agenda. Yet, despite the promises of the theory, the actual study remains a symptomatic reading of texts joined by the common term of "Bond," with some discussion of the sex of readers and their interpretations of various transformations of the text. The project indicates the "encrustations" of a text, another premise Bennett stresses, and this notion has enjoyed further applications. Using the work of Hans Robert Jauss, Bennett writes about the "pre-existing horizon of interpretations" (Bennett, 1982:6) that also influences readers' reception of texts and signifiers. This horizon of expectations seems similar to Hall's "framework of knowledges," and both are generally the basis for my insistence on context as the best explanation for what happens during the experience of a text (Staiger, 1992).

Another notable application of the encoding/decoding model is David Morley's ongoing research on television. From the mid-1970s, the CCCS had produced ethnographic studies of groups of individuals (Turner, 1990:131–80; see Hall and Jefferson, 1976). In 1978, Charlotte Brunsdon and Morley published an extensive symptomatic textual analysis of the British television program *Nationwide* for the purpose of establishing a "base line" for further studies "against which differential readings may be posed" (1978:v). Brunsdon and Morley wrote from a structuralist critical cultural studies position and assumed that *Nationwide*'s ideological goal was coherency, although that apparent coherency may not be fully in the employ of the state (Morley, 1980a:9–10). Morley then followed up in 1980 with an analysis of audiences for the program. Postulating that variability of interpretations was possible, Morley explains in his postscript to the study that the deviations he discovered seemed dependent on the "need-gratification structure of the decoder" (10). He states that this is not the same as a uses-and-gratifications hypothesis because (1) his social theory is critical rather than structural-functional (he assumes power differentials), and (2) his theory is social instead of psychological. "What is needed here [in the future] is an approach which links differential interpretations back to the socio-economic structure of society, showing how members of different groups and classes, sharing different 'cultural codes,' will interpret a given message differently, not just at the personal, idiosyncratic level, but in a way 'systematically related' to their socio-economic position" (12–15).

He refined the method further in *Family Television* (1986). Going into the homes of his subjects, he observed how interpretations and uses of the programs' materials occurred in "real" situations (Morley, 1986:14). The eventual analysis produced more information on sex and sex role differences than class ones, in part because Morley's sampling was mostly from a white lower-middle class to unemployed sector of South Londoners. However, the more significant implications were how the social situation may mediate any media effects from television. In family viewing, the father has great power to determine what is watched. Watching TV, moreover, is not a passive but a very active event. As Hall notes in his introduction to Morley's report, "Viewing is almost always accompanied by argument, comment, debate and discussion," and "the comment, far from destroying pleasurable identification, seems to be actually part of the pleasure." This family interaction "can forge solidarities, establish alliances between family members or just provide a much-needed excuse for cuddling up" (Morley, 1986:9). Morley's findings also include his emphasis on the multiple identities that an individual marshals up in any viewing experience: "We are not 'viewers' with a single identity, a monolithic set of preferences and repetitive habits of viewing. . . . We are all, in our heads, several different audiences at once" (Hall in Morley, 1986:10).

Scholars have criticized the model of three types of decoding—preferred, negotiated, or oppositional—for a number of reasons: (1) television and other texts do not necessarily reproduce dominant ideology in any coherent sense, so determining a preferred meaning is difficult; (2) a tendency exists to assume classes are unitary and unaffected by other identities and pleasures, making difficult the slotting of actual readings into one of the three categories (Morley, 1980b:172); (3) to read in a resistant manner assumes knowing the preferred interpretation (Maltby, 1986:22); (4) no evidence exists that an oppositional reading gives an individual any real social agency (Morley, 1992:29–32) or produces any social change; (5) as Hall himself (1989:273) notes, the model does not consider the decentered subject and pleasure; (6) oppositional might be defined anywhere from reading differently than expected to not reading at all; and (7) ultimately, then, most readings are "negotiations" (Hall, 1989:265). Thus, the system provides little felicity in describing what is occurring in any viewing event (Staiger, 2000b:31–32; also see Staiger, 1992:73, for an alternative model).

Although the schemata of three types of decoding produced a system of categorizing audience responses that has become fraught with problems, Morley's and others' research describing group viewing activities has produced important subsequent lines of inquiry. Scholars are now looking at the history of reading in groups (Long, 1993). As well, this perspective informs consideration of the television talk show (Livingstone and Lunt, 1994). A fascinating contribution that combines structural-functional and critical approaches is Daniel Dayan and Elihu Katz's *Media Events* (1992). The authors work from the proposition that a live broadcast media event may be a rite of passage (à la Turner). In some instances when the event can be predicted, the occasion is further transformed through turning it into a "festive" occurrence. People are invited to come to a single location (a home, a bar) and to be prepared in some ways (for example, to experience a particular emotion); large numbers of viewers are gathered; even if the viewers are scattered into smaller viewing pockets, a sense of a virtual community may exist; and the viewers are "focused"—despite all the discussion that may happen during the broadcast. Dayan and Katz write that different types of events (such as contests, conquests, or coronations) produce variable interactions (respectively, judging, witnessing, or pledging allegiance), although each interaction also has the possibility of being a preferred, negotiated, or oppositional response.

This sort of research has great potential for political analysis, as Dayan (1998) has neatly described in relation to diasporic groups. He points out that while scholars might consider global media systems valuable in maintaining homeland ties, another possibility is the construction of nationalisms and ethnicisms, which need to be studied carefully for their political implications. Indeed, the processes of identity building through discussions from viewing films and television participate in creating civil society. Combining this with narratology and applying it to two political crises in the United States, Jeffrey Alexander and Ronald Jacobs consider how narratives of "events and crises" may facilitate "the imaginative construction and reconstruction of more diffuse, but equally important collective identities and solidarities" (1998:23).

Other sorts of research developed from the CCCS's emphasis on social theory and ethnographically informed studies of people. Alongside Hall and Morley is Dick Hebdige, who is known for his study of youth cultures. Hebdige's work (1979, 1988) is a good example of how critical cultural studies would approach the matter of subcultures differently than the deviance theory of structural-functional cultural studies. Hebdige takes as a major influence the semiotics of Saussure and the anthropology of Lévi-Strauss. Considering working-class British youth as an oppositional subculture, he describes how clothing, behavior, and musical preferences of groups are both a bricolage and a structural homology that has internal consistency. Style sends a message; it is a signifying practice. Moreover, subcultural groups often speak to other groups as much as to the dominant culture.

Hebdige's work fits within the CCCS's articulation of culture, including "'maps of meaning' which make things intelligible to its members"

(Clarke et al., 1976:10). Moreover, Hebdige approaches youth as a class matter, not merely as a generational disjunction. The CCCS and other critical cultural studies scholars have been particularly attentive to the potential "othering" of subcultural groups as "deviant" (experiencing role dissonance) rather than representing their activities as due to structural inequities (facing power inequities). In *Resistance through Rituals*, CCCS authors chart relationships between media and social groups that wish to control nonconforming behavior (Clarke et al., 1976:75–79), and the authors develop a strand of research that critiques "moral panics" as symptomatic engagements with subordinated cultures. Hebdige (1979:94) not only discusses the demonization of subordinated groups but also describes another strategy for neutralizing the effects of these groups: incorporation through commodification.

Hebdige's work has been notable, but modifications of his conclusions have been necessary. Ken Gelder describes three concerns about *Subculture*. One is that not all subcultures are as spectacular in style as those Hebdige examined. Another is the need for a more complicated view toward the mass culture that is the source for the youths' signifiers. The third is the avoidance of assuming that subcultures are "authentic, original and vulnerable to incorporation into mass cultural production" (1997:146–47). These cautions are part of the sophistication of the critical cultural studies project.

Beyond providing an alternative to studying youth cultures, critical cultural studies has addressed other long-standing matters of media interpretation and effects, usually taking a mediation slant. For example, David Buckingham offers a different model for considering whether violent images in the media distress or impair children. Shifting the question from "effects" to how children "*perceive and make sense of [television violence]*" (1996:5, emphasis in the original), he stresses that children's interpretations and any effects are much more complicated as a result of their definitions of violence. How children respond will be influenced by input. In his conclusions, Buckingham proposes that parents discuss with children what they understand as real and disturbing while realizing that at different ages children work with media through varied conventional systems.

John Fiske has also dealt with television. Along with John Hartley, he proposes a theory of TV as "bardic," in which it serves cultural needs by addressing groups rather than individuals, providing oral, not literate, communication, offering a "centering discourse," and thus reproducing dominant "myths and ideologies" (Turner, 1990:102). This bardic model stands in contrast to Newcomb and Hirsch's cultural forum model of the medium: unlike the cultural forum view, the bardic model gives little agency to viewers. However, as Fiske develops his research, his faith in the potential for resistance has produced some of the most optimistic interpretations of what happens when subordinated groups encounter media texts with the potential openness that he considers television to have. Fiske stresses the evidence of this in readers enjoying irony, jokes, and excess in variable ways (1986; 1987:85). Fiske's view assumes media specificity; given that, readers with different identities will respond to aspects of the text. Thus, his model of effects is a mediation one.

Because of its initial recognition of class as significant in analysis, critical cultural studies has broached how national identities become involved in audience experiences of texts. An important study is Ien Ang's *Watching "Dallas"* (1982). In this investigation of the worldwide popularity of *Dallas*, Ang solicited letters from viewers and analyzes them symptomatically. Turning to Pierre Bourdieu's work on social distinctions and cultural capital, Ang postulates that if people recognize and enjoy in *Dallas* a tragic structure of feeling, they have a melodramatic imagination, tending to see the world as black and white and hoping for poetic justice to conclude the story lines. However, readers can negotiate or resist this experience by appealing at times to their ironical or critical knowledge of U.S. mass culture to criticize others engaged in the program and as a defense against their own enjoyments. Ang makes linkages to national contexts to sort out the responses.

Critical cultural studies has received its share of criticisms. An early one came from female members of CCCS who observed that *male* working-class youth occupied the attention of the scholars. This sex bias had a basis in larger social ideologies that considered young women were irrelevant to the economic scene; they worked in the home, and that did not count in the standard analyses of productivity. In their 1976 essay, Angela McRobbie and Jenny Garber expand on this bias. Since girls are "structurally subordinated," their experience is not similar to that of boys, who may be marginalized as youth but anticipate moving into the dominant class. To exemplify this, McRobbie and Garber point out that even when girls are involved in youth subcultures, they are subordinated through functioning primarily in sexual roles. They ask, "Do girls have alternative ways of organizing their cultural life?" (1976:219). Additionally, Andrea Press points out that some of the CCCS discussions assume "that resistance is rationally expressed," (1991:22), something feminist studies seldom presume. These comments have enlivened youth studies and feminism (which had also tended to ignore generational differences in its theorizing).

Other criticisms of critical cultural studies involve not only the problems of sorting readings into preferred, negotiated, and oppositional categories but treating all members of a group as if they were the same. Rather, people have multiple identities. Moreover, subcultural or other minority groups still function as groups—with all the potential for hierarchies and power differentials to develop (Gelder, 1997:146). For political economists, critical cultural studies fails to deal adequately with "economic, social or policy" issues (Ferguson and Golding, 1997a:xiii–xiv).

Finally, quandaries with human subject research exist. Ethnography as a method of gathering information has been targeted with accusations of elitism and unacknowledged subjectivity, as I noted in chapter 1. Motivations for studying subcultures may include a sort of fascination with the other, as well as a patronization of these groups. As Valerie Walkerdine asks in a self-examination of her method, is an implicit incentive of the scholarship to "'save' 'the masses' from the pleasures of imaginary wish fulfillment" (1986:168)? Bennett attempts to find an ethical standard to answer this. He suggests that the judgment derive from the intended use. Is the reason for the research to objectify the audience for the purpose of commercial gain (including publishing academic articles), or is it to secure knowledge helpful to providing agency for those studied (1996:149–50)?

Cultural studies in either the structural-functional or critical variety has first of all been interested in cognitive relations between individuals and media texts. However, like the revised social-psychoanalytical and cognitive theories, understanding and evaluating pleasure in relation to experiences and affects has occupied significant theorizing in the past decade. Where pleasure, affect, and taste exist in the model of media interpretation and effects is a significant contemporary problem. Structural-functional cultural studies tends to reinforcement and mediation propositions; critical cultural studies produces mostly mediation models of the relations between individuals and media texts.

Pleasure and Other Emotions

One of the major debates among revised social-psychoanalytical theory, cognitive psychology/syllogistic reasoning, and cultural studies is not how to handle the diversity of cultural experiences and social-psychological lives of spectators but how to explain affective and emotional responses to moving images. While linguistic theory did not offer any guidance to this, psychoanalysis's focus is primarily on that part of the life of an individual as it develops in relation to representations the individual creates of the world that is experienced. Pleasure, desire, anxiety: these are fundamental terms for psychoanalytical investigation. Cognitive psychology began as an attempt to explain how people organize conceptual information, but the matter of emotion was there from the start. Standard AI imaginings of what would count as a machine "thinking" included features of empathy, and science fiction forecast both the triumph and the dread of such an outcome (see *2001: A Space Odyssey* [1968]). Cultural studies has always had to reckon with pleasure and emotional responses intervening in cultural "maps of meaning."

In recent decades, the literature in several fields has addressed what writers variously refer to as affects, emotions, feelings, or sentiments. Each of these terms has different connotations. For my purposes here, I will generally be considering affects and emotions as distinguished by Birgitta Höijer: affects are natural "reactions present at birth or shortly thereafter, like surprise, joy, anger, fear, contempt and disgust," whereas emotions are more complex and develop in relation to "experiences of persons, objects, events and situations." Emotions include "love, anxiety and so forth" (1992:285).

As I shall discuss later, scholars are now aware of the cultural and historical dimensions to both affects and emotions. The recognition of the social construction of even so-called natural affects is partly due to feminist and cultural studies work on what social formations try to privilege as better. As Alison Jaggar points out, Plato and others held that emotions could be dangerous, even "subversive of knowledge." Reason, not emotion, was the way to understanding. In this formulation, reason is contrasted with emotion, making reason "the mental, the cultural, the universal, the public, and the male," whereas emotion is "the irrational, the physical, the natural, the particular, the private, and, of course, the female" (1989:145). Besides noting the sexing of the opposition, Catherine Lutz (1990:69–70) has studied discourses about emotion and points out that much of the time individuals talk about trying to "control" emotions. Both Jaggar and Lutz discuss how much current research indicates that emotions are interlaced with, and crucial, in reasoning and knowledge, and they emphasize that the regulation of emotion may be part of sex, race, and other cultural biases. Other scholars such as Lauren Berlant (1998) have also criticized normative cultural imperatives that produce a hierarchy of emotions: for example, failing to experience intimacy seems a personal flaw. Studying emotions is also avoided because they seem difficult to study (Plantinga and Smith, 1999a:1). If reasoning is interior, emotion seems even more subjective.

Discriminating against or within emotion is also evident in attitudes about specific cultural products. Neal Nehring (1997:xi) considers how aesthetic theory has linked emotional appeals to "the low or popular arts produced by the marketplace," suggesting a degraded experience. Or some contemporary critical theory assumes commercial interests have co-opted "natural" emotions, and this somehow makes affective and emotional experiences inauthentic (as though other encounters with popular arts are authentic). Following findings I am about to describe, Nehring argues that emotions are related to rational situations and may have very important political uses.

As early as 1972, literary scholars questioned the only recent hardnosed scientism then dominating textual analysis. Harold Pagliaro (1972) criticized W. K. Wimsatt and M. C. Beardsley's dictum against letting affect be involved in an analysis and evaluation of a poem. Pagliaro pointed out that it would be difficult to know if unconscious emotions were influencing interpretations and that, at any rate, subjectivity was assumed to have been part of the genesis of the poem. Excluding it in the analysis, being totally "scientific," was nonsensical. In another debate, Jauss (1974) argues against Adorno that emotional experiences of identification and catharsis are prerequisites for rational distance and aesthetic pleasure. Emotion precedes and permits reasoning.

For theories of media interpretation and effects, affects and emotions have had ambivalent positions. Most theories assume a bias against feelings, seeing them as a means of either reinforcing dominant messages or weakening resistance to bad images. Supposedly emotions seduce spectators. Even in a mediation model, a general suspicion permeates discussion of individuals seeking pleasure or gratification through media use. This is likely due to the strong cultural prejudice against consumption as distinct from production. As recent queer theory has noted, U.S. culture overwhelmingly privileges the latter. Thus, even when uses-and-gratification models recognize entertainment functions for media, questions arise about excessive use of television and film for these purposes. On the contrary, no one seems to worry much about extravagant amounts of media time devoted to work or study.

The place of affects and emotions in relations between media and spectators has required attention. For the social-psychological theory, based as it is on psychoanalysis, general discussion of some emotions is embedded in the descriptions of how individuals associate concepts and process information. Psychoanalysis assumes emotion is interwoven with cognition. Nearly any essay using this approach will discuss matters such as desire or anxiety, identification or dread. One useful example because of its particularity of detail is an essay by Linda Williams (1991) that combines psychoanalytical theory, variable emotions, and genres. In "Film Bodies," she follows up on a remark by Richard Dyer (1985:27) that "gross" movies are ones in which effects of the film may literally involve a bodily response. These sorts of texts are pornography (in the best case, an orgasm), horror (a physical turning away from the screen), and melodrama (tears). Connecting the three genres to structures of fantasy, she argues that each one provides a scenario for the spectator for, respectively, questions of sexual desire (the fantasy of seduction), sexual difference (the fantasy of castration), and the origin of the self (the fantasy of the family romance or a return to the origin). Psychoanalytical fantasies are utopian problem-solving narratives, and these genres participate in providing that story and resolution for the spectator—hence their pleasure, even in instances when a sadomasochistic pain also is involved.

Psychoanalytical theory has always focused on how emotions affect cognition and vice versa. By the 1990s, cognitive psychologists and media scholars were also addressing the matter of emotion. In their book *Passionate Views,* Carl Plantinga and Greg Smith (1999b) describe four psychological theories of affect and emotion: peripheral, central-neural physiological, cognitive appraisal, and social construction. At least the latter two suit well a contemporary cognitive psychological theory of affects and emotions. The cognitive appraisal approach considers how "emotions arise as a result of the way in which the situations that initiate them are construed by the experiencer" (Ortony, Clore, and Collins, 1988:1). In media studies, an example of this might be Dolf Zillmann's thesis (1991b) that suspense in a film derives from a spectator's empathy and moral reasoning or judgment in relation to the actions of the protagonist and villain.

A social construction approach would postulate a greater weight to socially derived codes of judgment. For example, one version is that cultures have "an indefinite number of emotions. That is, societies mould and shape many different emotions" (Crawford et al., 1992:33). Revising the cognitive appraisal approach, social constructionists emphasize that "emotions have objects" and "occur in specific contexts." While they give place to an individual's ability to self-appraise within the event, they also stress "social specificity," including socially constructed identities (33–35). A well-explained instance of an essay using this approach is Höijer's model (1992:290) of how people understand television narrative in which she includes not only standard schemata for conceptual interpretation but also an individual's "experience spheres," which affect and individuate the person emotionally.

From the general theory, media scholars using cognitive psychology then need to explain more specifically how emotional schemata become part of the spectator's repertoire for response. An extended application is Torben Grodal's *Moving Pictures: A New Theory of Film Genres, Feelings, and Cognition* (1997). Drawing on a typology of emotions, Grodal lays out how spectators should emotionally process various genres. Grodal, however, remains in the abstract—hypothesizing ideal spectators for each genre and emotion (also see Tan, 1996). As well, Carroll explores emotions in terms of the horror film, claiming "horror *also* essentially involves the emotional response of abhorrence, disgust, or revulsion in consequence of the monster's impurity" (1999:151, emphasis in original). The ground for Carroll's assertion about human response is the anthropological work of Mary Douglas and Edmund Leach on impurity.

Also turning to that discipline, Murray Smith invokes cultural anthropology's theory of "imagination" to give spectators both subjectivity and agency in which agency is a learned but quickly "automatized" goal orientation (1995:47–48). This feature to processing information may involve emotion as a combination of "affect and cognition" and explains for Smith spectatorial responses to characters within specific plot circumstances. Generally he avoids the notion of "empathy" to consider how texts solicit a "structure of sympathy" (60, 5). Viewers may align themselves with characters or even feel an allegiance.

So far, applications of cognitive psychologies involving affect and emotion parameters tend to run to the cognitive appraisal approach that implies a more individual psychology than the socially formed proposition of a social constructionist approach. Appeals to anthropology might create an opportunity for distinguishing responses in patterns related to social formations, but such a proposition needs to move from the general (e.g., an assumed cultural fear of impurities) to a specific analysis (why a culture constructs certain impurities as fearful). Given that a goal of media studies is understanding social and group processes, the particularity of a focus in its study of emotions is not surprising. As Jaggar describes it, the "dumb view" of emotions forwarded by positivists (behavioralists and likely those within Plantinga and Smith's categories of peripheral or central-neural physiological approaches) tried to separate emotions from what they were directed toward as well as how social evaluations came out of those emotional identities (Jaggar, 1989:148–53).

Cultural studies also has a continuing history of considering pleasure —as a potential means of both pacifying groups and urging group social action toward political goals. The examples are extensive, and, as they develop, more care is given toward claims. Mary Ellen Brown (1990a) concludes a study of women viewing television with the proposition that the social power in the interchange, if any exists, has nothing to do with "good" or "bad" representations of women but with the social aspects of talk among women about the representations. I have already mentioned Fiske's work in this area. While many compatriots believe he has a far too optimistic view of how pleasure can produce resistance from subordinated classes, Fiske has continually offered to cultural studies various theories of pleasure (1987:224–25).

Lawrence Grossberg has, too. In an essay about fans, Grossberg postulates that individuals use cultural objects to create "mattering maps" based on "affect" (defined by him as a "feeling of life"), "which direct our investments in and into the world; these maps tell us where and how we can become absorbed—not into the self but into the world—as potential locations for our self-identifications and with what intensities" (1992:57). According to Nehring's reading, Grossberg creates for affects "overarching structures or totalities" and derides affects as "inarticulate" expressions by fans that supplant actual political analyses (1997:47–53). The subtleties here are worth exploration, since they are intimately tied into propositions about media reception and effects.

Finally, the focus of cultural studies on youth cultures has involved many studies of popular music, a medium that is usually intimately tied to subjective feelings. Yet, as Sally Stockbridge cautions, any media theory that resides primarily on arguments based on vision and the gaze may have little to contribute to understanding even rock videos, which for fans invoke and involve "movement and dance" (1990:103) and plenty of affect.

While the examples that I have provided here suggest the sympathy with which cultural studies has dealt with theories of affect and emotion, I want to point out that recent critical anthropology has underscored "historicizing and contextualizing emotion discourse" (Abu-Lughod and Lutz, 1990:1). I have mentioned that emotion discourse can be biased, affecting negatively women and people of color (see examples in Jaggar, 1989:157–58) but also men. Additionally, as anthropologists have discovered, different cultures have emotions not easily equated with ones familiar to Anglo-American cultures. Moreover, the appropriateness of expressing emotions has changed. JoAnn Pavletich writes that at the turn of the twentieth century, "emotional inexpressivity" was expected for the dominant class (1998:57). Yet, in earlier periods, some emotional displays were obligatory. For example, Julie Ellison (1999) considers the functions of men weeping and "public emotion" in eighteenth-century literature.

The matter of history and emotion also leads to taste—which is intimately involved with affect and emotion. I mentioned Dyer's work from which Williams drew in her deliberation on gross genres. Dyer's initial essay (1985), which was about gay male pornography, underlined not only the emotional but also the cultural biases against media that appear more obviously to effect people. Tying an effect on the body to cultural positions of "low," Dyer displays the homology created with supposed intellectual effects and "high" culture. Taste is not an individual matter but socially sanctified (or not). This sort of recognition of how cultural products are imbued with affect and related to social distinctions has been widely discussed in the analyses of canons (in media studies, see as a start, Staiger, 1985).

The history of approaches to studying media interpretation and possible effects has produced increasingly developed propositions about how individuals operate alone and in groups with regard to media. The propositions at various points call up four general causal models—education, reinforcement, mediation, and power—to describe this relation. At almost every historical moment, most of the four models are in play within the scholarship. This is likely because fundamentally scholars hold different views of the general political and social environment. Are groups able to use checks and balances to secure needs, or are power relations exceptionally difficult to alter? Additionally, do individuals have agency? If so, of what kind? Once we determine the answers to these psychological, social, and political questions, answers to why people experience moving images and interpret as they do, and what the effects of that may be, will become possible.

4

Fans and Fan Behaviors

While all the theories of media interpretation and effects discussed in chapters 2 and 3 describe audiences and spectators in general, an area of special research has been fans and fan behaviors. This chapter reviews the general research on this topic, first describing some typical categories of fan behaviors and then reviewing explanations for this specialized mode of reception.

A Definition

In a survey of the source and use of the term *fan*, Daniel Cavicchi traces the word to at least three hundred years ago as a shortening of *fanatic* (1998:38–39; also see Jenkins, 1992b:12). The term disappeared but returned in the late 1800s in application to baseball enthusiasts. By the turn into the twentieth century, *fan* broadened to embrace multiple media, including movies. Scholars of film and television have tried, however, to define the term more rigorously and in doing so to imply explanations for the behavior. According to Henry Jenkins, a person is a fan "not by being a regular viewer of a particular program but by translating that viewing into some type of cultural activity, by sharing feelings and thoughts about the program content with friends, by joining a community of other fans who share common interests" (1988:88). Lawrence Grossberg also wants to limit the term from a general attraction to a media object to something more restricted. A fan has a particular "sensibility," an "affect or mood" that is a "feeling of life," an "investment" in something (1992:56–57). Grossberg believes that this affect has features of both quantity and quality and is "organized: it operates within and, at the same time, produces maps which direct our investments in and into the world; these maps tell us where and how we can become absorbed—not into the self but into the world—as potential locations for our self-identifications, and with what intensities" (57). These are "mattering maps."

Although what fans care about may have high value for them, their fandom often seems nonsensical to others. Scholars stress that taste cultures operate in making discriminations between official or high culture and fan culture. This helps produce pathological representations of fans. As Jenkins lists the depictions of fans, they run from "brainless," "infantile," and "feminized and/or desexualized" to "social misfits" and "unable to separate fantasy from reality" (Jenkins, 1992b:10; also see Hoberman and Rosenbaum, 1983:18–23, for examples of fans whose behavior might seem excessive). Joli Jensen (1992:9–10) agrees that pathologizing fans is a questionable representational move, pointing out that fans are contrasted unfavorably against academics and "aficionados or collectors" on the basis of the object of investment. Such binary thinking produces a stigmatization or a scapegoat, allowing some parts of the population to feel safe. She points out the "inherently conservative" elitism in this opposition.

Using Pierre Bourdieu's concept of cultural capital, John Fiske extends this social analysis beyond its class base into its potential intersections with "gender, race, and age" discriminations (1992:32). He notes that fan groups sometimes reproduce in their own communities the social hierarchy from which they are excluded. He also rescues fans, however, by declaring that official culture uses its information to discriminate or to "enhance or enrich the appreciation of the work," which increases the work's monetary worth, whereas fan culture uses its knowledge to participate in or to "'see through' the production process," which is not accessible to the nonfan (43).

Whether Fiske's optimistic view of fan activities is true in all cases, scholars trace the suspect fan behavior further back than the twentieth-century application of the term. Cavicchi notes that in the 1700s fans of literary authors "began sending letters to them, making pilgrimages to actual places mentioned in their books, and developing intense identification with the characters and settings of their various stories" (1998:5; see also Braudy, 1986:380–89, 481). Such involvement was, indeed, intense; in the mid-1800s baseball fans known as "kranks" would fight and even break up a game if it was not going their way. Serial fiction of the Victorian era produced large groups of people eagerly awaiting the next installment (Hayward, 1997:21). Followers of opera singers in the same era were equally devoted to their medium (Levine, 1988:108–9), and male theatrical stars were "matinee idols" to women audiences, with clubs for Harry Montague and Kyle Bellew as early as 1885 and public discussion from 1907 on of the focus by women on the male stars (Studlar, 1996:90–113). People eagerly sought souvenirs of Charles Lindbergh after his famous intercontinental flight (Braudy, 1986:23). Leo Braudy proposes that facilitators of this hero or celebrity worship after about 1880 included *Who's Who* (founded in 1898), photography, and mass media communications (491–98).

Already entrenched within other political and entertainment fields, people displayed what Jenkins and Grossberg define as fan behavior for U.S. films and broadcasting nearly as soon as movies and other mass media were widely available (Staiger, 1983). Even after radio ceased being a novel technology, people gathered at parties to listen to favorite programs (Butsch, 2000:215). At the first science fiction convention held in 1936, a fan "wore the first SF costume based on a visual media source —the Wells film *Things to Come*" (Bacon-Smith, 1992:9). Movies parodied female adolescent fans of movie stars as early as 1912 (Staiger, 1995:71). By the 1920s, people assumed a fan of movies to be of that sex and age (Scheiner, 2000:15–16). Movie magazines catered to fans, including publishing letters from them. Although research indicated that only a small segment of teens wrote to stars, in the early 1940s "nearly 90% of the fan mail studios received came from girls under 21" (Ohmer, 1991:12).

Finding star fandom of potential publicity value, movie studios supported it both by answering fan mail and by giving financial assistance to clubs that studios declared to be official. Georganne Scheiner indicates that one of the oldest national star fan clubs began in 1931, dedicated to Joan Crawford. These clubs developed local and international branches, and by the mid-1930s national "consortiums of fan clubs" held yearly conventions in Los Angeles (Scheiner, 2000:122–23; also see Thorp, 1939:96–102; Walker, 1970:250–51; deCordova, 1990:74–75). Scheiner (1998, 2000) has studied the Deanna Durbin Devotees, which was founded in 1937 after Durbin's first Universal film by four teenage women who produced a mimeographed newsletter, *Deanna's Journal*. Eventually three hundred locals existed, with Jay Gordon (a male) as president, membership cards, and club pins. A glossy magazine, *Deanna's Diary*, included studio photographs, a column by Durbin, "fan poetry or prose," and publicity about forthcoming movies. Durbin fans had privileges, including being allowed on the sets of films in progress. Scrapbooks and collections produced hierarchies of status among the community based on who had what memorabilia.

Like Durbin, Jeanette MacDonald also attracted young women fans. Mary Elizabeth Kracklauer (2000) reports that MacDonald's club members were mostly single working women with a high school or college education who spent much of their leisure time on their fan activities. They discussed MacDonald's fashions, created stories that were serialized in fan newsletters, and followed her from city to city during her concert tours in the 1940s. Club pins signaled "Jeanette's girls" and gave their wearers access to MacDonald in her dressing room after concerts. Thus a lively fan culture existed before television and the post–World War II increase in youth (and adult) leisure funds.

Types of Fan Behavior

The descriptions of pre-1950s movie fans contain most of the behaviors attributed to fan cultures. Detailing each of these more specifically will indicate where research remains to be accomplished and what debates exist in fan studies.

Jenkins's definition of a fan includes notions of particular behaviors, which he expands into five fan action categories (1992a:209–13; 1992b:277–80). These categories are useful ways for arranging this information, although I will add a sixth one. Jenkins's first category is **the adoption of "a distinctive mode of reception."** Most people select the film, television program, or performer they will watch on the basis of whatever is available. Bruce Austin's analysis (1981a) of audience movie selection is helpful to fan studies, since he organizes twenty-eight reasons for why college students attend movies into eight general categories and then compares these with how friends' comments influenced students' movie choice.

Fans, however, are much more purposeful in their consumption. They are attentive to the forthcoming arrival of a favored text or performer. They will be first to buy tickets and will plan to videotape. If the text is a serial program, they will view "faithfully." And they will rewatch. J. Hoberman and Jonathan Rosenbaum record the current world record in repeat viewings of a movie as of 1983: "Mrs. Myra Franklin, a Welsh woman is said to have sat through 940 screenings of *The Sound of Music*" (1983:16).

Rules exist that govern what fans should do during the movie, TV show, or performance. For films or TV, no talking occurs during the experience (Jenkins, 1988:88). For music, rituals of response are normal, such as routine responses to songs among Bruce Springsteen fans (Cavicchi, 1998:90–95).

The second of Jenkins's categories of behavior is **the constitution of "*a particular interpretive community*."** Fans usually have developed a network of colleagues, and these groups discuss, debate, and, for newcomers, teach perceptions of variation among the formulas, explanations for aspects of the text or performance, and predictions of future encounters with it. Cavicchi indicates that Springsteen fans will characterize a specific album or concert within his entire output, working toward a proposition about an "evolution of the various characters and themes" (1998:115–16) that have already been identified as part of Springsteen's authorship. Additionally, they make "aesthetic associations" to the larger musical art world, "political associations" to "social injustices" to which Springsteen often refers, "biographical associations" to Springsteen's personal life, and "personal associations" to the fans' own lives (110–26).

Jenkins notes that when groups negotiate readings of texts, debating strategies involve referring to "primary text episodes, interviews with program producers, or general social and cultural knowledge" (1992a:211; also see 1992b:86–119). Fans seem to seek coherency (they try to resolve textual contradictions), and they desire "emotional realism" (Jenkins, 1992b:107). He does find differences between two groups that he studied. *Twin Peaks* viewers on alt.tv.twinpeaks (mostly males) did not use personal experiences to justify argumentative positions as did the female fans of *Star Trek* (1995:62). These observations about classifying and debating within fan interpretive communities are good starting points; more research needs to be done to consider how diverse communities place different weight on certain forms of evidence or reasoning when an interpretation is in flux.

Besides rules for interpreting in the group, differences among reading formations for the same object exist. Barbara Klinger (1986) points out that three reading formations existed for the film *Written on the Wind*: the academic, the industrial, and the mass cultural. These formations proliferate if one considers the variable identities from which fans might come to a text. John Tulloch and Jenkins considered two groups of fans for *Dr. Who*: tertiary-educated social science students and technological/professionals. Tulloch concluded that the students assumed political communication from the program, but the technological/professionals did not (1995:67–85). Beyond that, Australian fans, young mothers, literary science fiction fans, high school boys, and high school girls all found different features of the text to foreground. Another example of such variable reading formations, even among fans of the same object, is Martin Barker and Kate Brooks's study of the fans of *Judge Dredd* (1998). Finally, Erika Doss (1999) recounts with great detail the variety of approaches to Elvis Presley that might explain why his image has likely replaced Jesus' as the most common American public icon. Fans see Elvis as a saint, an ambiguous sexual symbol, a white American, and a victim.

Certainly the "sheer diversity of [a text's] various elements," as Matthew Bernstein remarks (1999:15) about the 1997 film *Titanic*, means something is there for diverse interests. For that film, Bernstein notes that just the group of reviewers found intriguing five aspects of the movie: the framing story, the romance plot, actor Leonardo DiCaprio, the spectacle of the ship and its sinking, and the "nostalgic appeal to history" (16).

Studies of what attracts people to a specific text are plentiful. Most fan studies try to focus on distinct features of a text or performer as part of any explanation of fan attraction. In one of the major early studies of an interpretive community of fans, Janice Radway (1984b:119–56) points out that the readers of romance fiction whom she studied had very specific requirements for the formula, including a desire for an intense focus on the two main characters and no triangular relations. Fans of *Twin Peaks*, however, were interested not in the program's formula (something of a mixture of melodrama, mystery, and science fiction) but in the program's violation of formulaic television. Additionally, recognizing intertextual allusions was a major draw for that text (Lavery, 1995b:5–6).

Analysis of the young women who repeatedly watched *Titanic* indicates that the fan base was primarily for star DiCaprio but that the formula of desire for the "wrong" boy and rebellion, which is a female "coming-of-age" story, was likely equally important (Nash and Lahti, 1999). In this case of fan attraction, however, the women had to contend with DiCaprio's publicly stated rejection of himself as an icon for teen girls. The women's interpretive strategies to handle this included acclaiming him as an actor (rather than a hunk), disassociating themselves from the rest of the "herd" of girls (the authors note the crowd and animal metaphors used to describe teen DiCaprio fans), acknowledging their respect for his concern, and using other fans' interests to validate their own.

Part of the attraction of some texts or performances is fans' interest in or identification with characters or individuals. Although I will discuss in greater detail the problem of defining identification in chapter 5, here I would mention that research shows that identification affects interpretation. In a study of readings of *Coronation Street*, Sonia Livingstone (1990) found viewers clustered regarding whose side they were on, and that produced different views of motivations of various characters and evaluations of their actions.

Of course, most of this assumes something: that fans are semipurposeful in their media consumption. In studying readers of women's magazines, Joke Hermes concludes that not all readers read so intentionally. She raises the "fallacy of meaningfulness" (1995:16) but still claims that the habitual practice of magazine reading has other values for readers.

A third category of behavior proposed by Jenkins is **the constitution of "a base for consumer activism"** (1992b:278). This behavior is particularly in play when the fan text is unfinished because it is serially distributed. Hayward reports that reviewers of Charles Dickens's novels in serialization attempted to predict the ending of the text and even stated their "expectations about the way a plot should work" (1997:56). All parts should "weave" together, and poetic justice was a necessity. She indicates that evidence exists that Dickens responded to readers' commentary, altering the text in relation to their preferences (21–22).

In the case of contemporary television, fans make predictions based not only on textual information and senses of appropriate narrational outcomes but also on publicity about the production of the show that can provide reasons for temporary or permanent absences of actors (Hayward, 1997:186). Fans also use this extratextual information in other ways. They have orchestrated intense and highly organized campaigns to save favorite programs; a particularly successful example was the extension of *Cagney & Lacey* (D'Acci, 1994). Now an organization, Viewers of Quality Television exists to carry on organized audience campaigns (Brower, 1992; Harris, 1998).

More recently, fan preferences about plots, characters, and programming are visible not only to other fans but also to show personnel. Fans speculate (from good evidence) that serial program writers are now online, reading fan commentary in Internet chat rooms. Indeed, during the run of *Babylon 5,* its creator, J. Michael Straczynski, "correspond[ed] with fans on the internet but warn[ed] them not to discuss potential future plots lest he be sued for using any of their ideas" (Hunter and Kaye, 1997:9–10). However, this fan-author dialogue ultimately ended in hostility, with Straczynski withdrawing to a moderated list (Lancaster, 2001).

Fans constitute "a particular Art World" (1992a:211)—the fourth of Jenkins's categories of behavior. Fans make things. It is within this category that the scholarship insists on thinking about fans as not only consumers but also producers of culture, marking them out from just the general audience. I have already mentioned some fan productions: costumes, scrapbooks, newsletters, club insignia. Doss (1999:69–113) examines the construction of elaborate home altars to Elvis and Elvis rooms that seem to offer places of meditation for Presley fans. One major recent creative gesture is Web page building. Paintings and sculpture are common. Camille Bacon-Smith asked women involved in drawing illustrations based on science fiction texts about their motivations for choosing certain subjects. The women indicated their personal preferences for expressing some emotions or enjoying particular scenes was one factor. Financial recompense from sales at fan conventions was another reward, but one that then influenced their decisions in terms of what they believed would sell: idealized, romanticized images of certain characters (1992:69–73).

Fans operate within the constraints of a particular textual world. Part of the attraction to a movie or television program is the universe it offers. As Noy Thrupkaew puts it, art created within this constraint is an "ordered freedom" (2003:45). David Lavery speculates that *Twin Peaks* was successful in some measure because it was a " 'completely furnished world' " that permitted those involved to create trivia games, code words ("Peakspeak"), and quizzes (1995b:6). Fans now refer to these textual worlds as "-verses"—the Buffy-verse or the Zena-verse.

An area of fan art production that has attracted much scholarly focus is fan fiction, or fanfic, especially writing by women absorbed in *Star Trek,* but other universes have also produced this fiction (Jenkins, 1992b:162–77; Lancaster, 2001). Networks and systems of distribution are well developed among fans. Bacon-Smith distinguishes between zine and apa circulation (1992:44). A *zine* has a central editor who actually edits the journal; *apa,* or amateur press association, has a central collector of the material, but that person only collates for distribution to those submitting material.

Within a universe, formulas develop, and within formulas, hierarchies of status also have appeared. Bacon-Smith discusses several common stories within *Star Trek* writing, including the genesis of the "Mary Sue" formula (1992:94–102). Now somewhat lower in status, Mary Sue stories seem to be one of the first sorts of stories tried by new writers. These plots posit a smart, sometimes attractive, female who enters the textual world and saves the other protagonists, usually dying at the end of the story. Jenkins (1992b:162–77) provides an excellent list of the sorts of fiction produced. In his "Ten Ways to Rewrite a Television Show," he describes how fans expand given texts by providing new backstories for favored subordinated characters, shifting genres from adventure to romance, extending an unfinished subplot, and combining textual worlds by writing crossovers such as stories in which Dr. Who visits the *Planet of the Apes*.

"Slash" fiction has been of great interest. Written mostly by heterosexual women, slash stories posit a same-sex relation among male protagonists in some textual world. Called "hatstands" (which has connotations of homosexuality) in Britain, fan stories involving the two male leads in the BBC television program *The Professionals* appeared in the early 1980s. By 1993, fans had produced more than three thousand such stories and novels (Cicioni, 1998:157). Constance Penley states these had appeared in the United States "at least by 1976," and by 1991 had so proliferated that they produced "juried prizes (K/Star, Surak, and Federation Class of Excellence awards); . . . [a] house organ, *On the Double*; annual meetings . . . ; music videos (with scenes from *Star Trek* reedited for their 'slash' meanings); brilliant built-in market research techniques . . . ; and, increasingly, the elements of a critical apparatus, with its own theorists and historians" (1991:137–40; also see Green, Jenkins, and Jenkins, 1998). While the most famous pairs for slash fanfic are Kirk and Spock of *Star Trek*, Starsky and Hutch, Simon and Simon, Crockett and Tubbs (or Castillo from *Miami Vice*), numerous textual worlds have produced such fan efforts. Many of the stories are "first times" (Bacon-Smith, 1992:228–54) and for Kirk/Spock fiction have a formulaic narrative described by Jenkins as beginning with an initial relationship establishing some degree of desire, moving to a fear of rejection or self-accusations about proper masculinity and confessions between the two men, and concluding with "an erotics of emotional release and mutual acceptance" (1992b:215).

Although I shall expand on explanations for fan behavior later, it is worth noting that slash fiction has produced some specific debates. Penley (1991:154–59) believes that since science fiction has few females and the fan fiction often creates the males as androgynous, the stories are instances of fans making do with what they have. Additionally, the stories express a desire for a "retooling" of masculinity in the future in which men learn how to express their emotions. Jenkins (1992b:218–19) disagrees with her; he believes the fiction is a stronger critique of traditional masculinity. Bacon-Smith (1992:236–54) postulates that the fiction is sexually exciting for the women writers. Moreover, because the women identify with both characters, this fictional arrangement allows them to both be one man and have the other man. Finally, she notes that it is difficult to create a credible strong female character, so the men are surrogates for women in a relationship that has equality and good communication. Mirna Cicioni adds that the issues about equity may involve "the writers' tensions about heterosexual relations" (1998:155). Thrupkaew extends Bacon-Smith's views: "Slash enables its writers to subvert TV's tired male/female relationships while interacting with and showing mastery over the original raw material of a show (key for all fanfic)" (2003:42). Thrupkaew claims that such fiction produces a "richer sense of possibility than duplicating the well-worn boy/girl romances coughed up by most TV shows." She also thinks the fiction displays a strong feminist gesture: "They're not only laying claim to images of men but reconfiguring male behavior—a powerful way to make men their own, too" (42). As Thrupkaew argues, likely no single thesis covers all this behavior; rather, individuals are writing the fiction from the basis of several of these motivations.

Some members of the fan community dislike slash fiction, and Bacon-Smith describes working through other formulas before coming to it. Those who reject the genre dislike homosexuality, dislike pornography, think the fiction is unrealistic within the universe, and believe the fans should develop women characters instead (1992:222). However, slash fiction continues to be produced despite the disapproval by some members of the fandom. Furthermore, other sexually explicit materials are created. "Spooge" is like slash fiction but consists of "erotic stories or art in cartoon fandom" (Mikulak, 1998:204). Some of the art is homage, making explicit innuendos played upon in the original material; other work is satirical—going after firms such as Disney, which fans view as repressing their creativity through lawsuits against fans using its trademark material. The Internet has made distribution of such work exceptionally easy.

Fans also create "hackfic" or "suckfic." Those who dislike someone's creative works may hack the story, writing commentary that satirizes the original piece. When queried about the practice, these fans seem to be frustrated by what they think is "bad" writing or fiction that does not show a "true" understanding of the textual verse. Such hacking creates hierarchies among fans, marginalizes those hacked, and produces codes of fan conduct in the subculture (Carruthers, 2004).

Fan productivity includes not only fiction writing and art but also "filking" (creating songs), videos and music videos (reediting video material), and role-playing. Songs are sung solely and in groups at conventions, and people also produce music videos (Jenkins, 1992b:223–49). Mary Desjardins (1995) describes one fan video that has entered the canon of queer art: *Meeting Two Queens* (Cecilia Barriga, 1991), which combines footage from films starring Greta Garbo and Marlene Dietrich. While the video suggests a lesbian affair between the women (akin to slash fiction), Desjardins points out that it also works because of extra-textual information indicating real-life lesbian or bisexual preferences for both women. Moreover, the video plays with lesbian culture and creates Garbo as a butch and Dietrich as a femme. This might be viewed as out-ing the women, but Desjardins interprets the video to be more of a fantasy scenario for its audiences. A star system of these artists is developing (Jenkins, 1992a:215–31; also 1992b:250–76).

Costumes and games based on the universes allow fans to become the characters. Making costumes either for actual people or for action figures occupies many fans. Additionally, official products and fan-created fantasy games are very popular, and the growth of video and online gaming is noteworthy. Two types of role-playing exist. One is a sort of "hack-and-slash" fantasy that includes violence, leading to capturing treasure. The other is "character interaction and development" within the confines of specified characteristics, which allows improvisation and group development of story lines (Lancaster, 2001:xxiv; also see Hills, 2002:158–71). Fans police these universes for violations of credibility and taste, but most creative extensions are encouraged.

I would like to add a fifth category of behavior: **the extension of fan partialities into everyday living.** Bacon-Smith remarks that the women fans she met and studied fill their rooms and homes with fan-related material, sometimes pushing themselves out of their own living space. Two Presley fans have turned their entire home into Graceland Two—a mimicry of Presley's mansion that is open to fan visits twenty-four hours a day (Doss, 1999). Collections of material—books, videos, photos, everyday items such as cups with star images—make up a part of the physical world that a fan experiences in daily living. Fans of Springsteen and other musicians have a thriving exchange of bootlegged concert material and unreleased tapes (Cavicchi, 1998:74–76). Movie buffs collect multiple versions of films, and recent DVD technology provides these people with much insider information on alternative digital tracks (Klinger, 2001:132–51). Fans of TV programs indulge in massive tape exchanges to develop full collections of a show's episodes. Fiske believes that "collecting is also important in fan culture but it tends to be inclusive rather than exclusive"; he says fans operate on the principle of "as many as possible" (1992:44). This is certainly an area of research that deserves more exploration (see Staiger, forthcoming).

Collecting is one extension of the favored world into a fan's daily living, but others exist. Helen Taylor (1989:27–44, 220) describes women who were admirers of *Gone with the Wind*. They not only collected memorabilia but also named children and pets after characters in the book and film and took pilgrimages to Atlanta, Georgia. Visits to Presley's Graceland make his home the second most popular house tour in the United States after the White House (Doss, 1999:2). The practice of traveling to spots named in favorite fictional texts goes back two hundred years. Still, what draws people to some places rather than others is worth study. Roger C. Aden (1999:219–21) describes the phenomenon of people going to Dyersville, Iowa, to visit the Kinsella baseball field immortalized in *Field of Dreams*. Fans also take trips to contact stars and celebrities, or to visit and leave gifts at their homes (Cavicchi, 1998:60–72). Joshua Gamson (1994:140) believes the reason for this attempt to make personal contact is to confirm stars' authenticity. Matt Hills (2002:144–51) believes it is to make objective the text and perhaps even to enter it. He describes going to Vancouver to see *X-Files* being filmed.

People take their fiction seriously. Reception studies is developing histories of how earnestly people respond to texts in modes beyond their primary positions as fans. For example, mail to Frank Capra in the 1940s indicates that audiences viewed themselves as political subjects in the nation, with opinions about his movies and their relation to current affairs (Smoodin, 1996:111–29). Other research details audiences' vocal responses, fistfights, and exits from films before the end of a movie because they disagreed with the film's apparent political message (A. Ross, 1989). Martin Barker's research on *Judge Dredd* produced a response from one self-described "fascist." This individual indicated that he reads the comic for its "sociological" basis, and he and his friend avidly discuss possible social organizations based on scenarios within the universe of Dredd. Barker describes this as a "search for an ethical ideal" (1997b:28).

The political identity of fans is one overlapping subject position; Cavicchi finds some Springsteen fans describe their activities more as a religion than as fandom (1998:8). In fact, some people have reported paranormal relations to their objects of attachment. Stephen Hinerman (1992) has examined stories from people who claim to have experienced encounters with Elvis Presley—after his death. Analyzing the narratives these people tell, Hinerman concludes that Elvis is figured as a guide for resolving a trauma (also see Doss, 1999). Obviously, fandom exceeds the boundaries of being a leisure activity.

A sixth category of behavior, from Jenkins, is **the constitution of "an alternative social community"** (1992a:213). Fan clubs have always promoted group interactions, with all the sociological implications involved. Jenkins uses the term *alternative community* rather than *subculture* or *counterculture*. Given the ambiguities of definition as well as questions about whether fandom actually constitutes behavior that is not mainstream (perhaps today it is more mainstream than not), I shall follow Jenkins's terminology, acknowledging that the use of the word *alternative* does not imply nonnormative and, likewise, *community* is used loosely here.

Group interactions and shared activities are significant aspects of fan behavior. Internet technology has added another medium to in-person conversations, letters, and phone calls: methods used earlier to communicate and, from that, to form social orders that are labeled *communities* —although Hills (2002:175–82) cautions against seeing the Internet as merely a visible fan community. It is also a performance space for fans (see, for example, the hackfic described earlier in this chapter).

Talk of several sorts occurs among fans. Denise Bielby and C. Lee Harrington describe four kinds. One is *commentary*: "opinions or statements by viewers of what they find pleasurable, displeasurable, satisfying, or irritating" (1993:85). Such talk certainly establishes the interpretive community and opens the door to "'mutual self-disclosure' designed to initiate personal intimacy" (Jenkins 1992b:80, using theory from Deborah

Jones). Cavicchi notes that fans often tell each other "initiation narratives" (citing Bacon-Smith, 1992), although he prefers the term *conversion stories* for Springsteen fans. This is because, while for some people the fandom is an immediate, radical transformation, for others their involvement in Springsteen is a growing relationship that eventually involves proselytizing, using "him" for support, and is quite personal (Cavicchi, 1998:41–59). Commentary establishes group norms and deviations and may lead to inclusion and exclusion of members. In some instances, commentary also permits a performance such as "dishing" a program—providing sarcastic or campy commentary (Waits, 1997).

A second kind of talk is *speculation*: "gossip about a given program in terms of character development, story-line potential, plot twists, and so forth" (Bielby and Harrington, 1993:85). Extratextual knowledge can be presented here, especially about production of the text or events in the actors' and celebrities' lives. The third and fourth kinds of talk—*request* and *diffusion*—seem to me to constitute a pair. People ask for and receive information. Such exchanges create obligations and status. I believe a fifth kind of talk also occurs: *recognition* talk. This is the use of catchphrases or insider information that would identify the depth of knowledge that a "true" fan would know, creating a system of marking who does and does not belong to the fan community or establishing degrees of fan knowledge.

Thus, while talk is a basic cement for the community as a group, the community takes on features of any social unit. Individuals will adopt specific group roles, and, usually, hierarchies of status develop. Scholars have located some of the factors of status building: knowledge of information about the text or its production, knowledge of group norms or their history, articulation of or adherence to group taste preferences, leadership in group activities (Mikulak, 1998:201; A. MacDonald, 1998:136–39). Additionally, exclusion creates group identity. Fans distinguish between themselves and "mundanes" (Jenkins, 1988:88). In this opposition, fans "embrace pleasure; mundanes suppress or deny it." Fans are imaginative, childlike, doers, deeper thinkers; mundanes are shallow and shortsighted, adults, passive, and unaware (Jenkins 1992a:227–30).

Thus, if in the larger social formation fans are tainted because they enjoy unofficial culture, in turn they disparage elites as boring. Each group exercises representational power to denigrate the other, marginalizing and excising the other from their community and simultaneously solidifying their group. As Hills (2002:46–58) observes, where loss of cultural capital may occur, in fandom social capital may be gained.

As with any social unit, internal policing also occurs. I have noted earlier that members of some fan groups dislike Mary Sue or slash fiction and suckfic. Fans have labeled violations of universes as "character rape" (Jenkins, 1988:99–101). In *Beavis and Butt-head* chat rooms, assertions that the two cartoon characters are closeted gays produced vehement counterresponses including flaming, threats of personal violence, actual acts of cyberviolence (spamming those making the assertions), "traditional appeals to textual authority" and against subtextual reading strategies, and an attribution of "us" against "them" (Nash, 1999:16–19). Bacon-Smith describes the overt hostility in the forms of sexual harassment and actual physical intimidation that she experienced in attempting to enter a male space at a conference (1992:17–18). Thus, as with any social unit, equity and harmony are not always features of the alternative community.

Fan behaviors are many. Not every fan enjoys or indulges in all these behaviors, and at various points in his or her life a fan may take up a greater involvement in some of these activities. Considering the fans as always involved in either negative or positive behavior, however, would be much too simple. Rather, scholars need to sort out the implications of these activities within broader contextual theorizing. Turning to theories of why these behaviors exist is an important step prior to evaluating them.

Explanations of Fan Behavior

As I forecast in chapter 1, theories to explain audience behaviors run from psychological to sociological. This is apparent in the discussions around fans. While a Marxist might couch this phenomenon more fundamentally in the use-value that fandom has for individuals, beyond that exist a multitude of possibilities. In fact, ultimately, I would argue that any reasonable description of a complex of activities would need to turn to several lines of theorizing. Most authors actually draw on at least two or three fields of scholarship. For example, in her groundbreaking ethnography of romance readers, Radway argued that the women declared the functions of their reading to include learning historical facts, ratifying the world in which they lived, and providing a "declaration of independence" from their regular nurturing roles (1984a:479). She saw these functions as also including a return to a pre-Oedipal state in which the women could fantasize being nurtured by the romantic male protagonist of the story. In her analysis, Radway draws on sociology, uses-and-gratifications psychology, and psychoanalytical theory. Likewise, Cavicchi declares that the purposes of Springsteen fandom are "to release tension, reaffirm values, create a sense of self, and meet others" (1998:10). Thus, the concern here is not to find the correct theory that explains everything but to consider what possibilities exist. Of course, combining incommensurate or contradictory propositions must be avoided. I will start with psychological theories and then move to political and sociological ones.

Fantasy theory in psychoanalysis (not just the normal use of the term *fantasy*) seems to offer a very reasonable explanation for preferences in texts and interpretive strategies. An example is Lynne Joyrich's study (1993) of fans of Elvis in which she postulates that Elvis is a variable signifier of many things. As fans seek the authentic Elvis, their repetition in reading texts and listening to songs is pleasurable since it rewards an epistemophilia (the love of knowing).

Another lucid application in this vein is Cicioni's commentary on why straight women write slash fanfic: she states that the cause is "not discourses about homosexuality, but rather fantasies that articulate women's desires concerning relationships in which men are involved" (1998:154–55). As mentioned previously, Cicioni believes that slash fantasies respond to "tensions about heterosexual relations," but she also postulates, following Elizabeth Cowie's articulation of fantasy theory, that the fiction is a setting out of desire that expresses "a desire for a relationship that satisfies all the basic needs of the people involved." This explains why so many of the stories are about "the first time." The women are exploring how to transform "an emotional bond to sexual intimacy" (160).

A less rigorous psychological explanation, but a very old one, is the notion of catharsis. In his study of *Babylon 5* fandom, Kurt Lancaster theorizes that the reason for fans enjoying role-playing and other interactive performances "is to try to recapture—through participation and immersion—the original cathartic moment experienced during the first viewing of the originating material" (2001:xxxiv). Lancaster builds this proposition on the thesis that a universe capable of extensive interactivity is one that has mythical ties. Such a two-step thesis would not account for many fan behaviors or for a fandom that develops over time; however, either part of the theory—the event of catharsis or the proposition of a mythical feature to a textual world—has some explanatory power.

Psychological theories are also about building the self, and scholars have noted this as a potential account. Turning not to Freud but to William James, Cavicchi writes, "Various kinds of collecting and listening enable [Springsteen] fans to think about themselves objectively and to consciously shape a sense of who they are over time" (1998:140). Cavicchi cautions that fans do not identify with Springsteen. Rather, they use the content of his songs "as an ideal to guide their sense of who they might be" (140). Another version of this occurs in Stephen Duncombe's discussion of creators of zines. Duncombe postulates that the private culture in which these fan productions operate gives an individual space to search with less threat than if the culture were more official. This allows people to explore "without having to identify themselves—either positively or negatively—within mainstream culture" (2002:247; also see Katriel and Farrell, 1991). Additionally, Bacon-Smith has made a related proposition regarding writing as therapy (1992:93), and Hills (2002:90–113) provides a nice review of three psychoanalytical theories but opts for work by D. W. Winnicott on useful play.

Ad hoc or rigorous cognitive theories also explain behavior. Hermes describes two kinds of knowing—practical and connected—and posits that reading magazines provides tips to "ideal" selves and data about other people's emotions and problems that allow the reader to enjoy the "fantasy . . . of being a 'wise woman'" (1995:39, 45). A more complex situation such as group viewing of a television program encourages use of "framing" theory, a postulation that viewers use socially constructed knowledge frames derived from their own experiences and those of others to interpret texts (Fiske, 1987:77–80). Although often the term *schemata* is not invoked, something akin to that is implicit in the description. Grossberg ties affect into these frames in his discussion of "mattering maps" (1992:59–65).

Somewhere among the psychological, political, and sociological theories is the explanation that the preferred textual worlds and fan productions based on those worlds offer an imaginary transport to an alternative world, a utopia. Aden provides an extended and well-presented example of this proposition. Drawing on anthropological concepts (especially the work of Victor Turner) of rituals, flow, the liminoid, and *communitas*, Aden envisions popular stories as "alternatives to grand narratives, and sites of opposition to both the habitus and grand narrative. They are a means of . . . *hoping* for an idealized future" (1999:7, emphasis in original). When we read, we take a "ritualistic journey of the mind to spiritually powerful places where a vantage point that is anything but mundane affords us a reassuring view of an imagined promised land" (8). This is a more complicated and more well-supported version of the older commonplace that reading is an escape. Aden fleshes out the model by suggesting that both reading and actual trips (to concerts, conventions, special places described in the textual world) resemble ritualistic pilgrimages.

Such a model might be combined with psychological or psychoanalytical theory about why fans create certain kinds of fiction or artwork. Jenkins has postulated that women's pursuits in writing fanfic derive from inadequacies of the proffered textual worlds to emphasize the sorts of genres women prefer. Jenkins refers to scholarship by feminists and psychologists that does not hypothesize any essential preferences by women but instead discusses socially constructed predilections. Women rewrite the universe into other genres or specific formulas to produce the sorts of experiences they favor.

What is made politically of such imaginary transports or new fictions depends on whether any claim of effects from the experience is proposed. Envisioning an alternative world might produce political action. It might, however, be a pseudoactivity, as maintained by Theodor Adorno (1938:292). Likewise, the proposition that fan behavior is a poaching of mainstream products or a retooling of mass culture to turn a consumer into a producer is phrased in political terms, although most theorists fail to follow through on the implied analogy. To what degree is fandom generally or specifically really a threat (or support) to mainstream culture? (Also see Hills, 2002:27–45.)

Jenkins uses Michel de Certeau's term *poaching* when he writes that fan activities are "an impertinent raid on the literary preserve that takes away only those things that seem useful or pleasurable to the reader" (1988:86). Penley also uses de Certeau, drawing on his distinction between strategies (maneuvers available to the dominant) and tactics (guerilla responses by the subordinate). She claims that fans make do with what they have, in a sort of "hit-and-run" process. In describing one slash community, she writes about the women being able to "manipulate the products of mass-produced culture" (1991:137–39). Chad Dell also describes female fandom of professional wrestling after World War II as "a tactic [in de Certeau's meaning] to temporarily evade patriarchy and re-define the notion of 'appropriate' female behavior" (1998:87).

Whether the political effect is really insurgent, at times members of the dominant culture have viewed fandom as such a threat. When Beatlemania appeared, the phenomenon was described as revolutionary because it made explicit young women's sexuality (Ehrenreich, Hess, and Jacobs, 1992). Both fans and antifans of *The Simpsons* have expressed opinions that the antics of Bart Simpson evince "lack of respect for authority" (Glynn, 1996:61). Bacon-Smith introduces her discussion of the behavior of women fans as "subversive," "blatant civil disobedience," and "terrorism" (1992:3–6). Her claims derive from the fans' disregard of intellectual property rights. While her attributions may seem excessive in comparison with other sorts of possible crimes, a more detailed political analysis of the sociology of transgressions from a conflict perspective would illuminate how some aspects of fandom are very similar to other acts of social rebellion.

A major theory about fan behaviors involves creation of social groups or alternative communities, as discussed earlier. In considering the pleasures of watching *The Rocky Horror Picture Show*, Bruce Austin (1981b:53) concludes that "group ritual" is highly important. Hoberman and Rosenbaum (1983:15) turn to early functional sociology: Émile Durkheim's work on religion and cult gatherings for feasts to explain midnight moviegoing (1983:15; also see Telotte 1991a:12–15).

Cultural studies researchers look to anthropology and conflict social theory in subcultural and countercultural models to explain group phenomena around music and films (Hebdige, 1979; Marchetti, 1986). Bacon-Smith (1992:285–98) draws on Clifford Geertz's work on deep play for her explanations. Noting the similarities between men with their cockfights and women fans of science fiction, she points out that culture-building can occur under cover of apparently innocent recreation. Narratives, rituals, rules, mentoring—all these features underlie the subterfuge that nothing important is occurring, but for Bacon-Smith the women are creating an alternative social world based on friendship and feminist principles. That the women do perceive some risk in this socializing is shown through producing anonymous works, limiting distribution, and using fiction to maintain distance from the content (Bacon-Smith, 1992:207–19). Moreover, as I described previously, social groups develop internal hierarchies and boundaries, both protecting those inside the group and attempting to exclude and other those outside it.

The variety of explanations for fan behavior is exciting, for the variety of behaviors is also wide. Fans display interpretations and effects (activities) in their most observable form. While the phenomenon of fandom exceeds the typical, likely it points toward the more silent spectator—although probably almost everyone has been a fan in some way. As I have suggested, scholars describe fan activities as a mode of reception, a creation of an interpretive community, an activism, a production of new materials, an extension into the rest of living, and an alternative social grouping.

5

Viewers of Stars,
Cult Media, and Avant-Garde

This chapter will cover some modes of viewing that seem to involve a heterogeneous audience but are important sorts of viewing preferences for individuals. Most people pay at least some attention to stars in their engagements with media texts. Fewer but still large numbers of people engage in viewing movies in ways that are generally described as "cult" practices. I shall describe two of these behaviors as *paracinematic* and *camp* viewing. Additionally, many people engage in and enjoy art and avant-garde cinemas for which special strategies of engagement have been learned. For each of these sorts of experiences—stars, cult movies, art cinema, and avant-garde—some scholarship has attempted to determine who mobilizes the strategies and why. The answers indicate that audiences cut across traditional social scientific categorizations of individuals (such as age, sex, class, and so forth). Where information about who tends to partake in the practices is asserted, I will provide this. However, the chapter's focus is on the interpretive strategies, not the characteristics of the audiences.

Stars

Although fans are obviously fans of specific works of fiction or genres, most people associate fandom with attention to stars or celebrities. Because I am considering work in reception studies, I am not concerned here with who or what controls or creates stars or the "correct" (profitable) star image. Nor will I cover propositions about the functions of stars in representation in films or general hypotheses about ideological functions (for a survey of these theories, see Dyer, 1979; Staiger, 1997). Moreover,

I am not concerned with debates about differences between stars in films versus in television or "stars" versus "celebrities" or the criticisms of intellectuals as celebrities (see Alberoni, 1962; Cook, 1976; Langer, 1981; Ellis, 1982:91–108; Fiske, 1987:149–78; Burt, 1995). Finally, however, I will cover some of the work on specific audiences and their interest in individual stars.

Certainly, as others have noted, Richard Dyer's 1979 summary of star theory was an important intervention in media studies. Although much valuable research preceded his, his synopsis, which applied semiotic and cultural studies approaches to the area, and his hypotheses about why stars mattered to audiences transformed research agendas in the field. As Christine Gledhill (1991a:xiv) explains, he treats stars as texts that can be variably interpreted. Although Dyer (1979:11) considers matters of how stars are created and exist within production systems, he tends to discuss stars in relation to the term *image,* by which he means to cover various aspects of their lives and careers both outside and in movies.

Later commentators have questioned whether *image* is the most felicitous term, since it may hide matters of political economy. For instance, Christine Geraghty (2000) offers a breakdown of "star-as-celebrity," "star-as-professional," and "star-as performer." Paul MacDonald likes to analyze stars as "image, labor and capital" (2000:14). My preference is a four-part consideration, which might be lumped cautiously under the umbrella term of *image*: (1) the star *persona* (which may or may not be like the "real" person but which is the intertextually constructed notion of the star through a series of films or television programs and which is known, perhaps, only through watching fictional texts); (2) the star as *performer* (acting ability or how a star plays the roles he or she is assigned); (3) the star as *worker/laborer* (the professional life of the individual or how she or he negotiates work situations); and (4) the star in the domestic, *private* sphere (the so-called off-camera life).

A variety of materials construct these four parts of the star image. Dyer initially lists promotion, publicity, films, and criticism and commentary as the major sources (1979:68–72). Later he adds that impersonations of stars may extend or solidify the image (1986:3). I suppose that impersonations are a kind of commentary; as well, that fan material is now widely available on the Internet (P. MacDonald, 2003) does not disrupt but merely extends Dyer's initial list.

Because of the variety of sources constructing the textual persona and the star as performer, worker, and private individual, however, no coherent image may exist among these various parts. Indeed, Leo Braudy notes that even while Alexander the Great was alive he was described as contradictory: both "god and demon," city builder and murderer (1986:48). As I shall discuss later, differences between parts of the image may be fruit for praise or scandal. Additionally, some stars may lack parts of this typage. Animated characters such as Bugs Bunny and Mickey Mouse have personae but no private lives, eliminating typical fan questions about whether they are authentic (Wells, 2003; Hills, 2003, discussing computer graphics [CGI] but obviously this is an older phenomenon).

For most stars, however, audiences express curiosity or respond to relations made possible by the varied facets of the image. One relation that Dyer (1979:111–13) discusses is between a star's persona and any character in a particular text assigned to the star. For instance, multiple actors may play a Romeo-type role. What does the particular star bring to that type? Dyer hypothesizes that commentators may discuss the star as transcending the type and becoming "'utterly' individual." Or the star may maximize the type or inflect it or resist it. The last possibility becomes acutely significant for stars who may be categorized as minorities or for those stars' audiences. As I shall discuss in chapter 6, interpreting stars as resisting the roles into which they have been cast allows audiences to perceive the stars to be criticizing those (stereo)types and provides a moment of empowerment from such readings.

Another disjunction between facets of the star may have to do with the star's persona and the star as performer. A slightly different slant on Dyer's evaluation of star persona and character type is Henry Jenkins's list about a star persona, a star's performance, and the character's function within a narrative. In discussing anarchistic comedy, Jenkins (1992c:129–32) postulates that at times a performance may be integrated well into the narrative, but other performances may be in sharp stylistic contrast. A good fit may exist between a character and the star's persona, or it may not, such as Groucho Marx playing a country's president. In fact, writers have claimed that since the 1970s, some individuals have chosen deliberately to create a persona of an "actor," of someone who intentionally varies the sorts of characters played from film to film. This creates an image of star-as-performer as a "technician" rather than a "personality," which was the dominant strategy for both theatrical and cinematic actors since the mid-1800s (McConachie, 1990; deCordova, 1990; Kehr, 1986:9). As with audiences' evaluations of the persona and the character type, these fits or disjunctions may matter to the spectator.

Jean-Louis Comolli believes that spectators are not passively decoding films but playing games when watching actors perform the roles of historical figures: they "fool [themselves] for pleasure" (1977:46).

A key relation in the facets of the star image is between persona and private life. In Dyer's *Stars* (1979) and more so in *Heavenly Bodies* (1986), his thesis about the function of stars within society hinges on particular stars providing certain social and psychological gratifications for individuals. For instance, he studies gay men's identification with Judy Garland as having homologies with their own situation. Consequently, Dyer (1982:133) stresses that fans seek the "authentic" private personality of the star in order to understand that star as an individual (is the star really like the fan?) and to consider whether a performance is truthful to the private person performing it. If publicity about the real life of a star matches an on-screen character, the fan may read the performance as proof of the real life; for instance, a character's neuroses are evidence of the performer's. Richard Schickel (1985) argues that fans today are led astray; mass media provide so much information about the real lives of stars that people believe they know them. He calls this a phenomenon of the "intimate stranger."

Matching persona to private life is one goal of fans; unmatching is another. I shall discuss the postulated functions of scandal later (and scandals are almost always about private lives). Here, though, I want to mention two ways this can go. On the one hand, audiences may revel in disjunctions between supposedly respectable screen personae and unrighteous behavior in real life. Paul Cressey (1932:180) describes the exchange among urban youth of "pseudo-information" about stars as an example of how the youth could disassociate themselves from the apparently moral tales being propagated by classical Hollywood films of the period. On the other hand, such disjunctions may produce very different interpretations after some particular personal fact is discovered. Barbara Klinger (1994:97–131) considers this for the case of Rock Hudson who appeared during the 1960s to be an example of normative heterosexuality and later revealed himself to be gay.

Given the variable facets of the star, and given the potential correspondence and incoherence among these facets, observing that stars may serve multiple and variable functions for audiences is obvious. However, the possibilities need to be considered because of how they are individually inflected in star studies. As I mentioned, Dyer (1977–78) believes that stars speak to contradictions in society so as to appear to resolve those contradictions. Molly Haskell remarks about Marilyn Monroe that "if she hadn't existed, we would have had to invent her, and we did, in a way" (1973:255). Others talk about stars as compensations for people who lack real lives (L. Lowenthal, 1944; Merton, 1946; Ellis, 1982) or as distractions that corrupt "rational communication" (Schickel, 1985:ix). Stars function "charismatically," even supernaturally, for some people (Alberoni, 1962; Dyer, 1979; Marshall, 1997; Fowles, 1992:176). And stars may provide powerful images of nonconformity (Curry, 1996). In other words, almost any psychological or sociological function described already for particular audiences of media products may pertain specifically to stars.

Star studies has produced more fine-grained descriptions of audience-object (here star) relations. Reviewing three of these typologies is of value to beginning to think about the underlying premises of all descriptions of audiences and stars in a text. Dyer (1979:19) summarizes one produced by Andrew Tudor in 1974. Assuming that most audience members relate to stars of the same sex as the viewer, Tudor hypothesizes four possible relations: (1) *emotional affinity,* in which a person has a general involvement in the star's place within a plot; (2) *self-identification,* in which a person places his or her self in the same situation as the star; (3) *imitation,* in which the star acts as a model for the person; and (4) *projection,* in which the person not only mimics the star but wraps his or her life up in the life of the star. Obviously these are increasing stages of psychological and social investment by the audience member. The vocabulary also suggests a psychological theory underpinning the typology. Yet, as Matt Hills (2003) observes, Dyer's overall sociological theory (1979:26–37; 1986:17–19), which works off the basis of the Tudor typology, is basically about audiences' "love" of the star who reconciles social contradictions. Hills wants to broaden the discussion to affect as a whole. Not every audience response to stars is one of "love."

A second typology that Hills believes has more power is Joshua Gamson's recent ethnographic and sociological analysis (1994:146–85) of celebrities and spectators. Considering fans who have a moderate attraction to celebrities, Gamson finds five sorts of modes of engagement with stars in a text. One is the traditional mode in which the audiences take the star to be realistically deployed in a text; the second-order traditional understands the star as basically realistic but assumes some complexity between the star as enacted and the star in his/her private life. The postmodernist reads stars as purely fictional creations. The gossiper game player reads a text as semifictional, using the text for purposes of friendly exchange with other gossipers; the detective game player also considers the text semifictional but works to find the truth of the star. I find this typology better than the first one in that it presumes variable types of audiences, although it falls back into assuming that audiences are interested only in the relation between a star's persona and his or her private life.

The third typology is Jackie Stacey's (1994) in her psychoanalytically theorized analysis of the connotations of "identification" for British women's reminiscences of movie stars. Splitting up her respondents' remarks, Stacey sets out a very useful list of nine stances toward the star. A first group is a collection of attitudes of adulation: devotion, adoration (love at first sight), and worship (the star as in another realm of existence). The second group is the more normal sense of identification in which the stance is one close to taking on the star's identity: transcendence (mentally moving into the star's place, losing one's self in the character's actions) and aspiration. The third group is a stance with resemblances to an "idol of consumption" mode: pretending (mental fantasies of being the star), resembling, imitating, and copying—the last three being increasing stages of physical mimicry. This typology has real value in making important distinctions in human actions.

All three typologies—whether based on psychological or sociological theory—have some values and some deficits. In almost every case, at least part of the typology assumes a function of audiences building identities through the star. Edgar Morin captures this when he discusses stars as providers of dreams for people. Stars impart senses of fashion, models of behavior, and ways to live in "imaginary participations." This dream function, Morin writes, is middle-class (cinema is for the bourgeoisie) and is most effective for adolescents who are seeking ideals of who and how they should be (1957:166–77). Indeed, numerous studies have pointed to individual examples of such modeling in consumer choices (Thorp, 1939:106–12; Walker, 1966:115–16; Herzog and Gaines, 1985; Stacey, 1994:176–223). Additionally, the copying occurs in personality. As Dyer puts it, "Stars are also embodiments of the social categories in which people are placed and through which we make our lives—categories of class, gender, ethnicity, religion, sexual orientation, and so on" (1986:17–18).

Yet subtleties are necessary if one is employing this hypothesis. One is to think through what it means to have stars embody social categories. Judith Mayne objects to Dyer's thesis by observing that if the star displays social contradictions, then would the star serve as a "safety valve," shutting down radical potentials (1993:124–25)? As C. Wright Mills believes, celebrities may be "distracting images," hiding the real power elite (1956:92; also see Alberoni, 1962). Or, Mayne continues, could the star open up gaps between expectation and ability to secure what the star means, producing "anomie and alienation"? Moreover, Barry King also questions the hypothesis, wondering how an incoherent star image can reconcile social contradictions. Additionally, what serves as the model— the star as persona, private person, and so forth—may be different from person to person (1987:146). Finally, the term *identification* is often thrown around, with little finesse and fewer bits of evidence for whatever that relation is (Barker, forthcoming). In summary, the effect of any display of social contradiction is not guaranteed. Still, empirical work indicates that people do pick up information from stars in their various manifestations and apply this information to their own lives, even if not in any wholesale or coherent way.

A second subtlety required is to recognize that some of the earlier assumptions about where the modeling may be occurring require revision. In his study of audience preferences for stars, Leo Handel (1950:145) noted that same-sex preferences for identification outweighed cross-sex ones. This observation has informed some of the research (see Dyer on Tudor's typology, 1979:19; Stacey, 1994). However, Handel's actual finding indicates that men (76 percent) are much more likely than women (54 percent) to correlate preferences this way. Handel hypothesizes that the reason is due to "self-identification" (1950:145).

More recent attempts to follow patterns of identification during an actual film indicate that this is a potent field for research. For example, Carol Clover (1987) argues that the final victim in slasher films is an androgynous female; she theorizes that this allows adolescent males to identify with the victim in a scene that might have potential homoeroticism (since the monster is a male, this would produce male-on-male violence). Her claim is that of a necessary cross-sex identification. In an actual test of such potential cross-sex identification, Jeffrey Brown (1997) finds that people of both sexes and heterosexuals and gays and lesbians expressed identification with Jean-Claude Van Damme during one of his action films until the sex scene with the character played by Roseanna Arquette. At that point, women and gay men became "voyeurs," straight men identified with Van Damme's character, and lesbians desired Arquette's character, although not from the position of Van Damme. Although this study fits with what might be expected, further research to sort out the alliances and shifts in viewing patterns would be good confirming research. A recent cross-national study of the reception of *Lord of the Rings* (Barker, forthcoming) also suggests very complicated and unpredictable findings when people are actually pressed to discuss their relations with specific characters. (I will return to this issue in chapter 6.)

Finally, Hills's remark, noted earlier, that audiences' relationships are not always one of "love" is important. Jib Fowles's *Starstruck* points out that if the question asked is "What stars do for the public," then the answer must be "first and foremost, stars affect the emotional state of the audience" (1992:155). Broadening the possible affects studied should improve the findings. Stars (and the characters they perform) produce a wide range of emotional outcomes that may be what enjoins audiences to them: the ability to produce pleasurable or necessary affective experiences. Fowles even increases the functions stars may serve from the ones habitually part of the traditional array. Stars function in "surrogate form" (161); people secure "vicarious group membership" when they align themselves to particular celebrities. Stars are also life markers. "Fans often date what happens to them relative to what has happened to the star; they feel as if their lives and the star's have been woven together over the years" (175).

Yet if stars are so valuable, what happens when scandals hit their careers? I like the definition of a scandal provided by James Lull and Stephen Hinerman: "*A media scandal occurs when private acts that disgrace or offend the idealized, dominant morality of a social community are made public and narrativized by the media, producing a range of effects from ideological and cultural retrenchment to disruption and change*" (1997a:3, emphasis in original). They also underline that "the transgressions assume additional impact when markers of human difference such as race, gender, class, and sexual orientation are involved" (3). Lull and Hinerman's discussion includes excellent analysis of features of scandals, and they point out that scandals involving celebrities may be "relativized in terms of the moral character and boundaries of the star's complex image system" (22).

From the point of view of media reception studies, the questions such scholars would want to raise is how audiences understand and evaluate disruptions of norms in the private lives of performers. Certainly Hollywood has been replete with such transgressions. Kenneth Anger's collection of star scandals (1965) indicates the fan's obsession with alleged wrongdoings. Richard deCordova (1990:117) postulates that once stars' personalities were the focal point of publicity, the opportunity for scandals in their private lives developed. This is certainly true; however, attacking the private lives of public people dates back much further than the appearance of movies. Adrienne McLean gives the example of the 1828 presidential election that pitted "'profligate' John Quincy Adams against the 'adulterer' Andrew Jackson" (2001:3).

One approach in the scholarship has been to study the sorts of narratives told about celebrities. A major research project is Leo Lowenthal's "Triumph of Mass Idols" (1944). Using content analysis, Lowenthal examined biographies of "idols of consumption" and found a very routine story that was also contradictory. Actions that were none of the person's doing were mixed with examples of lucky choices. Such a contradictory depiction also appears in "the contrasts in lifestyle and appearance between the Hollywood star and the average working-class or middle-class" person (D. Mann, 1989:50; also Dyer, 1977; 1979:38–53; Ellis, 1982:97–98). Publicity tries to paint the star as normal, but all sorts of other texts belie such a picture.

Obviously, given both the contradictory image and the potential for disparity between the star's persona and private life, curiosity about the "truth" may develop (Hinerman, 1997), and various groups may find it profitable—economically or morally—to exploit evidence of private transgressive behavior. When public (especially religious) indignation over various events in the 1920s produced adequate pressure on the movie industry, the studios chose to protect their investments in stars in two ways. They added morality clauses to contracts, and they used threats of access (or not) to information to keep their stars or the press in line (Walker, 1966:136–37; 1970:195–208; McLean, 2001:4–5). After World War II, when the studios determined that long-term actor contracts were less advantageous than independent production deals, stars were on their own to negotiate the shoals of investigations into their private lives.

When a scandal occurs, one reason it may seem disturbing to the public is due to audiences' adulation of and identification with the star. Being humiliated is not pleasant—for the star or for someone who has associated with the star (McLean, 2001:9–10). A star's scandal confronts people's own self-identity. Elizabeth Bird (1997:108–16) notes that scandal narratives are nearly all melodramas with clear morals. Shortly after the appearance of such a scandal story, distancing through joking also occurs. In other words, one response is disavowal of having allied with the star. Connected to this is the phenomenon of Internet Web sites on which appear obviously fake nude pictures of stars. Paul MacDonald believes that this gives audiences "control over the stars" (2003:38), perhaps balancing somewhat the relationship between stars and their fans.

Moreover, the public does not view all scandals as equally transgressive because the public is by no means uniform in its opinion about various norms. In fact, some scandals seem merely harmless entertainment (McLean, 2001:5–6; Feuer, 1995:4–5). Others have actually revitalized careers (Dyer, 1979:69). Like Lull and Hinerman, Alexander Walker notes that part of the outcome may depend on where the star's image starts. He believes that Ingrid Bergman and Eddie Fisher had initial difficulties when their affairs became public because their images had been so bound to families. Bergman recuperated her career through an alteration in her image into someone who "'sacrificed all for love'" (1966:136–37; also see Damico, 1975); Elizabeth Taylor reentered public favor when her image became a "woman of instinct." In fact, Susan McLeland considers how Taylor, Jane Fonda, and Roseanne restored their star status, especially since their scandals were not merely about specific transgressions but ones associated with their "performance as a woman" (1996:2). Each star created a "radical embodiment" that focused on the "frailties of her human (and especially feminine) body" and produced "a narrative of victimization" (38). Finally, individuals in a minority position may see revelations about stars as actually affirming (McLean, 2001:5).

Star studies has become one of the major areas of research in media reception work because of the text/individual relation which seems so personal and because of potential importance to the person engaged with a star. Both psychological and sociological functions likely account for our attention to stars and celebrities; they become both models and friends of a sort. Certainly part of the parasocial experience of media, stars are one of the most complex of texts that we interpret and that may affect us.

Paracinema and Camp Viewing Practices

In her book *Guilty Pleasures*, Pamela Robertson quotes a motion picture exhibitor lamenting in 1933 that people would sit through a movie several times in a row instead of leaving after one circuit through the program. According to the exhibitor, this happened less for films with a good plot and much more frequently with stars such as, in this case, Mae West: "'It is when the star's personality is the attraction that seat-holding becomes a nuisance'" (1996:51). In an era before revival theaters or VCRs, here is a case of what we would now describe as a cult fan viewing practice.

In the study of media reception, scholarship on individual viewing behaviors started less with fans in general and more with a visible phenomenon that developed nearly simultaneously with the increase in university film courses. Midnight movies and the hoopla around the audiences for *The Rocky Horror Picture Show* from the mid-1970s drove media scholars to explain "cult" movies. James Monaco traced the activity of repeat viewing and appreciation of lowbrow, "trash" films to the late 1960s and movies by Roger Corman (B. Austin, 1981b:43), but J. Hoberman and Jonathan Rosenbaum convincingly argue that cult viewing occurs among the surrealists of the 1920s and 1930s and through the underground avant-garde cinema of the 1960s (1983:15–38).

From my perspective, cult movie viewing is merely a particularly visible form of fandom. Indeed, Hills declares that he uses the terms *cult fans* and *fans* interchangeably (2002:x–xi). I want to tackle part of the discussion of cult movies to review an important area of debate. Then I will delineate two related but distinct fan viewing practices: *paracinematic* and *camp*.

Essays about cult movies typically try to define something about the *texts* that might explain the viewing phenomenon most associated with them. I agree with Bruce Kawin that "the cult film has most often been defined in two ways: any picture that is seen repeatedly by a devoted audience, and as a deviant or radically different picture, embraced by a deviant audience" (1991:18). I usually put it just slightly differently in that cult texts are (1) texts in which individuals repeatedly view the same text or a specific formula (such as all slasher films), and (2) texts to which people wish to initiate others. These initiation texts may be classic movies such as *Casablanca, Gone with the Wind,* or *The Sound of Music.* Or they may be absolutely incompetent films such as *Plan Nine from Outer Space.* They may even be gross-out or gore movies such as *Evil Dead* or *I Spit on Your Grave.* Kawin classifies the repeat-viewing films as mainstream movies that are "inadvertent cult films"; initiation texts are often outside of the mainstream and become "programmatic cult films" (18).

What happens next is more questionable. Scholars try to find some essential features within all cult texts that would explain these viewing behaviors. In other words, the texts make the viewer into a cult viewer (a "power" hypothesis). For example, Umberto Eco asserts that the cult film has "a completely furnished world so that its fans can quote characters and episodes as if they were aspects of the fan's private sectarian world." Additionally, "naturally all these elements (characters and episodes) must have some archetypical appeal." Moreover, cult texts also are not perfect; they have a "ricketiness" (1984:198). Eco observes these features because they fit neatly with his theory of the cause for the audience behavior. The narrative formulas seem familiar to the audience, providing viewers with a sense of an "intertextual archetype" (200). Eco contributes a valuable observation about what some individuals might be doing in relation to some films, but the wealth of textual counterexamples to his hypothesis requires rejection of it as a theory that covers all cult viewing. Additionally, he cannot account for the fact that many people may see these films with no "cult" effect occurring for them.

Hills falls into the same trap. He argues that objects that develop a cult following have "family resemblances": "*auteurism, endlessly deferred narratives,* and *hyperdiegesis.*" A hyperdiegesis is "the creation of a vast and detailed narrative space, only a fraction of which is ever directly seen or encountered within the text" (2002:131, emphasis in original; 137). Hills explains cult fandom by turning to a thesis of the experience as "neo-religious" and as play, using D. W. Winnicott's theory of purposeful play as a psychological working through of personal issues. Barry Grant (1991) and Telotte (1991a) also postulate a common feature to cult films: transgression. Grant then argues, using work by Robin Wood (1979), that films that create a threatening Other render that Other contained, taking the viewer through transgression and into safety and well-being.

Again, each of these three theses of the text/individual relation has potential to explain some cult films and their viewers, but none of them covers every movie or television text that typically is thought of as able to produce repeat viewings or initiation gestures. Nor do the theories explain why only some individuals become cult viewers.

That said, within cult audiences two very specific types of viewing practices deserve special attention. Jeff Sconce has labeled the first one; *paracinematic* fans privilege films normally viewed as awful or bad or "trash." Sconce indicates that this is a "calculated negation and refusal of 'elite' culture" (1995:372). This viewing practice is prepackaged in the commentary provided in *Mystery Science Theatre 3000.*

Paracinematic viewing is not a *camp* (the other) viewing practice. Both paracinematic and camp viewers read parodically. They refuse to read the text as its makers intended. (Intent is, of course, a major philosophical problem; here, I am just asserting that traditional historical evidence would provide the evidence for a commonsensical decision about intent.) Both paracinematic and camp viewers exaggerate portions of the text as more significant than originally intended; they create double entendres; they focus on stylistic excess. A paracinematic viewer, however, does not exercise this viewing strategy on standard-quality Hollywood movies, as does a camp viewer. The object of cultivation is the obscure B movie or the off-off-Hollywood exploitation film.

Moreover, beyond the traditional parodic attacks, paracinematic viewers often use academic discourse to create their ironic commentary about these low-culture objects. Referencing auteur theory or specialized theoretical language, paracinematic viewers assert their intelligence and education. From his research, Sconce believes that most paracinematic viewers are "male, white, middle-class, and 'educated'" in film studies; they are also younger than the professorial elite whom they confront through their readings (1995:375–78). Greg Taylor's discussion of "cult" readers seems to coincide with Sconce's: "Cult criticism focuses on the identification and isolation of marginal artworks, or aspects and qualities of marginal artworks, that (though solely neglected by others) meet the critic's privileged aesthetic criteria" (1999:15). Both Sconce and Taylor emphasize that this viewing practice places a "high value on connoisseurship" (15), especially in the realm of style (Sconce, 1995:384–85). Paracinematic viewers even take their elitism further (as auteur critics did for directors); subgroups exist. Sconce notes that those around the journal *Film Threat* prefer confrontational trash avant-garde independent filmmakers, whereas those aligned with *Psychotronic* resurrect old poverty-row films.

Camp viewers resemble paracinematic viewers in terms of also being productive, parodic readers of a text; creating puns, allusions, and double entendres; and reveling in stylistic and generic excess. What distinguishes camp viewers is that their assumed reading position is a purposefully hypergendered one, often hyperfeminine but potentially also hypermasculine. The former is aligned with the traditional gay male subculture that has cultivated this reading practice for decades (and perhaps centuries). More recently, camp reading strategies have been disseminated into a broader cultural sphere.

I have just made a fairly bold assertion that needs justification. Scholarship on camp has tried to define camp through tracing historical examples of it or tying it to either essential sexualities (homosexuality) or historical circumstances (a recuperative act in the face of homophobia or an expressive style to communicate among gays). For example, David Bergman (1991) describes the activities of the Mollies Club in 1709 and public masquerades in 1717 as having features of a camp production. More recently, Thomas A. King has deftly studied the developing historical discursive relations in Anglo-Europe among aristocracy, homosexuality, "effeminate" body postures and motions, and cultivated taste preferences. He concludes that by the 1750s a serpentine body line in a man's posture connoted homosexual activity (1994:26–31). Other scholars have characterized camp as a response to social oppression, describing it as a "sensibility" (Babuscio, 1977:41; Bergman, 1991:92) or a "style" (Bergman, 1993:4–5).

Yet more recently, the emphasis has been to define camp as a purposeful production to avoid any attribution of camp to an "essential" homosexuality. The camp production may be through an artwork or a performance. It may also be through a "mode of perception." Andrew Britton (in a scathing criticism of camp) describes a camp interpretive practice as one in which "artifacts become the object of an arrested, or fetishistic, scrutiny" (1978/79:12). More positively, Michael Bronski depicts it "as a particular 'reimagining of the material world . . . which transforms and comments on the original. It changes the "natural" and "normal" into style and artifice'" (quoted in Klinger, 1994:135), although starting with objects that are already demonstrating "exaggeration, stylization, and tackiness" helps (134; also see Robertson, 1996:17–18; G. Taylor, 1999:16).

Camp interpretation certainly has an individual style for reimagining. Using Peter Stallybrass and Allon White's term *grammatica jocosa*, Bergman argues that, like carnival, camp operates to "'reveal erotic and obscene or merely materially satisfying counter-meaning'" (Stallybrass and White, 1986:10, in Bergman, 1991:100). It is a reading for the bawdy underneath the everyday surface. In a camp interpretive strategy, almost all the time, the constructed countermeaning relates to sexuality.

To create this production of sexual innuendo, the adoption of a sexualized persona is useful. Hence, I would argue, my definition that camp is an interpretive production from a hypergendered position is justified. Such an assumed identity is exceptionally useful to produce the bawdy sexual commentary.

At this point let me make a few distinctions. Undoubtedly, numerous reading practices may be parodic. Paracinematic and camp are just two rather well-studied ones. Second, the tone of the camp parodic production may be sarcastic ("bitchy") or affectionate. Nothing in a camp production requires a specific attitude about the text being reimagined. Third, an individual watching a camp production is not producing a camp reading but simply viewing a camp production. The person is merely seeing the preferred text. To *produce* a camp reading, an individual would need to take up a hypergendered position and interpret from that position a text differently than it intended to be read, to reimagine the text by emphasizing (or even creating) its artifice and surface and evoking a sexual subtext. Fourth, camp production has no necessary conservative or progressive politics (as I shall discuss later).

Finally, a camp reading is not equivalent to cross-gender or cross-sex impersonation. Most female or male impersonation has as its goal an illusion (Newton, 1972). Tricking the audience into accepting the performance as mimetic is the aim of such impersonations. Instead, someone producing a camp reading takes up a hypergendered position; the gender production is not mimetic but exaggerated in order to comment on and transform the text that is to be parodied. Drag performances (as a type of impersonation) may have the artistic goal of either mimesis or camp (or a bit of both).

This characterization of camp might help sort out the debates generated by the mass popularization of parodic reading of culture. In 1964, Susan Sontag published her "Notes on 'Camp.'" Looking back, her essay may have been as much symptom as cause. Avant-garde cinema (such as *Blonde Cobra* and *Flaming Creatures*), pop art, and general cultural skepticism toward elite/high art were popular among youth and the intelligentsia from the mid-1960s; in 1966, television brought the pop art program *Batman* into the living room of America (Torres, 1996; A. Ross, 1989:135–36; Penley, 1993; Erb, 1998:132–60). Mainstreaming of sexual double entendre and cultivation of lowbrow, fun art spread. Also in the United States, although movies had a spree of sex comedies in the early 1960s, the transformation of the film production code into a rating system opened up U.S. screens to explicit sexual content, culminating in the early 1970s with widespread viewing of soft- and hard-core films such as *Last Tango in Paris* and *Deep Throat*, the latter arguably a parody of pornography (also see chapter 7). Rock musicians from Elvis Presley to David Bowie played with gender roles. This cultural flurry trained youth to find sexual content everywhere and to adopt fearlessly exaggerated gender roles. Doing camp, no matter one's sexuality, was easy and popular.

Mainstreaming of parodic reading of conventional texts, however, may or may not produce a *camp* parodic reading. A parodic reading may be simply a bemused reimagining without the gendered stance. That is what seems to be the case for most of what Klinger calls "mass camp" (or others call "pop camp"), clearly a derivation from gay camp. In her discussion of some later interpretations of *Written on the Wind*, one of the Hollywood melodramas directed by Douglas Sirk, Klinger describes them as readings "trained on its absurd plot twists and hyperbolic Technicolor style." Mass camp "has encouraged a sensibility that views past Hollywood films as inadvertent campy send-ups" (1994:133). This mass camp, while perhaps uninhibited about gender roles, loses the hypergendered reading position in terms of how the text is reimagined: sexuality and bawdiness may not be beneath the text, but merely awkward filmmaking from present perspectives. Mass camp is also not the paracinematic mode of reception, since it is applied to objects once considered at least reasonably good moviemaking.

Another derivation from traditional gay camp besides mass camp is feminist camp, so argued by Robertson. Robertson believes that audiences need to be considered in terms of their related viewing practices developed out of similar experiences. Both gays and women, she points out, have reason to prefer some textual formulas because of their social construction as not heterosexual males. The appeal of gay camp for women has been its gender parody (1996:10). Using psychoanalytical theory, she believes some women have produced camp that might be argued to be feminist because of the women's productive critique of gender norms.

From my perspective, then, these women take up a hypergendered position to create their parody as do traditional gay camp producers. Robertson's primary example of such a woman is Mae West, who is not a "female impersonator" (as others have labeled her) but a female female impersonator, a woman creating an exaggerated version of femininity in order to parody gender stereotypes. Her argument works best for West, in my opinion (partially because of clear evidence that West was borrowing from gay camp), but Robertson also applies notion of feminist camp to Berkeley musicals, Joan Crawford in *Johnny Guitar*, and Madonna. Feminist camp also fits some productions in the 1990s: sections of *Designing Women*, two independent videos—*Joan Does Dynasty* and *Meeting Two Queens*—and probably more recent television shows such as *Xena: Warrior Princess* (Morreale, 1998).

Distinguishing among traditional camp, mass camp, and feminist camp helps sort out at least matters of stance toward the objects reimagined. It does not resolve problems of evaluating this mode of producing art or reception of texts. Camp has rightly been criticized as not necessarily politically progressive. One of the best statements of reservation about camp is Britton's. He vehemently argues:

> Camp attempts to assimilate everything as its object, and then reduces all objects to one set of terms. It is a language of impoverishment: it is both reductive and non-analytic. . . . As a gay phenomenon, it is a means of bring the world into one's scope, of accommodating it—not of changing it or conceptualizing its relations. . . . Camp is simply one way in which gay men have recuperated their oppression, and it needs to be criticized as such. (1978/79:12–14; also see Morrill, 1994:122–26)

Camp has also been accused of misogyny and gynophobia (Bergman, 1993:3–10; Flinn, 1995; Farmer, 2000:122–50). It "can be mobilized only within a very privileged setting" (Bergman, 1993:12). It is unclear whether camp is "disruptive" or easily assimilated into consumerism (9). And camp has discourses of morbidity laced through its objects of ridicule (Flinn, 1995).

Despite these justified criticisms, essentializing camp as one thing would be a grave error. Several scholars responding to the development of mass camp and to the criticisms of traditional camp have argued for the radical potential of camp production. Jonathan Dollimore believes that camp has the ability to attack a "depth model of identity" (1991:310). Moe Meyer makes a splendid defense of camp for "queer parody." Distinguishing between mass camp and "Camp," with a capital C, Meyer argues for its employment as a politically engaged "oppositional critique" (1994a:1).

As valuable as Meyer's agenda is, trying to recapture camp for one group is now impossible. Yet I would point out that even if most uses of camp, or mass camp, fail to attain any sort of social criticism, the very act of adopting a hypergendered stance, or even merely a parodic one, may open up some individuals to the socially constructed nature of our identities. That experience may have positive outcomes.

In considering paracinematic and camp viewing practices, some similarities exist. Both practices are learned; they do not come merely from the circumstances of one's existence but from psychological and social contexts. Both practices involve cultivation of bodies of information and, consequently, at least some level of economic security to permit investment in attaining knowledge necessary to practice these modes of reception. Research needs to investigate who engages these modes of reception and when. As well, are other viewing practices related to these and how? This is a rich field for research.

Art and Avant-Garde Viewing Practices

Greg Smith writes: "Film reviewing depends on a knowledge of tendencies within the appropriate national cinema, an understanding of the *auteur's oeuvre* and a film's place within it, an awareness of the star's constructed images, or a familiarity with the film genre's conventions. Film reviewing is a comparative exercise, construing the unknown (the new film) in terms of what one already knows" (2002:115). This list of strategies to interpret media texts is excellent, and it probably is applicable not only to reviewers of films and television but also to everyday audiences. It is likely also the first line of offense when someone is seeing an unusual film that does not look like a classical Hollywood movie or a network television program.

One of the research hypotheses that have intrigued scholars is how audiences deal with texts that fall outside the norms of the mainstream. Using his cognitive psychology/neoformalist approach to interpretation, David Bordwell (1985) has argued that beyond the viewing procedures for classical Hollywood cinema at least three other modes of texts and consequent viewing practices exist. These are the modes for art-cinema, historical-materialist, and parametric narration (see chapter 3). While the goal of a viewer of the classical Hollywood fiction film is to figure out the story from the information provided, the other three modes do not pose novel puzzle solving as their primary aim and, thus, a cooperative and knowledgeable spectator of those modes will need to respond to the textual narration in a different fashion.

Bordwell believes that art-cinema film viewers read these texts first for realism and, if that strategy fails, for a message from the director as the author. In the case of historical-materialist films (such as the films of the Soviet Union) and their viewers, the texts rely on well-known intertextual material about history and character types; viewers reference that information in their reception. For parametric narration (such as *Traffic*, directed by Jacques Tati), the story is easily understood, but the pleasures of the text involve patterns in style autonomous from the subject matter. A cooperative and knowledgeable spectator will enjoy focusing on those patterns during the viewing. Scholars using theoretical paradigms such as psychoanalysis have generally not approached this problem except to state that viewers are not interpolated into the fiction in the way they are for classical films.

Bordwell's distinction among modes of texts and viewing is a very valuable observation about the environment of media. I believe much more research and analysis of major modes is needed. In fact, his model might be extended to genres and other subgroups of texts as long as the research turns from the ideal spectator (Bordwell's cooperative and knowledgeable spectator) and cognition to incorporate actual viewers and other experiences such as affective ones. Some research has occurred in this regard directed toward the art cinema and the avant-garde (a category Bordwell does not consider). In this section, I will review the beginning work on these two modes of media texts and theories about their associated viewing strategies. Most of the work is preliminary, considering only what reviewers have done during encounters with these modes.

The term *art cinema* is used for texts that provide a narrative, characters, and narration distinct from the classical Hollywood cinema. This definition by opposition is not very satisfying (and Bordwell's attempt to define art-cinema films as having specific features distinct from other non–classical Hollywood films is very helpful and precise). However, in the everyday life of film culture, everything not Hollywood but still having a decipherable story is usually lumped together. In the United States, most of the time these films are also equivalent to foreign films, and even British films that concentrate on subjects of social concern might be categorized as "art cinema." Likewise, reviewers in other nations have decided and different attitudes about what makes movies "art cinema" (Barker, Arthurs, and Harindranath, 2001:15–25).

In the United States, the term *art cinema* appears to have been used as early as the 1920s when foreign films were shown in theaters dedicated to a different experience than privileged in the first-run, picture-palace houses. The "little cinema" movement offered foreign and avant-garde films, a smaller intimate environment, occasionally sans children, and often in a subscription format (Wilinsky, 2000: 46–55). After World War II, art-house cinema flourished in the United States.

Research on who attends art cinema indicates that in the 1950s art-house patrons expressed different preferences from the general population. For example, one study reveals that while 51 percent of the general population liked improbable happenings in the movies, art-house customers preferred realism and acting they considered to fit that attribute. Most studies indicate that art-cinema audiences had more education than the average population (Staiger, 1992:185; Smythe, Lusk, and Lewis, 1953). College towns usually had at least one art house where foreign films and revivals of some U.S. films functioned as part of the social scene (Lane, 1994; Wilinsky, 2000). In general, art cinema and "intellectual" were yoked together.

This image of the highbrow cinema was, however, mixed with one of less than high taste. Part of the realism and "not-Hollywood" that attracted the audience was also explicit discussion of social issues banished from Hollywood screens. Sex and violence were more likely on the screen than implied, leading ambitious exhibitors to promote these films as adult and daring (Wilinsky, 2000; DeAngelis, 1999). Barbara Wilinsky observes that conservative responses to art films in the late 1940s coalesced around the films' verbal obscenities, objectionable scenes that required excision before local screenings, and even accusations of communist propaganda and attempts to undermine the moral character of Americans (2000:25–27).

Other than Wilinsky's discussion of some social resistance to art cinema, the major research has involved how audiences interpret the films. All research to date (besides surveys conducted about preferences) has focused on reviewers and academics as the spectators. Still, those individuals may well fit the category of the typical audience member or may also be the trainers of other viewers. As Greg Smith (2002) notes, interpretive strategies usually involve contextual comparison with other known texts. One major background of texts for an interpreter is the national cinema in which the film is produced. As Smith's case study of the historical reception of *Rashomon* (1952) illustrates, reviewers compared the movie with what little they knew about Japanese and Asian cultural objects. Beyond that, they tried to resolve the film's four repeating versions of a story of rape from different participants' perspective by other common ways to make legible a difficult text: they compared it with modern art styles, claimed it reflected Japanese or all human nature, praised the camera-work as evidence of the director's choice, and considered the narrative as a philosophical discussion about "the nature of subjective and objective truth" (2002:115–24).

In fact, the latter two strategies are highly typical for art-cinema viewers. Bordwell believes that "when a spectator is confronted by non-Hollywood types of narrative form," he or she explains them as "either an 'objective' or a 'subjective verisimilitude'" and may impute the nonnormative narration as coming from the director (1979:59, summarized in Staiger 1992:180). Art cinema is certainly connected to the spread of spectators seeking an identifiable authorial source for the text and is related to the development of auteur theory in the 1950s (see Hess, 1974; Staiger, 1985; Knee, 1985).

In an attempt to determine the historical development of these viewing strategies, I studied the sequencing of reviewers' engagement with art cinema after World War II and concluded that attributing unusual narratives or narration as coming from directors-as-authors predated the 1940s. I conclude that the postwar foreign imports appeared to tackle serious subject matter compared with Hollywood's entertaining (and regulated) fare. Attributing a message in a serious film to an author was a logical move. Reviewers did not try to determine a final truth to ambiguous narratives, such as *Rashomon*, but indicated that the director was raising a point about subjective human knowledge (or failed to produce a consistent story). Soon, subjective realism was a solution to some narrations such as *Wild Strawberries* (reviewed in the United States in 1959) and *Hiroshima, mon amour* (reviewed 1960). Finally, with the appearance of *Breathless* (reviewed 1961), reviewers assumed a relation between the subject matter and the style, labeling the outcome modernist art from a director-artist.

Explaining difficult cinematography, editing, or mise-en-scène can be attributed not just to directors but also to a wider context: contemporaneous art trends. This is a common interpretive strategy for nonnormative texts. Michael Budd (1981) indicates that European critics of *The Cabinet of Dr. Caligari* in the 1920s turned to cubism to discuss the film, but American reviewers simply advised their readers that the strange sets and costumes become less noticeable as the mystery story picks up.

Aside from research that sorts out the naturalizing strategies for viewing art cinema is exploration of the reception of foreign cinemas in a country, accounting for national evaluations and exclusions, and the building of directorial reputations. Eric Rentschler provides an impassioned plea for a broader study of 1970s German film beyond the limited number of filmmakers imported into and praised within the United States and for an analysis that goes past a romantic "cult of genius" (1981–82; on the U.S. reception of François Truffaut, see Alfonsi, 1997). Robert Kapsis considers how auteurism helped Alfred Hitchcock achieve his goal of elevating himself into a top-ranked filmmaker. Placing Hitchcock within discourses on artistry, genre, and cinematic practice, Kapsis concludes that not only Hitchcock but also the genres in which he worked were reevaluated when auteurism accelerated: "Overall the evidence suggests that critics increasingly came to view the thriller (especially the adult thriller) as an effective vehicle for art not simply because of the change in attitude toward Hitchcock but mainly because of the adoption of auteurism, which resulted in a general upgrading of many other popular Hollywood genres as well" (1992:15).

The difficulty in interpreting art cinema is one thing; art cinema usually has a narrative that allows a viewer something traditional upon which to rely while coping with unusual cinematic narration or style. Avant-garde texts are those works that have either no narrative or one of so little use as to be negligible for turning to it to base on it an interpretive response. Viewers need to try strategies other than producing a chronological story textured by realism, authorship, national culture, art movements, and so forth. Here Smith's point about comparison and his list are once again useful. People dealing with avant-garde media typically turn to context or background sets: a national media history or art movement, the director-as-artist, and conventions of the genre. In any case, one significant goal is to create a unified explanation of the text. Jonathan Culler has pointed to four methods by which people try to find a coherency for a text: (1) noting how the text fits within a larger class (Smith's list is just such a list of possible classes); (2) arguing that in shifts of meaning, "what comes second is what is true"; (3) using context to argue meaning; and (4) "counting closings more than anything else" (1981:68–78).

Two discussions of what spectators do when attempting to make coherency out of a viewing experience of avant-garde cinema are those of Noël Carroll (1978) and James Peterson (1994). Like Bordwell and Smith, both scholars make use of cognitive theory and notions of a background set to establish their description (Carroll in more of an ad hoc way). Focusing on editing in general, Carroll's problem is to explain "what the spectator must do when confronted with an array of shots"

(1978:80). In the traditional text, the spectator uses each new shot to add information—within the bounds of cultural and narrative plausibility—to create a story. For nontraditional texts, Carroll indicates that cultural and historical contexts also assist. For example, "in order to comprehend the editing in *Text of Light* [directed by Stan Brakhage], the spectator must inductively identify pure chroma as the subject of the film" (88). Several other hypotheses also predetermine the reading: an assumption that the text is experimental (in the class of avant-garde) and that aesthetics is being foregrounded (as opposed to a narrative story being the more significant attribute). Beyond deciding what the subject matter is, the spectator is likely also to use familiarity with aesthetics as a guide, seeking repetitious stylistic patterns or contrasts (94). In short, once assuming the text is in the class of avant-garde, the spectator seeks its subject matter and then searches for aesthetic patterns complementing or creating the supposed subject.

Peterson also assumes (reasonably, I would guess) that most viewers who even go to experimental work primarily want "to make sense of the film." Making sense occurs "when they have established sufficient coherence among the film's elements by matching those elements to template schemata" (1994:21) such as the classes I have discussed here. What is "sufficient" coherency may vary for individuals. What Peterson contributes is a differentiation among types of avant-garde works as well as a study of actual historical responses to texts within his categories. Splitting post–World War II U.S. experimental work into the poetic, minimal, and assemblage groups, Peterson argues that coherency is achieved for the poetic when the film can be traced to the filmmaker's biography; for the minimal when the film can be related to some experience of viewing, a tracing of the process of the film's making, or an examination of the medium itself; and for the assemblage when the film's theme can be connected to a mood.

Investigations of both art cinema and avant-garde media have focused on cooperative and knowledgeable viewers, probably because watching these sorts of media really is optional. Those who have found these sorts of texts unpleasant do not have to return to them. What makes people predisposed, however, to find them enjoyable or worthwhile needs further investigation. Approaches using theories other than those well suited for philosophical or cognitive analysis may also provide assistance in illuminating how people engage with this work. Questioning presumptions that naturalizing or coherency (rather than sensuality, for instance) drives the experience might be worth considering. Finally, associating viewers of these texts with educational training or psychologies would provide much more detail about these viewers in comparison with the previous scholarly focus on spectators of mainstream narrative media.

Within reception studies, more specific questions than just broad experience of interpreting films or television shows have focused on viewers' engagements with stars, cult texts or texts susceptible to parodying, and alternative formal structures (the art cinema and avant-garde). Each of these particular strands of research indicates that variety and difference occur readily from the mainstream way people habitually engage in meaning-making. To enjoy stars means marshaling lots of extratextual information about actors' lives; to take pleasure in cult movies also may require extensive contexts; to produce a camp reading necessitates adopting a different identity and a ready wit; and to like art cinema and avant-garde means stretching into reservoirs of aesthetic, social, political, and cultural databases. Any one of these reading strategies is work, but obviously pleasurable work!

6

Minorities and Media

One of the major "mattering maps" for reception studies has been the relation of minorities to mass media. Fundamentally the reason for this is political: the cohesion or rupture of a social world depends on relations among groups who perceive themselves as disadvantaged either as a group or as individuals. Media are the sites of information and fantasy that may participate in the creation of these perceptions. In chapters 2 and 3, I discussed various theories of determination between media and individuals. In general, scholars believe media educate individuals, reinforce social views, function as mediation to the social world, or are so powerful as to overwhelm viewers. All these theses reappear when questions are raised about minorities. Additionally, the scholarship ranges through problems of how to treat individuals and groups both respecting aspects of essential features versus appreciating socially constructed characteristics. Agency is also a key issue.

In this chapter, I will review theses about identity groups as twentieth-century discourses have created such groups as pertinent: specifically sex, gender, sexuality, race/ethnicity, class, and nation. These sorts of identities have been researched because of their cultural, social, political, and, probably most important, economic significance (especially as targeted consumer groups). However, they have also been constructed: a reinforcing situation exists. For example, because the social world positions women in particular ways, women's experiences matter, making these individuals' designation as "women" noteworthy. Other designations (such as age, religion, and physical abilities) have been given some attention. However, I will focus on the identities that have received the most extended attention among media scholars. Other than a couple of general clarifications (at the beginning and end of the chapter), I shall cover these identities individually because often the debates have been somewhat internal to questions about a specific one. However, similarities and differences deserve note, and I will try to point these out throughout the chapter. For instance, for some groups such as gays and lesbians their sexuality is not visible, which is a different situation than for racial/ethnic minorities, whose visibility is quite obvious if their heritage is marked on their bodies but their existence in a social environment is not represented. Then, what happens if a minority is visible but as a negative stereotype or as a token?

I should emphasize that reception studies has not been interested in these questions for simple academic reasons. What is learned about the reception of media images has significant implications for the production of those images, particularly who produces them. Audiences are often well aware of the sources of their media, and contextual information about production circumstances contributes to interpretation and use of media. Simply discussing media or media images in the abstract as positive, negative, or whatever makes no sense.

Identity Debates

Most of the theory in chapters 2 and 3 assumes white heterosexual males as the "obvious," "it-goes-without-saying," dominant group. While many of those hypotheses are written with such an unstated assumption underpinning the propositions, social and psychological theory would point out that the hypotheses are also about what they do not always explicitly address: all others—those not fitting into the dominant roles (which would be functional sociology's explanation) or oppressed (conflict theory's view). Such deviations from the norm may be threatening. Solutions to that threat have been ridicule, marginalization, and exclusion. For all individuals who are not classified into the dominant, scholars have struggled to explain both the recognition of the features that have produced the marking of the individuals as not dominant and the history of that marking. For instance, while many cultures prohibit male same-sex acts, the creation of "homosexual" as a pertinent identity for an individual appears to be a twentieth-century innovation. Sex and race/ethnicity have long histories of relevance, but what counts as "woman" or a minority ethnicity has changed. In the British and U.S. cultures, the Irish were not always "white" (Ignatiev, 1995).

In chapter 3, I discussed three problems that existed for the cultural studies scholars: agency and consciousness, with hegemony as an explanation for why individuals might not always act in ways theorists believed would be most beneficial to them; an explanation of pleasure; and the politics of identity. Grouping people arbitrarily by externally created categories had theoretical drawbacks, especially if the individuals did not interpret texts through any sort of conscious recognition of that identity as pertinent. Grouping people on the basis of one identity that interested the scholar ignored other identities that might have been relevant to interpretations.

Yet, research indicated patterns of response that did not adhere to the hypothetical preferred way of engaging a media text. As Stuart Hall (1980c:135) questioned, how did selective perception develop? Moreover, what were the reasons for *patterns* of selective perception that scholars could observe? Was it demographics, as earlier researchers tended to assume, or perhaps "socio-psychological variables," as hypothesized by John Leckenby and Stuart Surlin, who coined the term to describe anomalies in interpretations of Archie Bunker in *All in the Family* (1976:483)? What are the origins of pertinent variables? Do they relate to traditional demographic categories? How and why?

Although cautions exist about the disadvantages of seeing identities and acting as though they matter, many individuals argue for a "strategic essentialism," a phrase promoted by Gayatri Spivak (1985:205). In an excellent survey of the investigation around "identity," Robin R. Means Coleman summarizes the current resolution to the research agenda as the following questions: "(1) who we are; (2) who we are in relationship to others; (3) how identity is formed and maintained; (4) how who we are is negotiated within varying contexts; and (5) how our identities can lead to struggle, resistance, or solidarity" (2002:4).

I would underline question 3: identities may shift in varying contexts. Considering how social spaces and person-to-person exchanges foreground particular identities has a bearing on specific interpretive outcomes. For example, Judith Mayne's (1982) and Miriam Hansen's (1991) thoughts about the spaces of the nickelodeon as pertinent for immigrant women's meaning-making (regardless of the content of the motion pictures) and Dick Hebdige's remarks (1979) about subcultural groups speaking not only to those in power but to other subcultural groups are part of what creates the effects of the media experience. Horace Newcomb and Paul Hirsch's concept (1983) of television as a cultural forum and Daniel Dayan and Elihu Katz's investigation (1992) of media events describe how media create and maintain identities through social dialogues around encounters with specific texts. Scholars (Gamson, 1997; Wong, 1998:91) have been considering the significance of gay and lesbian film festivals or local community groups' self-representation for producing identification within and among people.

Moreover, less mass and organized intercourse matters. Scholarship on gay, lesbian, and race/ethnicity subjectivities consistently emphasizes the function of informal, unofficial information about identities as pertinent to reading strategies (Becker et al., 1981:301–2; Weiss, 1991; Staiger, 1992:154–77; 2000b:161–78). Jennifer F. Wood labels it "Afrocentric talk" when African Americans use "oral tradition—story-telling, elaborate narrative construction, and interpersonal encounters" for "making sense of their world": "Afrocentric talk serves as a catalyst toward community building and the creation of self-identity and dignity. Therefore, Afrocentric talk is a shield against racism, both societal and internalized racism" (2002:106). That talk is context for minority media interpretation.

Right from the start of observing cinema audiences, writers sought variables based on perceptible identities. Mary Heaton Vorse observed in *Collier's* in 1911 that a German-speaking, Jewish woman sitting behind her in a theater articulated the plot's progress as it went along, warned the characters, and evaluated their actions. Karl Lashley and John Watson in their early psychological study of audiences in 1922 observed that when they showed a sex education film to a mixed-sex audience, some people provided flip remarks or statements of innuendo; this did not occur for a same-sex audience (1922:86). Paul Cressey noted the importance of gossip for the East Harlem youth he studied. Among their beliefs were that "Rudolph Valentino was not only a great Italian but . . . he died as a result of having too many 'affairs' with Hollywood beauties"; "Poli Negri served as Valentino's mistress"; and "many of the leading actors in movies are inverts or have unnatural sex practices which make it impossible for them to continue a marriage for any length of time" (1932:181). Cressey observed that for the minority youth such "pseudo-information," which was at odds with official stories, justified ignoring the moral endings of Hollywood films.

Contemporary cautions about identity politics particularly underline the heterogeneity of any one individual. Increasingly sophisticated studies attempt to account for intersectionality of identities and for matrices of domination. Patricia Hill Collins explains these concepts. Rather than thinking of identities as additive, they are interlocking:

> Intersectionality refers to particular forms of intersecting oppressions, for example, intersections of race and gender, or of sexuality and nation.

Intersectional paradigms remind us that oppression cannot be reduced to one fundamental type, and that oppressions work together in producing injustice. In contrast, the matrix of domination refers to how these intersecting oppressions are actually organized. (2000:18)

This approach to the heterogeneity of identities is recent. Most people credit the articulation of the concept to women of color in the early 1990s (Alarcón, 1990; Crenshaw, 1993). While some of the later work described below notes multiple identities, drawing out an intersectional analysis has yet to be accomplished.

Women

Second-wave feminism raised quickly the specter of another reader with different reading strategies. As Jonathan Culler pointed out, Elaine Showalter's foregrounding of the fact of a female reader disrupted traditional critical practice: "The *hypothesis* of a female reader changes our apprehension of a given text, awakening us to the significance of its sexual codes" (Culler, 1982:50). Although Showalter's observation had implications primarily for analyzing the production of literature, Annette Kolodny's criticisms noted further implications. Disagreeing with Harold Bloom's grand theory of artistic production (men battling their literary fathers), she notes that his theory only works if people assume that the artist and readers have the same texts as contexts. Women do not, for various reasons. She concludes, "Interpretative strategies . . . are learned, historically determined, and thereby necessarily gender-inflected" (1980:47). Moreover, Patrocinio Schweickart (1986:36–39) writes that a split needs to be made between feminists reading men's writing and feminists reading women's; in both cases gender and politics will enter the conversation.

In media scholarship, second-wave feminism created intense investigation of women's viewing, including discovering evidence that protofeminist "resistant" readings have existed throughout history (Staiger, 1992:124–39; Shingler, 2001:46–62). Some of this work has been fairly straightforward. In one intriguing instance of queries about women's emotional engagements with images, Sue Harper and Vincent Porter used a massive 1950s British survey to excavate what produced emotional responses for specific groups of spectators at that time. For women, "scenes which showed partings, unhappy children or cruelty to animals" or "death scenes and films about refugees" produced crying. While reluctant to list instances, younger men responded to "patriotism, self-sacrifice and heroism" (1996:157). Women "often misremembered a film in such a way as to *heighten* its emotional profile" (162), which is in line with what memory research would predict (see chapter 8). In another study, Jeffrey Brown (1997:129–33) reports that different sex and sexualities respond to different body parts; he claims that a male's butt is the focus for sensual arousal for women and gay men. Harper and Porter's work is historical and textual, analyzing questionnaires generated much earlier by social scientists. Brown's study, while contemporary, also uses textual analysis of self-reports from audiences.

In contrast, others have pursued this matter primarily theoretically. Some approaches have been via cognitive psychology. Mary Crawford and Roger Chaffin (1986) survey the concept of schemata for a theory of reading and then discuss how sex and sex-role identifications might alter standard practices. They theorize that women as a "muted group" may have either adopted male modes or created alternative ones. For example, "women's consciousness-raising" groups may have trained women in new schemata for reading to see sexism. The "muted group" approach would be applicable to other minorities as well. As such, Crawford and Chaffin incorporate historical contexts into their overall model, providing a flexible thesis that can account for both dominant and minority identities and group patterns in interpreting and responding.

Psychoanalytical theory dominated feminist film studies for at least a decade (mid-1970s through late 1980s) and still is a powerful explanation underpinning most debates. In chapter 3, I reviewed the application of Freudian and Lacanian theory to viewing cinema and pointed out that scholars raised the problem of the place of the female spectator particularly in terms of identification and desire. I noted that Stephen Heath (1978), Mary Ann Doane (1982), and others tended toward media models of reinforcement or power.

Unfortunately, this is not the book to summarize feminist film theory, but a glancing survey is necessary. Among the scholars influential for media feminists were not only Jacques Lacan and Jacques Derrida but also Julia Kristeva, Hélène Cixous, and Luce Irigaray. Their propositions about desire and the woman's body and the effects of both on the female's acquisition of language (and desired object choices) provide complexity to possible models for identification and desire that also eventually affect propositions about males (although note that in chapter 5 regarding stars I have pointed out that the concept of "identification" is a very troubled one).

Recall that both Christian Metz and Laura Mulvey initiated media application of these discussions by focusing on heterosexual male engagements with moving images. Mulvey upped the ante by foregrounding that dominant cinema was produced for the male gaze in that the male protagonist became the "ego ideal of the identification process" (1975:12). What, then, was the place for the female spectator? While Mulvey considered the filmic characters as different on the basis of their sex (men were causal agents; women were the objects of causal actions) and described how most Hollywood films were constructed to pamper the male viewer's desires and allay his anxieties, she treated "the spectator" and "audience" without regard to sex difference. In subsequent essays, when considering the female spectator, Mulvey offers disappointing answers such as that films with female protagonists produced for female audiences (such as Douglas Sirk's melodramas) offer "a fantasy escape" that raises more "contradictions than reconciliation" (1977–78:56). For a male-centered, male-addressed film, a female "may find herself secretly, unconsciously almost, enjoying the freedom of action and control over the diegetic world that identification with a [male] hero provides" (1981:12). Or the female spectator might also simply be "out of key" with the film. Mulvey notes that Freud defines post-Oedipal masculinity as the active drive of the libido (femininity is the passive side); thus, if a female identifies with the active/masculine male, it may be that she will "rediscover that lost aspect of her sexual identity, the never fully repressed bed-rock of feminine neurosis" (13). However, given that in our culture a woman's early masculinity has been reined in, "trans-sex identification is a *habit* that very easily becomes *second Nature*. However, this Nature does not sit easily and shifts restlessly in its borrowed transvestite clothes" (13).

In extending Mulvey's discussion, Doane (1982) claims that for dominant cinema a female spectator must (1) identify with the female character and become feminine/passive (which is to take up a masochistic position); (2) identify with the male character (which is the uneasy transvestite move proposed by Mulvey); *or* (3) flaunt her femininity, becoming an excessively feminine viewer, and narcissistically the object of one's own desire (which is labeled a masquerade). A slightly different extension of Mulvey's observations is Teresa de Lauretis's claim (1984) that the female identifies with both masculine activity and female passivity so that she engages in double identification.

Although I shall return to theorizing identification, several lines of research develop from these feminist propositions. One follows through on identification and desire for women (and other minorities); a second focuses on gynocentric forms—texts that address or construct a female or feminine spectator. Although not the first to ask about such textual relations, in 1984 Annette Kuhn provides an excellent articulation of a sort of ongoing binarism that had developed by then in media scholarship. She points out that film studies researchers were focusing on film melodramas, considering a psychic spectator, and using primarily textual analysis methods, whereas television scholars were looking at daytime soap operas, considering a social audience, and turning to social science audience research. She urges a merging of the approaches, arguing that the study of the Althusserian social spectator might be the way to do this. In any event, both melodramas and soap operas offered female viewers fluid but ultimately masochistic subject positions of femininity. Melodramas accomplished this through females identifying with a woman's renunciation; soap operas maintained this through females experiencing an endlessly differed resolution.

Such textual work on formal features of gynocentric texts did occupy film and television studies, producing important hypotheses about female spectatorship. Tania Modleski's work on soap operas had introduced the idea that not only their representations but also their form was significant. A fundamental feature of the broadcast structure was disruption by commercials: "Daytime television plays a role in habituating women to distraction, interruption, and spasmodic toil" (1979:100). Moreover, besides the lack of narrative resolutions, which she noted produced the "central condition of a woman's life: waiting," Modleski contended that women identified with multiple characters, acting as an "ideal mother." Although Modleski believed women unconsciously liked the villainess, Ellen Seiter and others (1989) argued that women consciously associated with the villainess as a strong character.

Seiter et al. based their argument on ethnographic work of actual audiences. In fact, from the mid-1980s, the impact of critical cultural studies turned feminist media theory toward attempting to verify psychoanalytical propositions about identification. Dorothy Hobson produced an extensive study of the British soap opera *Crossroads*, using in-depth interviews of women, and concluded that for the women, "soap opera characters were important points of reference in the maintenance of cultural identity" (summarized by K. Jensen, 1987:29; also see Hobson, 1990). As would be expected from critical cultural studies, such work cautioned that the explanation should not be some essential sex difference but socialized sex roles: women watched soaps and dramas while men viewed news and sports "not based on biological differences . . . or on a natural authority possessed by men. Rather, they are the effect of the particular social roles that men and women occupy within the home" (Hermans and van Snippenburg, 1996:140).

The need to verify theoretical claims through audience research also strengthened the complexity of the psychoanalytical options of identification. For example, Ien Ang's study of viewers' responses to *Dallas*, a prime-time soap opera, in various countries included analysis of identification patterns by women that supported earlier theoretical ideas. Ang concluded that although women identified with one of the major characters, Sue Ellen, "Just as the fictional character is not a unitary image of womanhood, then, so is the individual viewer not a person whose identity is static and coherent. If a woman is a social subject whose identity is at least partially marked out by her being a person of a certain sex, it is by no means certain that she will always inhabit the same mode of feminine subjectivity" (1990:84–85).

Providing for fluidity to subjectivity and identification did not answer political questions about the import of these engagements. Mulvey and Modleski were certainly unenthusiastic about women-centered, women-addressed forms. Modleski appealed to the Frankfurt school (as well as its extensions by Fredric Jameson) and concluded that soap operas and other mass-produced fictions for women supported neurotic experiences and provided false resolutions. A gothic was a "paranoid text" and the Harlequin romance, a "hysterical" one: both express "angry fantasies and fantasies of being wholly protected and cherished" but an "insufficiency of female selfhood" (1984:32–33). Janice Radway (1984b) also ended up ambivalent about the implications of women reading romances. Her textual and ethnographic study of forty-two women who enjoyed this literature concluded that the act of reading was somewhat an assertion of the self (the women stole the reading time from their family obligations), but the psychic pleasures were suspect. The literature provided a compensatory nurturing fantasy missing from everyday life. Likewise, Ang decided that soap opera viewers enjoyed the programs because of their "tragic structure of feeling" (1982:121), which did not seem to be a progressive outcome—psychoanalytically or socially. Still, Ang did not believe that this entertainment experience canceled out radical political behavior.

Given that all these writers are operating from theories that assume media effects of reinforcement or power, this unease about media is a logical outcome. Other scholars have considered that while the individual/text relation may have questionable political outcomes, the social place and surrounding circumstances also need inclusion in the analysis. Judith Mayne pointed this out in her discussion of immigrant working-class women in nickelodeons. The movies themselves might reinforce dominant values, but moviegoing could be a place of resistance to industrialization and the public nature of a working-class home at the turn of the century (1982:36–39; also see M. Hansen, 1991). Conversation among women as a consequence of viewing soap operas is also touted as a place for consciousness-raising (M. Brown, 1990a:183–98).

Media scholars have also raised the matter of women viewing media texts created by women. The debates around the singer Madonna may not be typical for how this affects interpretations, since her texts have been so problematic. She is a woman clearly authoring, but for whom and with what effects? The question always comes down to defining her intent or privileging an audience's appropriation (if its reading seems at odds with intent). Pamela Robertson neatly summarizes this by pointing out that the debates are even fodder for comedy in movies: "Jewelry thieves in Quentin Tarantino's *Reservoir Dogs* argue if 'Like a Virgin' is about 'big dick' or female desire. Hal Hartley's *Simple Men*, similarly, features generally laconic characters engaged in an extended discussion of whether Madonna's self-exploitation is exploitative" (1996:118).

E. Ann Kaplan initiated these debates as part of her feminist analysis of music video. In considering the subject of "the representation of the female body and the gender address in videos figuring female stars" (1987:115), Kaplan believes that Madonna is a "postmodern feminist heroine" in her video "Material Girl" because, while Madonna blurs boundaries, she "combines unabashed seductiveness with a gutsy kind of independence" (126), producing an idol for teen women. John Fiske also argues that Madonna provides her youthful female fans with a "pleasurable, empowering" image of being in control (1987:254). However, Fiske also discusses polysemy. Various identity groups view her differently: "So Madonna . . . is circulated among some feminists as a reinscription of patriarchal values, among some [heterosexual] men as an object of voyeuristic pleasure, and among many girl fans as an agent of empowerment and liberation. Madonna as a text, or even as a series of texts, is incomplete until she is put into social circulation" (1989:124).

While Fiske bases his claims on some audience research, as I observed in chapter 3, he has great faith in subordinate groups as resistant; here girls resist their place not only in the sex hierarchy but also in age differentials. Susan Bordo argues otherwise. She believes that the overall effect of watching Madonna's body does not produce an "abstract, unsituated, disembodied freedom [for viewers, but] . . . celebrates itself only through the effacement of the material praxis of people's lives, the normalizing power of cultural images, and the sadly continuing social realities of dominance and subordination" (1990:676). In other words, as in the case of women reading male-produced work for female audiences, readers can be suckered into harmful identifications and fantasies, reproducing dominant culture effects.

To test the meanings of Madonna, several empirical studies gathered evidence of individuals reading her music videos. Jane Brown and Laurie Schulze showed two Madonna videos to undergraduate communication students. Perhaps the most surprising finding was that for her "Papa Don't Preach" song, only 43 percent of the black males thought the narrative was about a teen pregnancy; the rest of this group interpreted "havin' my baby" as referring to a boyfriend. Although subsequent discussions have produced an onslaught of metatextual analyses of the discourses around Madonna (Schulze, White, and Brown, 1993; Andermahr, 1994: Robertson, 1996:125–29; Schulze, 1999), her productive output—especially as it has introduced themes of race and homosexuality—still elicits criticisms that the videos are complicit with nonprogressive politics or that her minority viewers are unaware of the dangers of the texts. Robertson (1996:134–36) lists some of the additional critiques by minority identity groups: Madonna lacks a recognition of her privilege; she creates a false sense of equivalence with other minorities, often by appropriating others' cultures; and she places herself at center stage.

Contributions to general media reception studies by feminist scholars considering the relation of media texts to women, feminists, and girls as minority identities have included important work on identification, pleasure and its vicissitudes, textual form and address in relation to identities, and contextual effects of authorship and postviewing conversations. Both men and women may identify across sexes (see chapter 5 on men's cross-sex identification), but the implications of such transgressive identification are different for those in a dominant versus a minority position. Identifying "upward" or experiencing an earlier authorized masculinity in a transvestite move is "uneasy" or perhaps even "neurotic," according to some theories or views about audiences and media. Such an identification does not ensure any sort of political power but perhaps produces nostalgia or an unproductive melancholy. In the later section on lesbian identity, I will return to matters of theorizing identification and will add new problems about desire. Additionally, these themes will reemerge for other minority identities.

Gay Men

As with the case of women, by the time media scholars turn to reception practices for gay men, the rejection of any essential "gay male" is established. Spectatorship is "a learned cultural practice" (Brasell, 1992:55), and gay men are complexes of identities without inherent or uniform reading practices (Staiger, 1992:154–78; Dyer, 1990:82–90, on race intersections). However, specific historical and social circumstances do create some patterns.

As Larry Gross (1991:217) tabulates, critical differences for gays and lesbians (and sexuality minorities as a whole) from other minorities such as women or people of color are that (1) people assume they are something they are not: heterosexual; and (2) no media images exist of what they are, or at least images recognizable to them—although this is a questionable claim for every person, even heterosexual males, and in the sense Gross means it, has perhaps been changing over the past ten years. Gross (1998) also observes that unlike racial/ethnic minorities, (3) sexual minorities are not born into families like themselves and do not live daily with others like themselves. They are isolated from others with the same identity and often do not even recognize this part of their identity until adolescence. Finally, (4) contemporary "good taste" protects other minorities from the worst features of discrimination. As a consequence of this social and historical situation, Gross believes sexual minorities take four responses to media: "internalization, subversion, secession and resistance" (1991:32). Subversion includes camp readings of dominant culture, and resistance involves creation of their own media.

Gross's list of responses is a possible alternative to the standard preferred/negotiated/resisting triad (see chapter 3), although it has its own frailties. For instance, is internalization (thinking that the image is accurate and incorporating it into one's sense of one's self) the only effect of a preferred reading? Does resistance require new media productions or just refusals of what is viewed? Where in this list should one place gay pressure groups such as the Gaylaxians, who have lobbied for explicit representations of sexual diversity in *Star Trek* (Tulloch and Jenkins, 1995:237–38)? Still, what Gross's list offers is more emphasis on the broader response by individuals to media (not simply what happens in the act of a specific engagement with a media text).

Gross's observations about the invisibility of sexuality, even to members of the same sexual minority, underscore the necessity for accounting for similarities in gay men's media spectatorship. Social theory has been very important to this study. Richard Dyer's solution has been out of the critical cultural studies tradition—determining "structures of feeling" that might account for why, for example, gays have enjoyed Judy Garland (1977; 1986:141–94). I have historicized that approach, arguing that structural similarities are created within specific discourses, often through circulating talk (1992:154–77), and Steven Cohan (2001) indicates that the Garland cult still exists among gay men although within a wider fan base. The importance for gay spectators of gay authorship parallels its significance for women, permitting readings of subtextual messages or gay aesthetics (Medhurst, 1991).

A significant part of the excavation of gay media spectatorship has focused on objects of attention or identification. Gays' interest in and use of specific females as stand-ins for themselves has been a major point of discussion, and, as for many fans, the star is often the point of watching the film or television show. Garland is iconic. So are other female stars such as Bette Davis and Joan Crawford. Martin Shingler has discovered that gay readings of *All about Eve* appeared by the 1960s. Gay men figure Davis as bitchy, a gay male in drag, which certainly seems a subversive reading (à la Gross), whereas lesbians use textual information about clothing and behavior to read her as "sapphic" (2001:56–59).

Such an appropriation of female stars has a broader tradition in gay culture. Opera queens, gay spectators of culture, have engaged in such a reading and life practice for a long time. Mitchell Morris (1993) describes this as a very cultivated critical maneuver that adds pleasure to the experience of the text and also to living around that experience. Among its reading features are a cult of the star; a preference for the text to be organized so that the star's performance dominates (that is, the better experience would be the music and drama existing for the star rather than vice versa); a cross-sex identification and subsequent engagement with the plot; and the privileging of the personal, and hopefully erotic, response to the text over any logical description. Compare this with paracinematic reading practices as described in chapter 5 for the general similarity of a performed connoisseurship but also the specificity in terms of what is preferred. Beyond this is the fan behavior around the experience. Morris describes the critical performance of the queen: in the same sentence may alternate "prissy diction and vulgarity" (190), and what might be taken to be insults are likely compliments in a campy inversion of all categories (also see Johnson, 1996, on "Janeites," devotees of the work of Jane Austen).

If Madonna is an exemplar for women's media spectatorship, Mae West is for gay men. Brett Farmer provides a recent and convincing explanation for why gays appreciate West not in a misogynistic act but as one of "emulative identification" (2000:138). Farmer chalks up a bunch of reasons: (1) West's stylization of her own character; (2) her excessive performance of her gender and of being a performer; (3) her preference for surfaces rather than depth; (4) her androgynous voice; (5) her "masculine" delivery; (6) her use of sexual innuendo; (7) her sexual aggression, which is transgressive; and (8) her use of the female grotesque and, in her later years, her age to critique norms of sexual decorum. I discussed gay camp in chapter 5 as a parodic performance from a hypergendered position. West offers gay men such a performance to enjoy. While West has been variably read and appreciated or denigrated (Curry, 1996; Robertson, 1996:36, even argues for interpreting her impersonation as an homage to African American lesbianism), the centrality of West in gay male culture until at least the 1980s is unquestioned.

Thus, social theory discussing gay men focusing on females as objects of attention and identification or enjoying or creating camp critiques of normative gender in historical context has been one explanation for the patterns of gay spectatorship. Recently, psychoanalytical theory is also presenting explanations. Farmer offers a "psychocultural" argument that the experience of gay men explains their particular way of responding to dominant cinematic texts. While carefully acknowledging that other features of the self exist, Farmer claims that the significance of sexuality and the force of social invisibility "make for specific forms of cinematic engagement and reading" (2000:7). Preferring to use the term "gay subjectivity" rather than "identity" in order to emphasize the psychoanalytical over the social, he uses Freudian commentary on homosexuality to argue that gay men in Anglo culture are psychically organized around matrocentricism. Gay men's phantasmic life (more on fantasy theory in the next section) is ordered to affirm an identification with the place of the mother and to refuse the traditional Oedipal structure for heterosexual men (53–67, 84, 168). Such a psychic structure explains the attention and identification with women.

Using this theory, Farmer runs through various well-known generic formulas associated with gay fandom. It is through "excess" that gays enter musicals. Musical numbers are themselves contrary to organized, Oedipal narratives. They are "non- or even anti-oedipal formations of desire" (83), creating viewing "positions that are aberrant, perverse, or just plain 'nonstraight'" (85; also see Davis, 2001–2). Melodramas are a second generic preference where gay men may indulge in matrocentricism. Identification with a phallic mother such as Violet in *Suddenly, Last Summer* or Norma in *Sunset Boulevard* is a fantasy that indicates refusal to submit to "patriarchal 'reality'" (Farmer, 2000:197).

Also turning to psychoanalytical theory to conceptualize gay spectatorship as more than camp readings is Michael DeAngelis. DeAngelis studies gay fandom of male (not female) stars, pointing out that gay men have been attentive to such disparate men as James Dean, Mel Gibson, and Keanu Reeves. Also using fantasy theory, DeAngelis points out that remaining "engaged in a scene of desire" (2001:5) increases viewing pleasure. In the case of melodrama, obstacles must be overcome in the search for origin and oneness. As the male leads in these films pursue their goal, gay men both identify with and desire the star. In the case of particularly famous stars, a career of well-chosen vehicles with this narrative formula aids in the process. An important part of this is to be sure that the credibility of the star's potential real-life availability as an object of desire not be destroyed. Evidence of the star's gayness is not required, but knowledge of explicit homophobia destroys the option of fantasizing.

DeAngelis joins other scholars who have considered gay spectatorship of males. Some of the requirements for objects of desire involve particular bodies or displays of bodies as "spectacles" (which contravenes traditional masculinity), but Steven Cohan (1997) and Daniell Cornell (1998) also think that costuming contributes to the creation of spectacle and thus queering of a male, opening the door for gay male voyeurism. Farmer also tackles this issue. Given that his argument involves a rejection of "paternal identification and phallic masculinity," Farmer believes that a "disidentification" occurs (2000:202–3), and gays appropriate certain specular, and thus feminized, males as objects of desire.

Disidentification is a concept that is gaining theoretical significance as a common experience for minorities. José Esteban Muñoz (1996) popularized the term, revising it from an earlier idea of "revisionary identifi-cation" in use by critical race theorists. Disidentification is an instance in which an individual sees another individual and both assumes some com-monality that might result in normal identification and simultaneously re-alizes that the two are not the same. These are "incomplete, mediated, or crossed identifications" (145). For example, Muñoz mentions Michelle Wallace's comment about Joan Crawford that "'she is so beautiful, she looks black'" (150). The key point is that Wallace does not wish she were white; she retains her identity as black. What she sees is the potential for sameness but also the differences that matter. Muñoz underlines that per-haps in cross-identity identifications individuals do not abandon their own identity as they "step" into the other person's subjectivity. Disiden-tification may have some power to contribute to the discussions by femi-nist media scholars about what options women have in viewing male-cen-tered narratives, adding to the array of masochist, transvestite, or mas-querade choices. At any rate, the concept will reappear in later sections.

Lesbians

As with other minority identities, whether lesbians have a specific and common experience is unlikely. Still, the question is raised about patterns. As one of the earliest second-wave feminists, Bonnie Zimmerman, put it, "Does a woman's sexual and affectional preference influence the way she writes, reads, and thinks? . . . Is there a lesbian aesthetic distinct from a feminist aesthetic?" (1981:200).

Like gay men, lesbians are invisible to others and, in their early lives, to others similar to them. Moreover, until recently, they were not explic-itly represented in texts either. However, research into lesbians' reading preferences does indicate some trends in negotiating their absences in mainstream media. In an early study, Caroline Sheldon (1977) deter-mined that lesbians were interested in the "strong" women of 1930s and 1940s Hollywood cinema, indicating that what drew them were women cross-dressing, especially Marlene Dietrich flirting with women in audi-ences as she performed and Katherine Hepburn in *Sylvia Scarlett*. Other scholars have noted female stars have stimulated lesbians to create fan videos such as *Dry Kisses Only* (1990) on Bette Davis (Mayne, 1993:135–36). Lesbians have also been fans of opera divas (Castle, 1993:200–238).

Cheryl Dobinson and Kevin Young argue that lesbians interpret popular film "informed by lesbian-specific life experiences and cultural competencies" (2000:97). As with gay men, social theory involving a homology between self and other is a robust and logical explanation for why this pattern exists. Research on lesbians reading films without apparent lesbians in the representations is fairly consistent in its findings. First of all, lesbians "identify with or desire" "strong" and "self-reliant, resilient female characters." This identification/desire may even lead into privileging the "outlaw," the "bad girl," or the "defiant/deviant" woman (Dobinson and Young, 2000:101; Whatling 1997) or elevating a secondary "lesbian" character to protagonist (Ellsworth, 1986). It may be that this is a more recent variation. In one of the few attempts to determine older historical preferences, Andrea Weiss (1991) believes she has evidence from historical context that lesbians in the early 1930s viewed androgyny as "liberating" and also enjoyed the stars later lesbians have looked to for viewing pleasures.

In any case, cross-dressing such as by Dietrich, Hepburn, or Greta Garbo in *Queen Christina* (1933) plays into the delight, as viewers enjoy "inadvertent lesbian verisimilitude"—from touching to body posture to eyeline glances (Ellsworth, 1986:54; Weiss, 1991; Dobinson and Young, 2000:111). Interviews with lesbians indicate that anything that would "violate conventional gender codes" helps (Dobinson and Young, 2000:107).

Also useful to a lesbian reading are female friendships. In a valuable argument about appropriating images for lesbian or "queer" use, Alexander Doty considers women pairs or friendships in film and television, describing how to "make" them into lesbians, which is not too hard. Often the texts themselves make joking allusions to the potential for a lesbian relationship (1993:39–62). Marilyn Burgess (1990/91) argues that a 1940 National Film Board documentary about wartime women's troops easily opened itself to lesbian pleasures on the basis of scenes of women together in sensual activities such as swimming.

Beyond features of the texts, lesbians also use gossip about stars or knowledge of a history of the stars portraying unconventional females to justify the projection of a possible lesbianism into the text. As with other minorities, they may seek out the history of creators of the text, reasoning that individuals with their same identity could produce texts with an appeal for them or even insert secret messages. They then search for such a homosexual or lesbian textuality in passages of the work (Hennegan, 1988).

These readers are actively using reading strategies that defy normative procedures. Alison Hennegan (1988) indicates that even as a child she identified with male characters so she could desire women. With a possible lesbian character, readers "resist a 'straight' ending" (Dobinson and Young, 2000:102, referencing Ellsworth, 1986). Heterosexual scenes with imagined lesbians are ignored as a cover-up. These readers even admit to a tendency to "force" "dyke-ness" into a scene (Dobinson and Young, 2000:111–16).

If a lesbian does appear in the text, lesbians may still need to work on the image if the text does not produce a pleasurable outcome (Traub, 1991), especially given the negative representations of lesbians in media. Elizabeth Ellsworth's analysis of lesbian feminists reading *Personal Best* indicates that the minority group read it differently from the dominant press in order to produce pleasure and political information. Using a "structures of feeling" thesis, Ellsworth emphasizes that feminism supports such an appropriation of a dominant interpretation:

> Social actors may experience these patterns [of hope, anxiety, and desire] initially as private, idiosyncratic, even isolated responses to cultural forms like films. But through material practices like consciousness raising [*sic*] groups, women's studies courses and feminist film reviewing, feminist communities collectively develop interpretative strategies for making sense of these structures of feelings, moving then into the sphere of public discourse by giving social, semantic form to anxieties and desires. (1986:46)

In other words, part of the explanation for these patterns must lie in social exchange among minorities. Additionally, evidence exists that some minorities enjoy maintaining subtexts as just that: subtexts. Fans of *Xena: Warrior Princess* indicated that they really enjoyed the lack of an explicit indication of any lesbian relation between Xena and Gabriel (S. Ross, 2002).

Scholars have used social theory and textual analysis of interviews, questionnaires, and historical documents to excavate and describe lesbian viewing practices. One of the most important recent debates, however, has occurred within psychoanalytical theory. As I noted in chapters 3 and 5 and earlier in this chapter, psychoanalytical approaches to minority-identity viewing practices emphasize identification and desire. Recently, questions have developed about the efficacy of merely asking with whom a reader identifies. Part of this questioning developed as a result of the discussion of Mulvey's work, stimulating theories of identification as masochism, (an uneasy) transvestitism, and masquerade. Scholars note that double identification and cross-sex, cross-sexuality, and cross-race identifications seem to happen. Even the definition of what would constitute "identification" is undecided.

To begin to sort this out in a new way, Jackie Stacey (1994) discriminates among nine different attitudes that fans have toward stars, ranging from worshiping them, to finding similarities between their fictional characters' concerns and the individuals' own, to imitating their clothing or behavior in everyday life (see chapter 5). As part of her argument, Stacey turns to Elizabeth Cowie's work (1984; also 1997) on the Freudian theory of fantasy. Cowie stresses that desire develops in a scene; it takes place in a "'mise-en-scene of desire'" (Cowie, quoted by Stacey, 1994:30). Moreover, in Freudian theory, an individual may take up multiple positions (that is, "identify") in a scene. The classic case is the "child is being beaten" story in which the individual may take the positions of observer, child, and the one doing the beating. Freud offers that at least three fantasy scenes are very common: ones of sexual desire (the fantasy of seduction), sexual difference (the fantasy of castration), and the origin of the self (the fantasy of the family romance or a return to the origin), which, as I noted in chapter 3, Linda Williams (1991), following Richard Dyer (1985), has pointed out correlates neatly with three major film genres (pornography, horror, and melodrama).

Following Cowie, Stacey argues that identification is not easily separated from desire and is likely related. Identification with the other is important in the formation of an ego. So is recognition by the other. About an "ideal love," she writes, this is a "'love in which the person seeks to find in the other an ideal image of himself [sic]'" (Stacey, 1994:174, quoting Jessica Benjamin). Research on lesbian viewers (and others as well) indicates that all sorts of permutations of these positions and affects exist. Jeffrey Brown (1997) surveyed responses to a famous *Vanity Fair* cover in which the model Cindy Crawford is shaving K. D. Lang, who is publicly a lesbian. Lesbians indicated that they both desired Crawford or Crawford and Lang and identified with Lang or Crawford and Lang.

Recently, however, de Lauretis has questioned the elision of difference between identification and desire. In her book *The Practice of Love* (1994) she argues for maintaining a strict distinction in order to understand the particular psychic and social place of a lesbian in self-identity and desire (see Hollinger, 1998, for a review of the debates). This discussion will be an important one to follow.

An additional cautionary move has occurred. Judith Halberstam points out that just as it is necessary not to confuse a "masculine" female with a lesbian, scholars should not assume only two genders or two sexualities. At the turn of the twentieth century, many nontraditional female identities existed: tribade, hermaphrodite, romantic friend, Sapphist, Tommy (1998:51). Even now, as gender and sex reassignments are easily possible, creating hypotheses about patterns of audience response needs subtle distinctions.

Study of lesbian viewing practices has much in common with that related to other minorities, but feminist and queer media scholars considering this identity have produced important interventions in the larger research area.

Race/Ethnicity

Unlike sexual minorities, individuals who are born visibly different from the dominant stereotype—here in Anglo-land as light-skinned, with northern European features—encounter tacit and explicit racism. The effects of this are apparent in the negative or noncomplex representations in media when these minorities are even present. Exclusion from representation is another method of marginalization. As for women and sexual minorities, it has mattered to race/ethnic minorities whether the members of their own group or others produce these representations—or, even if dominant groups are the primary producers, whether the representations open up to minorities mobility opportunities by providing acting jobs.

Research indicates that blacks will support their own product, evaluating it better than whites do for comprehension and other factors (Birtha, 1977). However, this is not always the case: African American audiences have at times preferred Anglo-produced fare even when black-produced product was available, if the Anglo movies were slicker (Carbine, 1990:20–21), which they certainly became as the film industry developed and minority ownership or control declined. Still, black audiences in Chicago between 1905 and 1930 also enjoyed surrounding that white product with black music and live entertainers, potentially creating a complex experience in terms of meaning.

Additionally, black journalists have attempted to raise the quality of African American and Anglo media through sharp criticism. Several scholars (Griffiths and Latham, 1999; Everett, 2000, 2001; Regester, 2001) have studied extensively the commentary of the black press at the turn of the twentieth century. Lester Walton, entertainment editor for the *New York Age* beginning in 1905, criticized racist and sensationalist representations of African Americans in white-produced movies, urging boycotts even prior to the major attack on *The Birth of a Nation* from 1914 on. He particularly went after images of blacks being lynched and other such melodramatic fare that he believed exploited audiences through sensation rather than reason. Walton also scolded black audiences for failing to support black-produced work. Study of contemporary minority criticism of minority-produced work remains conflicted: Should minorities create "positive" images or "real" ones, and what might the dominant race think about "real" images if they are not positive (Cornwell and Orbe, 2002)?

Anna Everett labels Walton's critical distance from the movies, his localization of parts of the film for his censure, and his nonstandard interpretations to be a "transcoding" (2000:31). Associating transcoding with the reception strategy of "talking back/black" described by bell hooks, Everett believes this is a widespread phenomenon among African Americans. Everett's transcoding and hooks's talking back/black should not be confused with the widely discussed "call-and-response" practice of providing oral commentary during a movie in black and other audiences. While call-and-response may have a critical edge, it is employed to create laughter and focus attention on the individual producing the commentary or to create a socially bonded audience; in this way it belongs to other normal fan reading practices. Rather, transcoding is a recoding or translation of what is occurring on the screen into a politicized black perspective. I shall return to this later.

The use of black actors in white-produced media roles that seem to be negative stereotypes has produced mixed responses from blacks. For example, in the 1930s Paul Robeson played both heroic and stereotypical black roles in music, theater, and film. Dyer records that whites and blacks mutually saw him as "the representative of blackness" (1986:73), but African American evaluation of his work was mixed, with only some black approval. Likely part of this lack of a uniform response is traceable to splits in black politics or to class differences. Whether African Americans should pursue an assimilationist or upwardly mobile solution to their oppression or opt for a separatist and revolutionary stance affects perception of the value of working as an actor within dominant media. Thomas Cripps (1983) points out the options well in his study of black debates about the 1950s television program *Amos 'n' Andy*. This choice is also apparent in Norman Friedman's study of black criticism of black-centered television shows when these journalists castigated the white-produced programs for "negative stereotyping" and "lack of ethnic uniqueness and/or realism" (1978:89). Anita Bodroghkozy finds the same thing for the late 1960s television program *Julia*. Black viewers who saw the show as "unrealistic and who found Julia to be a 'white Negro' had difficulty identifying with any of the characters" (1992:159). Debates over the black-produced *Cosby Show* in the 1980s produced the same result (Staiger, 2000a).

In a sort of reverse situation, Chon Noriega (2001) explains why *Born in East L.A.* has a strong Chicano/a scholarly following; such viewers are used to reading mise-en-scène because that is where much of the progressive political commentary exists in forms of posters and other visual remarks. Much like the difference between women and women feminist spectators, political perspectives may split configurations of response within race/ethnic identities, producing subgroups that develop similarities in interpretations and evaluations. Sylvie Thouard (2001) finds several subgroups based on nationality and feminist politics for audiences responding to Lourdes Portillo's documentary, *The Devil Never Sleeps*.

Not only politics but also sex may create schisms in patterns of race/ethnic minority response. Cheryl Butler and Jacqueline Bobo have considered African American reactions to Steven Spielberg's adaptation of Alice Walker's novel *The Color Purple*. Protests occurred over the filmic representation of the black men as historically inaccurate (and unfaithful to the novel) and denigrating to black men, who also have been victims of their social circumstances. However, some black women "defended the film, suggesting that it was a realistic depiction" (Butler, 1991:64) in terms of the lives of African American women and was a rare instance of making black women central to the story (Bobo, 1995:61–132). Bobo explains this variation among the African Americans as a consequence of the bonding of black feminist women into an "interpretive community," allowing them to "bring an oppositional stance to their interaction with mainstream media" (1995:27; also see Bobo, 1988).

Indeed, the specificity of race/ethnic minority interpretations has produced extensive theorizing about both their methods of engaging and disengaging with dominant and minority media and the intersectionality of their minority identities. This theory has been one of the richest contributions to media reception studies. Drawing from the early observation by W. E. B. Du Bois that blacks have a "double consciousness"—they grow up seeing the world through the eyes of other people who judge them, and they constantly reflect on whether they live up to those expectations (Gaines, 2001a:12–13)—scholars have extended and debated what this means for race/ethnic identities and minorities' reception of media.

The idea of an "oppositional gaze" comes from hooks (1982). By this she means that since blacks were traditionally forbidden to gaze on whites, the opportunity to look at them in environments such as the movies has produced a critical gaze. In addition, hooks explicitly rejects describing the oppositional gaze as a resisting interpretation (in the sense employed by Stuart Hall). Instead, she defines it as more of an alternative reading practice. For instance, African Americans see race and racism where whites do not.

A lovely example of this is the case study of "Ti-Rone," who did radio updates for a local African American community on the CBS afternoon soap opera *The Young and Restless* in the early 1990s. Gloria Abernathy-Lear (1995) describes this DJ's sassy commentary, which provides plot information but ridicules white manners while foregrounding story arcs involving black characters, citing it as an example of a classic race/ethnic bilingual life in which an individual moves between dominant and minority communities. (Also see Nakayama and Peñaloza, 1993; Cooper, 1998; and on whites' race-blindness, J. Lewis, 1991:110–15, 159–202.)

While African Americans and other racial/ethnic minorities have watched and interpreted media through a transcoding or an oppositional gaze, they have also identified with, or sought to identify with, characters. Karen Alexander (1991) uses autoethnography to describe how she hunted for black female stars but was disappointed to discover that women such as Dorothy Dandridge had serious problems with their careers. Anne duCille tells much the same story, recounting her internal struggles: "My attempts as a child to define myself against such images [of blacks as portrayed in Hollywood cinema] haunted me as a kind of double fault, a shameful shame that ate at the core of my black identity and challenged my credibility as an authentic African American" (1998:30–31). Another reading strategy in the face of negative roles for minority stars has been to interpret the stars as resisting the roles into which they have been cast. Thus, if the actors are covertly criticizing those types, the audience can enjoy a moment of empowerment for the stars.

Lacking individuals with similar racial/ethnic identities for identification produces a certain amount of cross-racial appropriation by minorities, although justified by gossip (Wallace, 1993). As I mentioned earlier, Michelle Wallace tells about observing and identifying with Joan Crawford, who was rumored to be black. Jane Gaines (2001b) also analyzes James Baldwin's reminiscences of his cross-race, cross-sex engagement with white female stars. Following Muñoz, she thinks this is an instance of disidentification (although I am unconvinced that Baldwin is making the second step of retaining his pride in his black identity and thus "disidentifying").

Identification for race/ethnic minorities has prompted additional theorizing from the minority perspective. In an important essay on the question, Manthia Diawara (1990) postulates that the basic dynamics for identification with characters exist for all spectators regardless of identities. However, if textual ruptures occur, a spectator might recognize a personal identity (such as black, Marxist, gay) that is separate from the characters with whom the spectator is identifying. Thus, following traditional psychoanalytical theory, textual features determine spectator activity; however, what happens as a consequence of the break would be specific to the individual. This would explain when and how a minority becomes a resistant spectator.

Recently, Jacqueline Stewart has questioned both Diawara's resistant spectator and hooks's oppositional gaze theories. She believes that from the start the discussion must include spectators' senses of a "public self" (2003:666). For racial minorities, the modern public self is different from the white privilege of the flaneur or the surrealist. While at times minority spectators may take up the spectator positions offered, when they do resist images, a better way to think about this is as talking back/black (from hooks) or transcoding (from Everett). Stewart says the minority response is "reconfiguring . . . racist hierarchies by subverting the pleasures that Hollywood films anticipate" through a "sardonic laughter" (675–76).

More Matters

Class probably was the first major identity for scholarly investigation. The critical cultural studies group organized to follow up on earlier Marxist concerns about how economic oppression and hegemony operated. That group also concerned itself with age (youth) and sex (boys and men). I have covered some of this research in chapter 3 and alluded to it earlier in this chapter. Still an important identity, class has sometimes been relegated to a secondary variable with primary focus on another identity. However, the results have indicated that class makes important differences.

Andrea Press's research provides a good example. Using critical cultural studies and feminist perspectives, she assumes potential diversity based on class and age in women's responses to representations on television. In one study she determines that "middle-class women are more apt than working-class women to identify overtly with television characters on a personal level and to use these personal identifications to work out problems concerning interpersonal relationships in their lives" (1991:96). However, for the high-spectacle prime-time soap opera *Dynasty*, middle-class women thought the show was "quite fantastic" (Press, 1990:165), although they could identify with some characters and situations. Working-class women found the show "realistic" (164). A second finding was that working-class women tended to "express this reception of television using terms that are first related to their experiences as members of the working class and secondarily related to their experience as women per se in our society" (Press, 1991:97). Finally, if the working-class woman had aspirations for a middle-class life, her responses to some matters (such as representations of abortion) differed from women who conceptualized themselves firmly now and in the future in the working class.

Other recent work on class produces the same sorts of phenomena: class identity intersects with other identities in ways that suggest patterns of intersections result in variations that need to be noted. In a study of *The Cosby Show*, Justin Lewis determines that "middle- and upper-middle-class viewers tended to see the show as class-specific (i.e., a show about people like them), while working- and lower-middle-class viewers often referred to the show as classless and universal (i.e., also about people like them)" (1994:28). John Gabriel's study (1996) of British responses to *Falling Down* (1993) indicates both class and race identities rise up at various times in reactions to narrative events.

Age likely needs to be factored in. Karen Riggs (1996, 1998) has found that individuals in retirement have viewing preferences that she believes relates to their changed life circumstances. She thinks that predilections go toward texts that provide more closure and ritual continuity.

Also needing to be factored in are religious, national, and political allegiances. Some cross-cultural studies have produced the unsurprising results that people recognize the source of media texts and that this may influence responses. The studies by Tamar Liebes and Elihu Katz (1990; also Katz and Liebes, 1984; Liebes, 1988) are well respected. Using the method of gathering data via focus groups and theory from psychoanalysis and structural-functional sociology, Liebes and Katz considered how five cultural groups in Israel interpreted the U.S. prime-time soap opera *Dallas*. They discovered that in retelling story lines, three types of narration occurred: linear (event by event), segmented (highlights), and thematic (story morals). In their groups, Arab and Moroccans did linear retellings; kibbutz members and Americans produced segmented readings about personalities and changing situations; Russians stressed the moral or message of the program (Liebes, 1988). Other examples of such research are Ang, 1982; Norden and Wolfson, 1986; Crofts, 1992; and Puri, 1997.

Intersectionality theory, which developed in critical race studies, has not yet advanced enough to provide models for how to engage in the aspects of studying interlocking identities. While social science methods have attempted to use statistical packages to consider pertinent and nonpertinent identities, those methods cannot tackle complex bodies of evidence such as texts from focus groups or self-generated essays. Intersectionality theory also emphasizes historical variables. When we are dealing with reception of media texts, self-perceptions of identity and minority status are also likely to be pertinent.

Consistent within the work on minority identities has been some attention to whether "essential" features of being a minority matter, how other aspects of identities influence experiences with media, and what is or is not available for the minorities' pleasure. Threads of theory involve minorities' variable engagements and disengagements with the images producing appropriation or disidentification. Traditional questions of identification and desire are also consistently raised. Finally, contextual knowledge makes a difference. Minority (and majority) viewers often know who produced the media text and the circumstances around its availability. Social conversations in social places play into interpretations.

7

Violence, Horror, and Sexually Explicit Images

A major issue in reception studies has been fears of effects, especially couched in language about unformed, ill-formed, or weak minds, most often projected as belonging to children, the working class, immigrants, and women. As I discussed in chapter 2, initial research on media effects and reception derived from such turn-of-the-twentieth-century social and political concerns. Moreover, from that point on, events produced moral panics, and new cycles of attention toward this question have occurred, with government funding often supporting extensive research projects. Additionally, a belief in at least general outcomes from media experiences has resulted in significant governmental discussion and planning. G. Tom Poe (2001) describes how U.S. policy makers sought to contain possible widespread defeatism and depression feared as an outcome of the 1959 release of the nuclear holocaust saga *On the Beach*. So both media in general and specific texts have concerned those in power.

Particularly in the late 1950s, questions of effects on behavior and attitudes topped the agenda for academic mass communication theorists. Behavioral psychology and cultivation theory supplied education-model views that media exposure could produce short-term or long-term differences for viewers. Uses-and-gratification theory was more sanguine, taking a mediation view that other factors contributed significantly to individual choices in media consumption and that those factors, not the media images themselves, were salient. Likewise, social-psychoanalytic theory, cognitive psychology, and cultural studies (either structural-functionalist or critical) have postulated a variety of theses about media effects from education through to power views. However, to date, no thesis about direct behavioral effects from watching media images is accepted.

Certainly, we do have anecdotal reason to assume some relationship between media images and human beliefs, if not behavior. For instance, stories exist of movies influencing important choices in lives. One woman looking back on her career selection as a psychiatrist of children's traumas attributes it to seeing a documentary about Hiroshima at a Saturday matinee at age nine (Pillemer, 1998:25–26). While the viewing of such horrific images had an immediate negative effect for her, the overall outcome for society might be considered positive. Additionally, our identities or cognitive schemata or psychological profiles are constructed in part from various environmental experiences that do include film and television. Thus, dismissing altogether the idea of effects from media would be obstinate. The questions are how to find a reasonable ground between competing claims of significant or no implications to watching and listening to media and how to distinguish between apparently negative and positive outcomes.

In chapters 2 and 3, I provided fairly extensive reviews of the basic premises of the major approaches to media effects, including those effects from violent and sexually explicit materials, and I also outlined key theoretical and methodological criticisms of these theories. In this chapter, my goal is to sketch out several historical exchanges in order to indicate generally where debates about media effects from these sorts of images are at this point. Some premises have been revised or dropped as scholars have adjusted to the difficulties of proving media effects. Although the broader theories should apply regardless of the content, different issues have concerned researchers for violent, horrific, and sexually explicit media. Thus, I will consider each separately.

Violence in the Media

The first and strongest claims for effects of media have been that watching moving images can cause unsocial behavior. Richard Maltby reports on a Columbia University professor who in 1929 studied effects of movies on children:

Joseph L. Holmes published the results of a two-year study. . . . Holmes found no evidence of harm, a result he attributed to a combination of the consistent presence of pictures of a "highly moral ending, the ultimate punishment of the sinner," and the children's poor memory of the movie, even immediately after they had seen it. (Maltby, 2001:123)

For every supposed example of movies creating behavior that Holmes reviewed, "'the cause was found not in the movies but in an individual's history of imbecility or unwholesome home environment and training'" (124). This is the classic causal conundrum: What causes what?

At this point, claims that movies or television viewing causes unsocial behavior have not been proved. It is not even clear that people who act unsocially have as great an exposure to violent images in their lives as the general population. In an excellent and sympathetic review of the literature within a behavioral psychology perspective, Barrie Gunter (1994; also see Linné and Wartella, 1998:5) defines five hypothesized behavioral effects of watching violent images and summarizes the state of research for each possible behavioral consequence. He concludes that not much evidence exists for **catharsis**: that people might discharge aggression while watching violence (also called the "hostility catharsis" premise). **Arousal** may occur, but it can happen for all sorts of images, not just violent ones. Some evidence exists that **disinhibition**, reduction of normal social controls, may occur. The classic proof is that people may be more aggressive in a controlled laboratory setting, for instance, permitting someone to hurt someone else. However, this finding has yet to be repeated outside such an artificial environment. Children especially show some evidence of learning (**imitation**) from watching movies, but children also gain knowledge of social restraints (as Holmes notes in 1929). Finally, repeat viewing of violent images may lead to acceptance of violence, the so-called **desensitization** (or cultivation) hypothesis.

The proposition that violent movies produce unsocial imitative behavior has had great media attention and equal critical scholarly rejection. For example, Victoria Harbord notes that the British press reported that ten murders were "linked" to the film *Natural Born Killers*. Investigation later showed that none of these connections were plausible (1997:137–38). Proving such a link will always be difficult. As Graham Murdock enumerates the problems, (1) finding an unimpeachable case example is difficult because witnesses are often unreliable; (2) other causes are easily turned to as explanations for any specific instance; and (3) correlation is as easily the relation as causality (1997:75–86).

Moreover, studies of juvenile offenders indicate that their media viewing habits are not dissimilar from those of all schoolchildren. In some cases they even watch fewer movies and less television. In one study, *Groundhog Day* was one of the delinquents' top five movies (Gauntlett, 1995:4–6). As David Gauntlett summarizes, "Profiles of the most frequent offenders reflect lives of deprivation rather than depravation" (6). The *New York Times* reviewed the histories of one hundred "rampage killers" and determined that "cultural" influences were small: only eleven people reported liking violent television, and only six played violent video games. However, forty-seven had a history of mental health problems ("Rampage Killers in 100 Cases," 2000:A13).

Disinhibition with an increase in aggression from watching violent images has some small credibility. Because the argument that viewing mediated violence directly begets violent behavior could not be sustained, scholars revised their claim to one that seeing aggression (real or mediated) lowered social constraints against it (i.e., disinhibited it). Experiments in controlled environments within a social-learning theory perspective in the 1960s (Albert Bandura's work) indicated that children would imitate violent behavior in that situation. However, the lab setting and cueing the research subject might have been the cause as much as the violent content (Cumberbatch, 1989:32–39). In 1978, a team of researchers attempted to transfer laboratory results into a natural setting. While watching a violent movie did produce higher verbal aggression among a group of juvenile offenders, repetition of viewing made no difference to behavior. This led the researchers to conclude that the aggression was "short-lived" and that disinhibition from repetition might also produce "satiation or habituation" (Sebastian et al., 1978:164). An exchange in the mid-1980s indicates that further studies in laboratory and natural environments could not produce greater results than the small, short-term effect of general stimulation of the subject (Freedman, 1984, 1986; Friedrich-Cofer and Huston, 1986; also see Durkin, 1985).

By the 1990s, media specificity arguments also attacked a "linear-effects" approach to viewing and behavior. Sporadic exposure to film had made it difficult to sustain causal claims, but the habitual, ubiquitous environment of television is different. The disinhibition thesis was mostly directed at television violence. However, even behavioral psychology (the theory most invested in stimulus-response models) concluded that, while television might have extensive instances of violent images, behavioral theory required that the stimulus actually come to the attention of the subject. In the real world of television viewing, this was a chancy situation. Daniel R. Anderson and John Burns (1991) point out that viewers attend to the image for only about two-thirds of the time, and even then their looking is limited to short glances. Certain content, style, and identity features (such as age and sex) make a difference in viewing behaviors, but taking these variables into account is necessary when making claims about what people are actually experiencing in real environments.

If it has been difficult to prove behavioral effects from watching mediated violence, some people believe that attitudes or beliefs about the world might be affected, indirectly producing behavioral results. Whatever the theory of how we acquire our selves, observation of exterior settings does matter in our development as children and in our lives as adults. Whether biological, social, or psychological underpinnings are postulated, somehow affective and cognitive views develop, and cognitive scripts or psychoanalytical scenarios form cores to our daily interactions with other people. Refusing to acknowledge that children (and adults) may have nightmares from violent (or frightening) images of real or fictional sources is not a productive engagement with the question of media images.

Still, what can be said about the causal relations between violent images and attitudes or beliefs is vague. One way to handle the lack of findings from violent images to behavior was to redirect the disinhibition thesis to effects of images on beliefs about reality. The central statement of this is found in cultivation theory, led by George Gerbner's research. Gerbner's various research projects have produced extensive and at times incredible findings about the amount of violence represented in film and television. For instance, a 1980s study showed that Saturday morning children's programming produced almost three times the number of incidents of violence as did prime-time television, rising to an average of twenty-one acts per hour (Signorielli and Gerbner, 1988:xii). Study of viewers indicated a "pleasing positive correlation between the amount of television viewing and 'fear of victimisation'" (Cumberbatch, 1989:31).

Others have challenged this relationship and what it implies. Rather than seeing viewing as causing a belief, it may be the reverse: people who hold the belief use viewing as a way to reinforce it or to stave off anxieties as they survey their environment (Gunter, 1994:183–87). Watching crime may even produce crime-prevention (instead of violent) behavior (Cumberbatch, 1989:32).

Part of the viewing-creates-attitudes/beliefs proposition involves describing what it is that people are watching. As I noted in chapter 1, content analysis is a favored technique if causal or correlation theses are posited because counting seems to produce objectivity. The cultivation hypothesis (and other mass communication theses) is based on content analysis (twenty-one violent acts per hour). Not only were the causal claims about violence and attitudes/beliefs challenged during the 1980s; so was the supposed transparency of the content of the texts. With the introduction of linguistic and semiotic textual studies in the 1970s, thinking about the function of violence within the larger narrative changed. As I noted in chapter 2, from the start of film analysis, pointillist and total-picture theories of interpretation vied for credibility. Just as television viewing environments complicate claims of attention (and stimulus-response), so does narrative studies.

Violence exists not on its own but within complexes. As John Cawelti (1975:523) points out, these complexes include generic conventions, cultural stereotypes, and specific treatments of motives, acts, and emotions. Although young children will need to learn these complexes, adolescents and adults know them. More important for the point here, violence is not an isolated act for a total-picture theorist. Violence may occur as punishment for wrongdoing and may be emotionally satisfying if it upholds social contracts (Sumner, 1997b:1). Moreover, people perceive and define acts as violent on different grounds: they distinguish between "playful" and "authentic" violence, and their response is regulated by a sense of fairness (Morrison et al., 1999).

Where is the violence in the narrative? No theory of viewing can afford to decontextualize violence from its place in the text. Among the sorts of distinctions possible would be type of violence (murder, sacrifice, self-defense); perpetrator (criminal, victim, law enforcement official); legitimacy (has a social group affirmed its use, as in the case of war?); affirming of the status quo or revolutionary; individual or mass; discrete or spectacle; on or off the screen; by which social identity against which social identity; real or fiction; straight or parody; and so forth. Gauntlett (1995:4–6) also points out that violence is not the only content produced in media; one content analysis that counted the number of pro-social acts versus violence in American television recorded an average of twenty pro-social acts per hour, compared with eight instances of violence.

What people are watching also includes how they interpret the complexes of violence. By the 1990s, studies indicate that audiences do not interpret violence as content-analysis researchers see it (Gunter, 1994:190–97). Thus, even if media violence is part of the experience of creating our attitudes and beliefs, the outcome is not a given from specific tallies of violence in texts.

One possible influence on interpretation of violence is identification. As I have noted in chapters 3 and 6, theories of identification are complex. Anyone might identify with a victim in a narrative, and psychoanalytical theory suggests that representations—even of violence—are structured for scenes of fantasy and wish fulfillment that may be very personally idiosyncratic. One study of how women interpret violence indicates, reasonably, that women who have experienced violence are more able to identify with a narrative victim (Schlesinger et al., 1992). Still, identity differences involving race and class could make such identifications complex and discriminating, and films that the women viewed as using violence as a ploy "to entertain by producing fear" were not even taken seriously.

Such a transformation from direct viewing hypotheses of violence creating attitudes and beliefs to more sophisticated theories of interpretation and methods of considering textual features makes claims about violence creating attitudes and beliefs not invalid but complex. Take, for instance, Neal King's argument in his *Heroes in Hard Times* (1999). Attempting to account for the function of racial/ethnic minorities as sidekicks in cop action films of the last couple decades, King argues that these nonwhite males exist as foils and ideal egos for the white heroes to work through their own anxieties about women and minorities. With most of these films featuring whiter-than-white villains, the heroes align themselves with women and minorities as victims, thus making the heroes' initial violence acceptable while trying to deny its existence. Now, assuming such a description of this (very violent) genre is fairly faithful to the narrative content, the numerous ways actual viewers might engage with the violence in these films is quite complicated. Furthermore, deciding whether these films are reinforcing old views and attitudes or rearranging them into new ones depends on the sort of overall theory of media effects. Whatever is the case, it is not a simple one of violent images creating attitudes/beliefs.

Debates about media violence not only have considered possible bad effects but have hypothesized good effects beyond the notion of hostility catharsis from viewing. Depictions of violence are not inherently immoral if such images also function as social control. Cawelti's (1975) study of the formulas using violence was a proposition about lessons involving crime, revenge, honor, and regeneration, although more pessimistic assessments of some films' contributions to the public good also exist (see Elsaesser, 1976).

In the last several years, scholars have turned the questions about media violence away from the effects-oriented approaches popular among theories of education, reinforcement, and power and toward how mediation theory prefers to consider reception. In this case, they ask, how do already formed individuals engage with texts that include violence? As early as 1973, Richard Dembo employed an ethnographic study to consider the "uses-gratifications" of violence for "aggressive" and "non-aggressive" boys. Of his twenty-six categories, six fall into media use as "exciting." Escaping worries or the humdrum seems quite pertinent as well. Indeed, Leo Charney argues that 1980s and 1990s action films and their violence are satisfying because they give people a sense of lost presence. He claims, "The force of violence externalizes and renders as a kinaesthetic effect the rolling hunger to face the present, to feel it and see it and re-present it. But this effort fails" (2001:49).

Two extended studies present similar mediation-theory treatments of violence in media. Annette Hill's *Shocking Entertainment* (1997) and Martin Barker and Kate Brooks's *Knowing Audiences* (1998) are valuable contributions to this approach to media effects and violence, and both employ interview methods to produce their results. Hill believes that people have "portfolios of interpretation." These "contextual and individual factors form the viewing experience" (Hill, 1997:4–5). Barker and Brooks study audiences for *Judge Dredd* and conclude that six "patterns of involvement" (1998:153) explain the more local interpretations of the film. These patterns of involvement involve why the individuals choose to attend the film and what expectations they held. Some went because they liked action-adventure movies; others were fans of the comic book, of science fiction, or even of Sylvester Stallone, who played the lead role. Given the premises or possible uses of the film—Barker and Brooks list sixteen (143–45)—the viewers' responses to the movie and its violence followed from that.

Although claims of direct effects from watching violence in film and television continue to occur, scholarship about the effects of violent images has evolved into questions about how to understand violence within narrative contexts as creating or reinforcing already held attitudes or beliefs. The text is also no longer taken for granted as a transparent object susceptible to content analysis. Violence within narrative context and viewers' premises about the reality or entertainment value of the text are considered. Additionally, attention (the effect of not watching television even though it is on) is not assumed. Finally, work is veering more toward mediation approaches to watching violence. While assuming violence has no effects—behavior, affective, or cognitive—is scarcely a credible position to take, even less credible is any sort of simple equation between images of violence and actions by individuals.

Horror

Horror is obviously related to violence, but the academic debate has been more concerned with the potential implications (negative or positive) of the pleasures of being frightened. Violence in movies does not necessarily create spectator terror. Thus, the issue for horror is, why do people willingly subject themselves to experiences that create this sensation?

As with violence, researchers viewed children's consumption of this encounter with concern. In 1941, Mary Preston published a "clinical study of children's reactions to 'movie horrors and radio crime'" in the *Journal of Pediatrics*. According to David Buckingham, she described the shows as "indigestible mass" and "addictive," arguing that the exposure led to insensitivity and delinquency (the behavioral effects of desensitization and imitation) (1996:96–97). As Buckingham notes, the history of the early research was one of pathologizing fans of horror, describing the genre in general and vague terms, assuming spectator responses, ignoring the matter of pleasure, and treating the genre as though it were consumed willingly only by males. Not only did mass communication scholars such as Preston view horror as socially dangerous; so did second-wave feminists, who similarly assumed imitative effects. Marjorie Rosen in her early study of images of women in Hollywood movies, for example, describes a set of 1940s films in which men persecute women, "undermining" and "terrorizing" them (1973:233–38).

One of the main developments in the history of discussions about horror has been the variety of textual approaches to films and television programs that elicit the affective response of fright or fear. Most textual approaches use the findings to present universal claims about the effects on a spectator. Indeed, this happens for all sets of moving images; I raise this here to point out that the same could be said for any such grouping —comedies, melodramas, romances. But for horror, some researchers believe that the affective response is potentially dangerous, unlike the experiences of laughing, crying, or fantasizing love. The same judgmental problem exists for sexually explicit materials, where sexual arousal outside the bounds of heterosexual coupling has disapproving dominant social value (or at least used to have).

Many people doing content analyses of horror films generally do not express disdain for them; in fact, studies done after the heavy production of slasher films—movies with high incidences of sudden, violent killings —often seem designed to disprove common misrepresentations of films. Basically in an attempt to separate out myth from actuality, these studies refute ad hoc claims about women being killed more than men and sexuality or rape figuring in most of the violence. Four useful essays conclude that both sexes are treated equally in terms of likelihood of being killed and that "direct acts of sexual aggression are not commonly portrayed," although the films do contain many violent acts of "extreme brutality or sadistic victimization" (Sapolsky and Molitor, 1996: 41–42; also see Cowan and O'Brien, 1990; Weaver, 1991; Molitor and Sapolsky, 1993). Gloria Cowan and Margaret O'Brien point out that women who do not engage in seductive behavior are more likely to survive; in fact, they are "more androgynous, less inane, and less physically attractive than nonsurviving females" (1990:195).

As with the case of violence, such information about films has some use in providing a notion of what is "there," but it may not reveal much about what a spectator is seeing. Other means of textual analysis may seem more impressionistic but actually may be more faithful to individual perception and interpretation. A long history exists of alternative methods of describing horror, along with claims about audience engagements. Several of these are worth reviewing to point out the various psychological and sociological explanations provided for why some people like to experience fright.

One still quite influential approach is a psychoanalytical one proposed by Robin Wood (1979). Working from a Frankfurt school position, Wood argues that while some repression is basic and necessary for society, other repressions are "surplus." In our culture, certain sexual energies are repressed, such as bisexuality, homosexuality, and child sexuality. Monsters are "others," which must be annihilated or assimilated. Horror brings these monsters to our cultural consciousness, displaying these repressions and allowing us to work through them. Thus, the experience of a horror film is much like a dream in which the pleasure is negotiating our fantasies.

Most psychoanalytical analyses follow much the same premise for why spectators place themselves in the way of what frightens them, although both the psychoanalytical authorities and the explanation for the engagement may vary. For instance, Steve Neale's discussion of *Halloween* works from arguments about filmic texts proposed by feminists and Lacanians Jacqueline Rose and Kaja Silverman to consider the affective trajectory as a matter of fluid spectator identification with both the killer and the victim, producing "the masochistic enjoyment of the infliction of aggression, pleasure in subjection to another, or rather a masochistic pleasure in combination with its sadistic opposite" (1981:342). Dennis Giles employs fantasy theory to discuss a staging of desire in horror to see but not to see too much: "While fantasy is the *mise-en-scène* of desire—of the wish—it is also produced by the subject's defenses *against* desire" (1984:41). Giles points out that looking too long at horror causes a dissipation of its effect.

Two more psychoanalytical analyses have been important: Carol Clover's book *Men, Women, and Chain Saws* (1992) and Barbara Creed's book *The Monstrous-Feminine* (1995). Clover's discussion of various sorts of horror formulas emphasizes the possibility of cross-sex identification (e.g., male spectators might be identifying with the androgynous female victim of a slasher film in a scenario that represses potential homoeroticism), thus complicating any straightforward feminist criticism of horror films as sexist. Likewise, Creed runs through numerous sorts of representations of women as abject figures and argues different monstrous figures involve different psychological fears. Since some of these figures relate to pre-Oedipal terrors, sex and sexual identity (formed during the Oedipal phase) may have little to do with the psychic dynamics.

Psychoanalytical theory, and the symptomatic textual analysis associated with it, is only one broad explanation for audiences putting themselves in the way of being frightened. In terms of the list of possible behavioral effects, most of these writers assume a sort of catharsis or arousal effect from watching horror. None of them is suggesting any change of attitudes or beliefs as a consequence of the viewing. Although also using psychoanalytical concepts, James B. Twitchell argues a structural-functional sociological theory that suggests an imitation effect: horror films are "formulaic rituals coded with precise social information needed by the adolescent audience. Like fairy tales that prepare the child for the anxieties of separation, modern horror myths prepare the teenager for the anxieties of reproduction. . . . They are fables of sexual identity" (1985:7). For Twitchell, the pleasures come from having watched terror and survived, seeing "'the return of the repressed' or the compulsive projection of objects of sublimated desire," and vicariously undergoing "a more complicated rite of passage" (65).

A third broad theoretical approach to horror is a cognitive psychology one. In something of a joint cognitive/philosophical proposition, Noël Carroll (1990) queries two "paradoxes": Why are people afraid of things they know not to be real, and why do people expose themselves to something unpleasant? Carroll's answer is that audiences experience the emotions of the characters; in doing so, they have a physiological response (arousal effect) that produces affective experiences and cognitive thinking about the impure and repulsive monsters. Thus, the pleasure comes from new ideation. This is also generally the view of Cynthia Freeland, who wants to extend Carroll's theory to a broader range of feelings and intellectual awareness: horror films "are designed to prompt *emotions* of fear, sympathy, revulsion, dread, anxiety, or disgust. And in doing so, they also stimulate *thoughts* about evil in its many varieties and degrees" (2000:3, emphasis in original).

Yet all these theories are propositions about abstract and undifferentiated spectators, the sort of complaint that cultural studies had about both psychoanalytical and cognitive theories of film spectatorship. Scholars who have directly studied audiences draw on the same social and personal theories as I have discussed here but would be best categorized as part of the current mass communication approaches of behavioral or uses-and-gratifications theory. (Cultivation theory would treat horror as it does violence, with a concern for desensitization; script theory is the mass communication variant for cognitive psychology; see Tamborini 1991.)

For example, behavioral theory has asked the same question: Why do people like to be scared? Dolf Zillmann and colleagues (1986) turn to social theory and argue that mastery over fright is important. Moreover, success in this challenge is related to sex roles and sex-role socialization (an imitation effect). Splitting their subjects into men and women, they determined that men enjoyed horror movies most with distressed women and least with women who displayed their own ability to hold their own in the face of terror. Correspondingly, women enjoyed horror most with men who seemed in control of their responses and least with those who were distressed. As summarized by Mary Beth Oliver, "Gender-role expectations may be important factors in the enjoyment of horror" (1993:30). Follow-ups to Zillmann and colleagues' 1986 study extend these findings (Sparks, 1991; Oliver, 1994; Zillmann and Gibson, 1996; Zillmann and Weaver, 1996).

As I indicated in chapter 2, uses-and-gratifications theory tends to create lists of reasons for using media. Seeking thrills and adventure constitute major motivations, although Ron Tamborini claims that "boredom susceptibility" is the only real predictor for horror spectatorship (1991:314). One study of self-reporting produced two sorts of gratifications: "identifying with film characters and using audience reaction to facilitate enjoyment" (Lawrence and Palmgreen, 1996:161). While identification figures significantly in earlier theories arguing via textual analysis, the introduction of the social environment as part of the reason for engaging with frightening material is notable and also central to Zillmann and colleagues' arguments.

This emphasis on the social experience of horror has appeared in textual analysis–based arguments as well, possibly also due to the influences of cultural studies on traditional psychoanalytical film scholarship. For instance, in an otherwise classic psychoanalytical reading of the pleasures of horror, Rhona J. Berenstein writes that what is at stake is performing screaming: "I assume . . . that viewing is a social activity in which conventional gender roles get displayed" (1996:37). Horror offers optional gender embodiments. Appealing to the idea of the performative in which spectators can enact identities that may be other than ones they traditionally perform, Berenstein argues that audience members should be thought of as spectators-in-drag (38). (See Sullivan, 1997, for a good critical review of Berenstein.)

While identifying with characters and enjoying the social environment for either learning social roles (Zillmann et al.) or trying on different ones (Berenstein) are two possible gratifications, other studies expand the lists of why people watch horror. Oliver (1993) reports on a 1990 study that correlates motivations for watching with individuals' levels of empathy and adventure seeking. Watching for thrills compares positively for both characteristics; rebel watching occurs for those with low empathy but high adventure seeking; and gore watching is the motivation for people with low empathy, high adventure seeking, but also low levels of fear, suggesting that these people may be identifying with the aggressors in the movie. A follow-up study by one of the authors, Deirdre D. Johnston (1995), revises the motivations to four: gore, thrill, independent (formerly, rebel), and problem watching. The new category, problem watching, is viewing to escape isolation or anger.

Part of the study of the pleasures of horror is distinguishing responses on the basis of various identities. While Zillmann et al. and others discuss sex differences, scholars have pointed out that a built-in presumption is that women do not like to be frightened. Isabel Cristina Pinedo (1997) and Brigid Cherry (1999) have criticized this hypothesis. Certainly, while women may enjoy men acting like men (per Zillmann et al.) and may know enough about their own sex-role performance to act as women "should," this does not equate to finding no pleasures in the genre for the other reasons hypothesized.

The same concerns exist for young children's viewing of horror. As Twitchell (1985) notes about fairy tales, children do enjoy hearing and reading stories that frighten them. Morris Dickstein also appeals to this characteristic of youth in his discussion of horror: "Children create games around the very things they most fear, as a way of subduing those fears and gaining control. Horror films are a safe, routinized way of playing with death, like going on a roller coaster or parachute jump at an amusement park" (1980:69).

Since it is out of protection of children (and others) that social concern over horror films exists, scholars study the effects of frightening images on them. Joanne Cantor notes that children do experience both "immediate emotional response" and longer effects of "anxiety, distress, and increased physiological arousal" (1991:170). How to judge the implications of this is complicated by the ethical problems of doing experimental research, especially on young people. Cantor remarks that while most children report being frightened by fictional texts, most children also indicate they enjoy it and take pleasure in scaring others as well (Buckingham, 1996). Cantor conjectures that the reason for the pleasure is that the children know the experience is not dangerous and that the texts are fictional. Still, she cautions parents that reminding children that such stories are not real does reduce affects of fear.

Like violence, concern about watching horror has resulted in multiple speculations about the experience, but the discussion has been focused on why people voluntarily subject themselves to experiences that create what would seem to be a potentially negative sensation. Effects postulated run the gamut from behavioral ones (such as catharsis, imitation, desensitization, and arousal) to affect and cognitive ideation. Most recently, differences among viewers are attracting most of the research attention.

Sexually Explicit Materials

Arousal, imitation, disinhibition, desensitization: all of these behavioral effects are feared—at least by some people—as possible consequences of watching sexually explicit materials. However, other people believe that such responses may have benefits! In debates more heated than even for violent images, scholars have attempted to determine the behavioral, attitudinal, and cognitive effects of viewing mediated sex. Because of the controversy, it seems most honest to be up front from the start about my opinion. I believe that most sexually explicit materials are either harmless or possibly helpful to their viewers, the major exceptions being representations of underage participants (because of the participants' lack of ability to consent) and sex scenes with excessive sadomasochism (because of the violence rather than the sex). The latter case may be more a matter of aversion on my part than any justified theoretical opinion.

Because of my opinion and the degree of controversy over this topic, I wish to start with a discussion of the current state of knowledge about what sexually explicit materials in film and video look like. One development as a result of the debates has been extensive textual analysis of this genre. (The ability to show sexual acts rather than imagine them means that media specificity matters; see L. Williams, 1989.)

First of all, outright sexual aggression—rape—is rare in sexually explicit materials. One of the major textual scholars, Joseph W. Slade, notes that if the point is to see the sex act, then rape would be the fastest way there: "That ravishment is not a common enabling device suggests that it is inherently antithetical to the stag's intent" (1984:153; on rape narratives in dominant cinema, see Projansky, 2001). In a content analysis of pre-1970 hard-core pornography (hard-core is defined as occurring when genitals and penetration—the "meat shot"—are visible), Slade finds only 5 percent of 1,333 examples using any violence, and fewer instances involving force; only 1 percent is bestiality. In instances of violence, men are mostly the victims, although Slade does observe more violence in the later decades (1984:148–63).

In fact, the typical stag (one-reel, about twelve-minute, short film) and feature-length narrative begin with an adult female's sexual voraciousness; she wants sex (Slade, 1984:154–58). This attention to female sexual desire can be interpreted ambivalently, however. Considering this from a Foucauldian perspective, Linda Williams, another major textual scholar of this cinema, argues that sexually explicit films are indicative of "the modern compulsion to speak incessantly about sex" (1989:2). She believes that the narrative focus on the woman is to investigate and explain her because, for men, her pleasure is "alien" and unknowable, since it is not readily apparent via ejaculation (2–3). Williams describes the formulas for both stag and feature-length films, arguing that the latter have greater narrative coherence and a requirement of visible ejaculation—the "money shot" (72–74; Slade, 1993:76). Filling up the text are sexual "numbers," akin to the songs and dances found in musicals (Willeman, 1980:64–65; Williams, 1989:126–28).

Most sexually explicit materials include some same-sex coupling (usually between two women rather than men) and multiple-partner sex (Knight and Alpert, 1967; Waugh, 1992). This may be because, until the arrival of home video, a socially situated audience viewed sexually explicit films. Currently, sexually explicit materials are almost entirely a private-couple or single-person viewing experience—altering both the context and the representations (Slade, 1993). Subsequently, scholarship on pornography addressed to gays and lesbians has noted similarities with and differences from heterosexual-addressed texts (Pajaczkowska, 1981; Goldstein, 1984:19; Dyer, 1985; Waugh, 1985; Mary Conway, 1996; Stevenson, 1997; Champagne, 1997). Additionally, criticisms based on race and ethnicity and class have explored questions of representational bias or critiques (Fung, 1991; Ortiz, 1994; Kipnis, 1996; Penley, 1997). Moreover, the function of humor in pornography has received attention (Willeman, 1980; Penley, 1997).

Even if sexual aggression is not at all common and a woman's desire is the ostensible focus, that does not make sexually explicit films untroublesome to their critics. As with any symptomatic reading argument, surface information may have little to do with what viewers make of the material. Here I want to follow a line of historical argumentation that informs contemporary thinking about effects of these images. In 1957, the court case *United States v. Roth* changed standards for finding a book or movie obscene to requiring the consideration of the text as a whole (rather than just part of it) and "community" standards. During the next decade, the U.S. Supreme Court several times reaffirmed this position. Although some restrictions were initiated in *Miller v. California* (1973), on the whole only hard-core pornography is illicit in the United States. By merely putting a framing narrative around sex acts, a film could be argued to meet the criterion of "serious, artistic, political, or scientific value" (Copp and Wendell, 1983) and thus evade prohibition. These legal revisions opened up "adult-film" production and exhibition.

Moreover, during the 1960s, public discourses contributed to authorizing viewing of hard-core pornography among intellectuals, women, and middle-class people (A. Ross, 1989:171–208). New York intellectuals associated sexually explicit materials with radical underground cinema (Staiger, 2000b:125–60); prominent literary theorists discussed pornography as a genre of high-art aesthetics and radical ambitions (Sontag, 1967; Michelson, 1970; Carter, 1978); second-wave feminists declared that female orgasms were sexual rights; and liberals and leftists equated censorship of sexual materials with repressive attitudes and strategies of the Nixon administration. The widely popular showing of *Deep Throat* in 1973 earned a *New York Times Magazine* article titled "Porno Chic" (Blumenthal, 1973).

Even as these pro-pornography views were expressed, others argued that women were degraded in sexually explicit materials. As early as 1969, Roxanne Dunbar and Ti-Grace Atkinson vigorously attacked these materials (Dunbar, 1969; Atkinson, 1970; for detailed histories, see Stern, 1982; Echols, 1989). A seminal statement came from Robin Morgan in her essay "Theory and Practice: Pornography and Rape" (1974), along with books by Andrea Dworkin (*Woman Hating* [1974]) and Susan Brownmiller (*Against Our Will: Men, Women, and Rape* [1975]). The argument in brief is that pornography creates women not as human characters but merely as objects for male sexual gratification. Thus, sexually explicit materials teach men that they may use women as they will. In other words, this imagery provides conceptual ideas that will produce behavioral effects: not treating women as people or even abusing and raping them.

Psychoanalytical film theory and symptomatic textual analysis reinforced this radical feminist claim. Laura Mulvey's essay "Visual Pleasure and Narrative Cinema" (1975), discussed in chapters 3 and 6, provides a general theory about the woman as object of the male gaze in mainstream narrative cinema to strengthen these claims. Scholars within that school then turned to sexually explicit materials and considered what psychic operations might be occurring. For instance, Giles (1977) employs a sophisticated Lacanian psychoanalytical method to argue that in pornography a woman is not a woman but a projection by a male of what he fears about himself—being feminine and having uncontrollable, excessive, and perverted sexual desires. The "woman" is thus a place of desire and dread. The penetration and withdrawal scenes so ubiquitous in sexually explicit materials prove male manhood and also indicate his sadistic attitude toward her: she is nothing to him.

Other strong examples of this approach are "Sexual Violence and Sexuality" (1982), in which Rosalind Coward stresses that many images of women in submission construct woman as associated with death, and "Pornography, Ethnography, and the Discourses of Power" (1991), in which Christian Hansen, Catherine Needham, and Bill Nichols point out how the genre "others" its object of attention by using distance as control, creating differences as inferior, and claiming the possibility of assimilation through explication. (Also see Ellis, 1980, and the criticism of the psychoanalytical approach by Prince, 1988.)

This conjuncture of opinion did not last long. Although Alice Echols (1989:289) believes that radical feminists thought the pornography issue would unify women across class and race, several events hindered this. For one, feminists and Christian fundamentalists both testified against sexually explicit materials during the 1978 Meese Commission study of these images, causing some people to question how the interests of the two groups could be conjoined. Additionally, Dworkin and Catharine A. MacKinnon worked to pass an antipornography ordinance in Minneapolis on the basis of the supposed causal relation between the images and violence against women; courts struck down this law, but, as I shall detail later, many people questioned such a direct-effect claim as well. Most important, however, many feminists differed on women's rights in relation to sexuality.

One of the signal rejections of the antipornography movement occurred during a conference at Barnard College in 1982. There and elsewhere at about the same time, anti-antiporn advocates raised the following points:

- Antipornography criticism did not acknowledge the variety of uses of sexually explicit materials.
- This position did not account for complexity of imagery and thus complications of fantasy and individual interpretation.
- This position disregarded the experiences of many women who enjoyed pornography or felt empowered by it.

- Conservatives, who were otherwise often antifeminism and anti-gay/lesbian/bisexual/transsexual, held this position, viewed as a troubling alliance and potentially a reproduction of patriarchal ideologies of protecting women.
- The relationship between sexually explicit materials and violence was not proved.
- Censorship was the end result of this position.
- In some ways this position required women to be "feminine" and "good" and excluded sexuality that might include promiscuity, sadomasochism, bisexuality, and pre-Oedipal pleasures (B. Brown, 1981; Pajaczkowska, 1981; Stern, 1982; Rubin, 1984; Kleinhans and Lesage, 1984; A. Ross, 1989; Vance, 1989; Prince, 1990).

As early as 1982, Lesley Stern called for "an examination of fantasy and a development of feminist erotica or pornography" (1982:47). By the middle 1980s, several women were producing women-addressed sexually explicit materials.

That the anti-antipornography position is now fairly dominant is also because of the failure of producing any significant direct-effect linkages between viewers and behaviors. The findings for audience studies of actual users of sexually explicit materials repeat the pattern I have recounted earlier in this chapter for violent images and horror.

Let's face it: sexually explicit materials that do *not* produce a behavioral effect of arousal are not good pornography. However, psychologists find no evidence that sexual arousal causes sexual deviance or criminal acts (Cairns, Paul, and Wishner, 1970; Howitt, 1989:63–65). In fact, a 1965 study indicated that women reported more sexual arousal from hard-core obscene stories than did men (Cairns, Paul, and Wishner, 1970:8). Moreover, while it is based on self-reporting, no differences in use of pornography occurred for criminals, noncriminals, and sex offenders (9). Edward Donnerstein and Daniel Linz (1986), two of the major behavioralists approaching this problem, question whether a relationship exists between represented sexual violence and aggressive behavior toward women. While violent images may produce a short-term arousal, it is the violence, not the sexual content, that may correlate with aggression.

In fact, as rape has been more recently conceptualized, it is now understood to be about control of the victim rather than desire. Lynne Segal points out that "studies of convicted rapists found them to have had less exposure to pornography during adolescence . . . than the control group." Other empirical work suggests "a *negative* correlation between access to pornography and sex crimes" (1990:33–34, emphasis in original). Recent research indicates that "men's 'usual response [to depictions of sexual cruelty] is . . . one of anxiety and depression, of revulsion rather than arousal'" (McNair, 1996:96).

It is the case that, unlike for violent images, the social inhibitors for sexually explicit materials are fewer. With the "proper" partner (currently still primarily heterosexual coupling), imitation is an approved behavioral response. A 1973 study determined that couples who viewed pornography had more sexual activity (although the self-reporting may have also produced this outcome). However, no evidence of new or unconventional sexual behaviors developed; rather, attitudes toward sexual acts remained stable (J. Mann et al., 1974). During the heyday of porno chic, a national survey on attendance at theatrical exhibitions of sexually explicit materials indicated that most of the audience was young and that "attendance increases for those in the higher educational levels" (Klenow and Crane, 1977:76). The authors of the study speculated that the viewers were using the films as sex education materials, a conclusion supporting Charles Winick's study (1970) for the 1970 U.S. Commission on Obscenity and Pornography.

A 1989 study did conclude that some changes in attitudes occurred after watching sexually explicit materials, with viewers becoming more tolerant of nonmarital sexuality and "deviant" practices (Gross, 1996:169–70). Increased tolerance of difference may be a positive outcome. However, other research indicates that some pornography spectators are less inclined to consider rape a crime that deserves a significant prison term; the authors hypothesize that this might be due to an assumption that women are "hyperpromiscuous" (Bryant and Zillmann, 1982:4). Moreover, if sexually explicit materials are also about spectators' anxieties (of performance or competence), then these films "offer viewers not only materials for constructing images of their sexual desires but also opportunities to face their imagination of sexual disaster" (Rollin, 1982:3).

Ultimately, the claim by the antiporn advocates is that sexually explicit materials shape individuals' worldviews (Dines, Jensen, and Russo, 1998:5), a view also held by the opposition. The difference, as Brian McNair summarizes, depends on one's theory of reception:

On one side [are] the radical feminists, strongly antiporn, who believe it capable of being accurately read only one way—as the essence and exemplification of male sexual pleasure. For a woman to challenge this reading is to be complicit in her own oppression, and to share responsibility for the survival of patriarchy as a social system. On the other side are those pro-porn feminists who assert the multiplicity of meanings and readings to be derived from mainstream male heterosexual pornography; the importance of fantasy and play in sexual desire and behavior; and pornography's subversive potential to challenge dominant sexual values (which, all feminists agree, disadvantage women). (1996:97–98)

As I have outlined it in this book, this difference is also a question of an education, reinforcement, or power model of media effects, on the one hand, and a mediation thesis, on the other.

On the contrary, Michel Beaujour underscores the possibility of perversely reading even "exemplary novels." While some authors write to produce lessons for their readers, it is all too common and easy to misread: "Misreadings, indeed! The libidinous little reader will have his hands bound until his head is expurgated by an experienced exorcist" (1980:346). Pornography is ultimately and also an assault on the aesthetics of distance: "Pornography crosses the boundaries not only of law and institution, and of subjectivity, but of the critical act itself. Pornography undermines a pretense to critical distance" (Wallen, 1998:102).

While scholars may calmly discourse on all sorts of claims about the reception of media, sexually explicit materials remain a key test case for any theory of media. Sexually explicit materials are not transparent; the potentials for reading them in variable ways are high; reading nonpornography in ways unfriendly to women also exists. If one takes the position, as I do, that mediation theories of reception are the most accurate to what happens in a spectator's encounter with media, looking at the spectator's identities (psychological and social) and the texts themselves within a context of watching sexuality explicit materials is the best way to determine whether pornography has effects, and what those personal and social effects might be: conservative or progressive.

8

Memories

Research on memories has significance for media reception studies in terms of both methodology and findings. Scholars use memories for almost all their raw evidence. Asking someone with whom he/she identified during a movie to plundering diaries or scrapbooks of early filmgoers—each of these excavations of response rests on the declared recollections of individuals. Consequently, since textual analysis is applied to the data of memories, considering features of that data is necessary. This is particularly pertinent in that researchers often invoke memories to argue for or against effects. In chapter 2, I indicated that early arguments about movie effects rested on anecdotes of children seeing crimes and repeating the behavior. Also, in chapter 7, I noted the story of one individual who recalled seeing a film about the bombing of Hiroshima and who believed that that single film experience significantly affected her childhood and her adult career. If these causal claims, or something close to them, are valid, understanding features of personal event memories will assist researchers in devising appropriate instruments to solicit memory and help historians in interpreting biographical accounts of the past.

In this chapter I will review general assertions about the social and personal functions of memory. Although I will briefly discuss social (or collective) memory, my focus will be on personal event memories that are the sorts of memories pertinent here. In that discussion I will mostly review cognitive psychology's current hypotheses, but these conjectures at least open the horizon to the sorts of issues media reception studies should take into account even if other theory develops to map personal memories. Finally, I will survey several studies of media reception that directly address memory.

Memory Matters

Contemporary scholarship on memory generally distinguishes among habit memories (those sorts of skills we learn through repetition, such as riding bikes, that are so ubiquitous as not to require any conscious attention on our part); cognitive memories (facts and such that do not require us to remember how or when we learned them); and personal memories (information that we attribute to sometimes unique experiences during our own lives; Connerton, 1989:22–23). While habit and cognitive memories have an obvious value to survival, personal memories do not. Yet personal memories are intimately influential. Personal memories provide continuity, accretion, and, as groups of individuals remember, social identity, authority, solidarity, and political affiliation (D. Lowenthal, 1975:5–15; Zelizer, 1995:215–18). People act on narratives of the past, and beliefs about the past produce social norms (Knapp, 1989:123). As Barry Schwartz summarizes it, "To remember is to place a part of the past in the service of conceptions and needs of the present" (1982:374).

Because memory and representations of the past are so influential on the present, psychologists and sociologists have attended to their production. Schwartz (1996) traces the analysis of the social sources of memory from Charles Horton Cooley's *Social Process* (1918), George Herbert Mead's *Philosophy of the Present* (1932), Émile Durkheim's *Elementary Forms of the Religious Life* (1915), Stefan Czarnowski's *Cult of Heroes and Its Social Implications* (1919) to the pivotal work by Maurice Halbwachs, *Collective Memory* (1950). Halbwachs emphasized the role of the group in the construction of memory, even personal memory: "The experience of time and memory is socially constructed" (Preston, 2000:11). In Halbwachs's view, conceptual schemata (personal and social) already in place shape memories, although those schemata can be transfigured by the materialization of evidence of the memory (how the past is commemorated) and the strength of the group trying to preserve the memory in a particular way.

All scholars recognize that the present influences the representation of the past: "Instead of remembering exactly what was, we make the past intelligible in the light of present circumstances" (D. Lowenthal, 1975:31). Schwartz suggests that it is valuable to distinguish between chronicling—putting down dates and facts in an order—and commemorating. In the latter case, social groups mark specific events as "ideal," as an instance that "embod[ies] our deepest and most fundamental values" (1982:377).

In this marking, iconography is used not only to symbolize meanings but also to create a sacred notation. Commemoration cannot (usually) create historical facts; selection is its modus operandi. Selection occurs on the basis of " 'practical value in solving situational problems' " (Schwartz, quoted in Gregory and Lewis, 1988:215). Facts congruent with the proposed solution are privileged, although pragmatism and pleasure may also be considered.

Social or collective memories are public; however, here I am more concerned with personal memories that are the sources for evidence of audience relationships with media images. As with public memories of the past, personal memories are functional and operate in the service of the present. Remembering our personal past, "autobiographical remembering," has adaptive functions (Barclay, 1994:66). These include giving selves "a sense of coherence," "a means of regulating their own feelings," a way "to explore possible selves . . . or the nature of other selves," a method "to relate one's personal memories to cultural events," and an opportunity "to establish and maintain intimate interpersonal relationships" (66–67).

Personal memories may be couched in general or specific language of recollection. Although we hold many images of our lives, we may take some of these to be ideal: they are not tied to a specific time but are exemplar of life at that period. For instance, I have memories of playing in certain environments as a preschool child; I would not tie these to a precise moment in my life. However, other memories are very discrete; I believe they happened only once. Cognitive psychologists have focused much attention on the latter sorts of memory. Although reception scholars retrieve both general and event memories, the latter has a body of research worth our notice.

In a valuable book, *Momentous Events, Vivid Memories*, David B. Pillemer summarizes the work of the past couple decades on "personal event memory" (1998:50). Such a memory has the following features: (1) it is a memory of "a *specific* event that took place at a particular time and place"; (2) the person can provide a "*detailed* account of the rememberer's *own personal circumstances* at the time of the event"; (3) the memory has "*sensory images*, including visual, auditory, olfactory images or bodily sensations, that contribute to the feeling of 'reexperiencing' or 'reliving'" the event; (4) "memory details and sensory images correspond to a particular *moment* or moments of phenomenal experience"; and (5) "the rememberer *believes* that the memory is a truthful representation of what transpired" (50–51).

Obviously, not all our personal memories are so stunning. However, these sorts of memories are the ones that we often use in creating our autobiographies. They are ones we feel, or have decided, were eventful to us, making us who we are, when we tell our personal event histories. They are the ones we claim are causal. Pillemer's definition provides the bases for characteristics that he believes are generalizations about what produces these sorts of memories. These characteristics are important to be aware of when using memories as reception evidence.

One characteristic of personal event memories is that the original event will have been "delimited" in its occurrence to a specific time and place. Moreover, if the original event was sudden or brief, that may increase its sense of being "momentous" (Pillemer, 1998:26). If it provoked an emotional reaction, that also increases its impact (Pennebaker and Banasik, 1997). Surprise enhances the recollection (R. Brown and Kulik, 1977). At a certain point, these become "flashbulb memories" (a concept to which I will return later). If the event is strong enough, an individual will rehearse it, adding more narrative detail. Research indicates that these sorts of single-time events can have lasting effects on behavior. Although cognitive psychology expends much energy on describing general schemata, rules, and scripts as the foundations for individuals' actions, Pillemer (1998:12–15) argues that a single event can have the same effect.

Still, that single event will already be an abstraction from the actual incident. As Jerome Bruner cautions, "What is 'laid down' in memory is not some aboriginal encounter with a 'real world,' but is already highly schematized" (1993:40). Scholars following Freud on memory agree: "The process of memory [is] one of continuous revision or 'retranslation,' reworking memory traces in light of later knowledge and experience" (N. King, 2000:4).

Additionally, its abstraction is into an image, sensual as that may be. Indeed, Walter Benjamin's remark that "history does not break down into stories but into images" (quoted in White, 1996:17) may be more accurate than metaphoric. Such a memory, while an abstract sensual image, will also be oddly concrete. The self may be bound up in the place of its occurrence (or its like) as a consequence, which may explain why physical sites and other sensual materials produce emotional resonances.

A second characteristic of personal event memories is that both personal trauma and public tragedy may produce these memories with their effects (Pillemer, 1998:28). The archetypal example for most Americans of the baby boom generation is the assassination of John F. Kennedy. If truth be told, for some people that public event has had as much significance as more obviously personal ones.

Third, quite reasonably, events that matter more to us will be remembered better. Pillemer provides the example of a study showing that African Americans remembered more than did Caucasians of the assassination of Malcolm X (1998:36). What matters more is an individual affair—here, race makes the difference. Pillemer's survey of the research indicates that sex, culture, and personality differences produce diversity in remembering, sharing, and representing personal event memories (1998:21, 177–212).

Additionally, what people take from an event can be quite disparate. Pillemer lists the outcomes as "memorable messages," "symbolic messages," "originating events" (events that people view as starting a new path), "anchoring events" (ones that are a "touchstone for a continuing set of beliefs about the world"), "turning points," and "analogous events" (1998:65–83). Some events will seem critical—life changing— while others, just as vivid, will not.

The fourth characteristic is that a personally experienced event will be recalled more consistently and more accurately than if one only heard news about an event (Pillemer, 1998:36). This attribute raises the subject of forgetting. In the psychology of memory, theories have been advanced as to why people remember some things but not others. Henri Bergson postulates that every experience is ultimately available to us; as Mary Douglas explains, "forgetting is due to obstacles, remembering is the removal of obstacles" (1980:5). Halbwachs believes that "forgetting is due to vague and piecemeal impressions and remembering a process of fitting them together under suitable stimuli" (Douglas, 1980:5). Freud's theory of repression of some memories is a cornerstone of psychoanalysis. Pillemer argues that the explanation for children being unable to remember early life experiences is their lack of narrative tools to script the events into viable memories (1998:65–83).

In some instances, whether a memory is vividly accurate matters; recollections for the purposes of assigning criminal responsibility are a foremost one. Although Pillemer attributes a child's lack of memory of an event to "inadequate cognitive understanding and narrative assimilation"

(135), he also believes that narrativizing by others can create an explanation for what is recalled (also see Neisser, 1994:5–6). Thus, he cautions about false or "recovered" memories.

In most other cases, the belief that something happened as it is recalled is all that is pertinent. Unfortunately, the so-called flashbulb memory is no longer credible as Roger Brown and James Kulik first postulated it in 1977. Brown and Kulik believed some events were so startling and personally significant that they were engraved into the memory in a sort of arrested image, hence the "flashbulb" metaphor. The memory's detail was due to the individual repeatedly describing the image. To test this thesis, in 1981 the renowned cognitive psychology theorist Ulric Neisser compared the audiotapes of President Richard Nixon's office against the testimony of John Dean in the Watergate trials. This was a good case study because Dean's accounts of the White House conversations were particularly dramatic in details. Neisser concluded that Dean's details were often off: Dean placed himself into the center of the events more than actually occurred; he recalled praise for his work that was not given. However, fundamentally, Dean was accurate about the gist of the state of affairs.

Subsequently, Martin Conway (1995) has tried to rescue at least part of the original flashbulb thesis. Conway argues that people have these sorts of memories; however, they depend not on rehearsals of what happened but on the events' original personal significance. These memories are more coherent than normal autobiographical memories, and they are "core" memories because of their extraordinary meaning. Conway does accept that details for flashbulb memories change over time.

Cognitive psychologists all agree that personal event memories have some foundation in real happenings but that memory is active, with details being altered (Neisser, 1994). As Pillemer puts it, you will remember that a car (not a mountain) hit you, but you may not remember the color of the car or the day of the week when it happened. Prompting can create false childhood memories, but if an unprompted memory exists, it is likely to be "generally truthful" (1998:55–56). In any circumstance, however, an experience of personal significance will have some degree of consistency and "truthfulness" to the original event. Research indicates that grief and other emotional responses to traumas never go away; aspects may soften, but they are not forgotten (Frijda, 1997:104–5). Moreover, as I noted about the laying down of any memory, the details are already being abstracted and revised.

Having personal event memories, what do we do with them? Part of the study of these memories also involves how people share and narrativize their selves. This is particularly important for reception researchers because we often come upon diaries and autobiographical statements and thus need to be alert to how people string together personal event memories. Moreover, we need to recognize that our own critical method will affect how we analyze the narrative. Scholars working from a psychoanalytical perspective will treat narratives with a symptomatic textual analysis, seeking structuring repetitions and metaphors that might lead toward repressed core memories, or poststructuralist "unsaids." Those working from a cognitive psychology perspective tend toward neo-Aristotelian critical approaches. This is likely in part because Aristotelian narratives are canonical for telling stories; people who learn how to tell stories learn to tell them as Aristotle modeled as appropriate.

In point of fact, in an attempt to write a "coherent, temporally ordered life history," a person often moves from "landmark to landmark" (Pillemer, 1998:96). Although episodic or general personal memory serves as part of the material of any autobiography, individual events are also there. This constitutes one main feature to these narratives.

A second is the protagonist of the narrative. Central to identity is the self. Daniel Albright points out, "As Neisser notes, anyone who asks himself the question Who am I? will offer not only social and physical information—I am so-and-so's husband and I have a scar on my right hand—but also historical information" (1994:21). From all accounts, this "remembered self" is fragile. We construct it on the basis of need, in the context of asking such a question. Our autobiography is highly related to any dialogue in which the self needs to be represented (Barclay, 1994:63; also Bruner, 1994:41; Neisser, 1994:9). Beyond the context of need, determinants for telling about selves include "our intentions, . . . the interpretative conventions available to us, and . . . the meanings imposed upon us by the usages of our culture and language" (Bruner, 1993:38; also Barclay, 1994:59).

While we are the protagonists of our own story, we may or may not have agency. The wishes and desires we have drive the story, but the story may be of us as victims to others. In fact, Bruner states that stories are usually "thickly agentive," with outside forces changing us. Neisser writes that unpleasant events about the self are remembered better than others (1994:13). Perhaps we tell stories to deal with this, learning from the past.

Bruner describes other features to self-narratives. They have "turning points" that produce a "new and intense line of activity" (1994:50). These turning points seem to be a way for us to "'debug' the narrative in an effort to achieve clearer meaning" (53). The stories are "drenched in affect" (50). Our culture has rules for stories that include a "valued end-point" (Gergen, 1994:91). Thus, incidents are selected to contribute toward the foreseen moral of the tale. Some sort of causal linkage between the incidents is expected. Finally, as the end is reached, self-narratives engage in "evaluation" and a "coda," a return to the present situation (Langellier, 1999:126). Just as people of different sexes tell stories differently, they tell self-narratives in patterns related to their sex (Bruner, 1994:48). Presumably cultural and other differences also affect attributes of autobiography.

Understanding personal event memories and knowing the features of self-reported memories are requirements to using this sort of information in media reception research and may also help us look for memories.

Media Research and Memories

Many media researchers have considered how movies represent the past, creating the potential for collective memories. The ability to characterize the past for the public has not gone without struggles. One or two disputes occur each year about how a film or television program has depicted an event or era. The public debates over Oliver Stone's film *JKF* provide an example of studying the reception of conflict over representing the past (Staiger, 2000b:210–28). However, my focus in this chapter is primarily on media reception research on personal memories. What research has been produced should now be fit into this larger analysis of memory.

Some media scholarship indicates that an experience with an individual film or star can create a personal event memory. Pillemer describes one example of a student recalling seeing *Platoon* and then studying the Vietnam War intently. As Pillemer cautions, however, "countless other college students viewed the same movie without experiencing it as a directive" (1998:87). As I noted in chapter 5, people do describe movie stars serving as "life-markers" for them. That a single event or person might have such an impact on an individual is not only possible but common. What cognitive psychologists do not know is why this happens to those to whom it does. All that can be determined is that the individual seems already to be in a life situation in which they are actively seeking a sign (see Pillemer, 1998).

Asked to produce self-narratives about their experiences with movies or television, people can generate "frozen memories" and self-narratives. Jackie Stacey's study of British women's recollections of watching films during World War II conforms to the expectations. As she analyzes the stories from a psychoanalytic perspective, she determines that the teller creates the self-narrative from her current perspective and weaves a tale of met or unmet utopian fantasies, with movie moments as transformative (or, in Bruner's term, a "turning point"; 1994:63). Likewise, Sue Harper and Vincent Porter's recovery of 1950s responses to movies indicates that people assess their memories on the basis of the "intensity of response" rather than "narrative or visual pleasure" (1996:153). If personal significance is a major feature in laying down a personal event, this makes sense and correlates with Bruner's remarks about self-narratives being "drenched in affect."

One of the most extensive studies of personal event memories in relation to media viewing is a recent publication by Annette Kuhn, *Dreaming of Fred and Ginger* (2002). Attempting to reconstruct the experience of filmgoing in Britain in the 1930s, Kuhn describes several ways people portray that past: recalling doing things repeatedly ("general" personal memories), producing individual anecdotes (a personal event memory) and impersonal observations about situations, and describing in the "past present." Cognitive psychology indicates that in the instance of a particularly vivid memory, people will articulate the story as if they are actually reliving it, drawing detailed sensory images. Thus, Kuhn's evidence indicates that these are strong personal event memories. Kuhn also emphasizes that her informants for her ethnohistory told stories with spatial features. Of course, part of her question was about going to movies, so this is a prompted recollection. Physical space provides linkages and helps string story events together. Given that the narrative goal for her respondents is to arrive at the movies, the variant spatial organizations she outlines indicate how much more we might be able to learn about canonical self-narration.

Solicited memories such as the ones gathered by Kuhn are more need-dependent on the side of the researcher than the narrator. Still, other research conforms to the outline produced by the cognitivists. Sonia Livingstone examined individuals' recounting of an event in the television program *Coronation Street*. While the start of the retelling had no clear point of departure, as the narrators progressed, they moved toward coherence to explain the event, often bringing in information they knew from watching the show over the years. Livingstone's respondents focused on "feelings rather than actions" (1991:293); they wanted to speculate about the characters' emotional states. Livingstone accounts for the inaccuracies in remembering the episode as being due to the viewers' expectations about the program and their own sympathies. In other words, the memories of the television episode had been laid down in abstractions.

Another study of solicited memory is Lynn Spigel and Henry Jenkins's analysis of adults' memories of having watched the television show *Batman* in the 1960s, when they were children. The overall results are predictable, but that is good; they point to the validity of the model. For example, the respondents used the memories "to evoke their own personal identity and explain their particular relationship to the social world" (1991:136). The memories were "transitional moments, rites of passage, through which people moved from child to adult, from family to larger social meanings" (137).

However, perhaps more valuable are several specific findings that extend the cognitivists' research. For one, some respondents in Spigel and Jenkins's study "tended to construct vivid images of themselves watching the program as children" (134). While the vividness of the memory is expected, the structure of the people's point of view seeing themselves in the image is notable. This is not surprising from the perspective of Freud's remarks about how we place ourselves in various positions in our mental imaginings (see chapter 6); perhaps cognitivists can attend to this question in their work.

Additionally, the respondents not only watched themselves watching but also placed themselves into a collective group (likely more probable for television viewing in the 1960s, before the proliferation of television sets and private viewings in households). Their memories were "expansive." They had associations to *Batman* that were part of their overall personal memories. Finally, perhaps because the memories were solicited, they were general personal memories rather than event ones. As described by Spigel and Jenkins, the recollections were "isolated but recurring images" (135). I pluck out this finding because researchers need to distinguish between self-generated memories of media versus solicitation of memories of specific programs. Differences between these two requests may produce diverse sorts of responses.

While scholars have asked about specific television programs or movies, they have also looked at memories of types of media. Again, the findings conform to the hypotheses about reporting personal memories, but more research may be useful. An important question is how people interpret and remember news stories, since such ideation should be part of overall personal views of the social world. Justin Lewis gives the distressing results that most viewers in his study remember only a general abstract meaning that is categorized into a standing belief (1994; also see Gunter, 1991). Dirk Eitzen (1995) also cautions that while people know the difference between documentaries and history, facts and fiction, they care about the emotional pull of a film more than explaining a complex past. Likely this is no surprise.

Given that how we interpret and create memories and how so much of reception research relies on recollections, as the field of inquiry continues, memory studies will be a primary area for further work. Both psychoanalytical theory and cognitive psychology can contribute to this, as will sociological analysis in its work on collective and social remembering. Textual methods of analyzing these narratives also need to be recognized as influencing what might be argued to be known. It perhaps is reassuring to me that individuals often struggle against official histories, finding them not to conform to their personal memories or sense of the import of significant events. Then, how media construct, mediate, or reproduce personal memories also carries some weight in our engagement with reality.

Selected Bibliography

I regret the exclusion of all the articles and books that I did not cover or reference specifically but that might have been included. This bibliography is selected to reflect what is noted in the text.

Abercrombie, Nicholas, and Brian Longhurst (1998). *Audiences: A Sociological Theory of Performance and Imagination.* London: Sage.

Abernathy-Lear, Gloria (1995). "His Name Was Not on the List: The Soap Opera Updates of Ti-Rone as Resistance to Symbolic Annihilation" in Dines and Humez (eds) *Gender, Race and Class in Media.* Pp. 383–93.

Abu-Lughod, Lila, and Catherine A. Lutz (1990). "Introduction: Emotion, Discourse, and the Politics of Everyday Life" in Lutz and Abu-Lughod (eds) *Language and the Politics of Emotion.* Pp. 1–23.

Aden, Roger C. (1999). *Popular Stories and Promised Lands: Fan Cultures and Symbolic Pilgrimages.* Tuscaloosa: University of Alabama Press.

Adorno, Theodor W. (1938). "On the Fetish-Character in Music and the Regression of Listening" rpt. in Arato and Gebhardt (eds) *Essential Frankfurt School Reader.* Pp. 270–99.

——— (1967). "Culture Industry Reconsidered," trans. Anson G. Rabinbach, *New German Critique,* no. 6 (Fall 1975): 12–19.

Adorno, Theodor W., and Max Horkheimer (1944). "The Culture Industry: Enlightenment as Mass Deception," trans. John Cumming in *The Dialectic of Enlightenment.* Rpt., New York: Herder and Herder, 1972. Pp. 120–67.

Alarcón, Norma (1990). "The Theoretical Subjects of *This Bridge Called My Back* and Anglo-American Feminism" in Anzaldúa (ed) *Making Face, Making Soul.* Pp. 356–69.

Alberoni, Francesco (1962). "The Powerless 'Elite': Theory and Sociological Research on the Phenomenology of the Stars," trans. Denis McQuail, in McQuail (ed) *Sociology of Mass Communications.* Pp. 75–98.

Albright, Daniel (1994). "Literary and Psychological Models of the Self" in Neisser and Fivush (eds) *Remembering Self.* Pp. 19–39.

Alexander, Jeffrey C., and Ronald N. Jacobs (1998). "Mass Communication,

Ritual and Civil Society" in Liebes and Curran (eds) *Media, Ritual, Identity.* Pp. 23–41.

Alexander, Karen (1991). "Fatal Beauties: Black Women in Hollywood" in Gledhill (ed) *Stardom.* Pp. 45–54.

Alexander, William (1981). *Film on the Left: American Documentary Film from 1931–1942.* Princeton, NJ: Princeton University Press.

Alfonsi, Laurence (1997). "La réception de François Truffaut aux Etats-Unis: Les conditions de sa popularité," *Canadian Journal of Film Studies* 6, no. 1 (Spring): 3–17.

Althusser, Louis (1970). "Ideology and Ideological State Apparatuses (Notes towards an Investigation)" in *Lenin and Philosophy and Other Essays,* trans. Ben Brewster. New York: Monthly Review Press, 1971. Pp. 127–86.

Altman, Rick (1999). *Film/Genre.* London: British Film Institute.

Andermahr, Sonya (1994). "A Queer Love Affair: Madonna and Lesbian and Gay Culture" in Holmes and Budge (eds) *The Good, the Bad, and the Gorgeous.* Pp. 28–40.

Anderson, Daniel R., and John Burns (1991). "Paying Attention to Television" in Bryant and Zillmann (eds) *Responding to the Screen.* Pp. 3–25.

Ang, Ien (1982). *Watching "Dallas": Soap Opera and the Melodramatic Imagination,* trans. Della Couling. London: Methuen, 1985.

—— (1990). "Melodramatic Identifications: Television Fiction and Women's Fantasy" in M. Brown (ed) *Television and Women's Culture.* Pp. 75–88.

Anger, Kenneth (1965). *Hollywood Babylon.* Phoenix, AZ: Associated Professional Services.

Angus, Ian (1993). "Democracy and the Constitution of Audiences: A Comparative Media Theory Perspective" in Cruz and Lewis (eds) *Viewing, Reading, Listening.* Pp. 233–52.

Anzaldúa, Gloria (ed) (1990). *Making Face, Making Soul, Haciendo Caras: Creative and Critical Perspectives by Women of Color.* San Francisco: Aunt Lute.

Arato, Andrew (1978). "Introduction" in Arato and Gebhardt (eds) *The Essential Frankfurt School Reader.* Pp. 3–25, 185–219.

Arato, Andrew, and Eike Gebhardt (eds) (1978). *Essential Frankfurt School Reader.* New York: Urizen Books.

Arnheim, Rudolf (1933; rev. 1957). *Film as Art.* Berkeley: University of California Press, 1957.

Atkinson, Ti-Grace (1970). "Individual Responsibility and Human Oppression" rpt. in *Amazon Odyssey.* New York: Links Books, 1974. n.p.

Austin, Bruce A. (1981a). "Film Attendance: Why College Students Chose to See Their Most Recent Film," *Journal of Popular Film and Television* 9, no. 1 (Spring): 43–49.

—— (1981b). "Portrait of a Cult Film Audience: *The Rocky Horror Picture Show*," *Journal of Communications* 31: 43–54.

—— (ed) (1985). *Current Research in Film: Audiences, Economics, and Law,* vol. I. Norwood, NJ: Ablex.

—— (ed) (1986). *Current Research in Film: Audiences, Economics, and Law,* vol. II. Norwood, NJ: Ablex.

Austin, Joe, and Michael Nevin Willard (eds) (1998). *Generations of Youth: Youth Cultures and History in Twentieth-Century America.* New York: New York University Press.

Austin, Thomas, and Martin Barker (eds) (2003). *Contemporary Hollywood Stardom.* London: Arnold.

Babuscio, Jack (1977). "Camp and the Gay Sensibility" in Dyer (ed) *Gays & Film.* Pp. 40–57.

Bacon-Smith, Camille (1992). *Enterprising Women: Television Fandom and the Creation of Popular Myth.* Philadelphia: University of Pennsylvania Press.

Bad Object-Choices (ed) (1991). *How Do I Look? Queer Film and Video.* Seattle, WA: Bay Press.

Barclay, Craig R. (1994). "Composing Protoselves through Improvisation" in Neisser and Fivush (eds) *Remembering Self.* Pp. 55–77.

Barker, Martin (1984). *A Haunt of Fears: The Strange History of the British Horror Comics Campaign.* London: Pluto Press.

—— (1997a). "The Newson Report: A Case Study in 'Common Sense'" in Barker and Petley (eds) *Ill Effects.* Pp. 12–31.

—— (1997b). "Taking the Extreme Case: Understanding a Fascist Fan of *Judge Dredd*" in Cartmell et al. (eds) *Trash Aesthetics.* Pp. 14–30.

—— (1998). "Film Audience Research: Making a Virtue out of a Necessity," *Iris,* no. 26 (Fall 1998): 131–47.

—— (forthcoming). "*The Lord of the Rings* and 'Identification': A Critical Encounter."

Barker, Martin, Jane Arthurs, and Ramaswami Harindranath (2001). *The Crash Controversy: Censorship Campaigns and Film Reception.* London: Wallflower Press.

Barker, Martin, and Kate Brooks (1998). *Knowing Audiences: Judge Dredd, Its Friends, Fans and Foes.* Luton, UK: University of Luton Press.

Barker, Martin, and Julian Petley (eds) (1997). *Ill Effects: The Media/Violence Debate.* London: Routledge.

Barthes, Roland (1970). *S/Z,* trans. Richard Miller. New York: Hill and Wang, 1974.

Baudry, Jean-Louis (1970). "Ideological Effects of the Basic Cinematographical Apparatus," trans. Alan Williams, *Film Quarterly* 28, no. 2 (Winter 1974–75): 39–47.

Baughman, Cynthia (ed) (1995). *Women on Ice: Feminist Essays on the Tonya Harding/Nancy Kerrigan Spectacle.* New York: Routledge.

Beaujour, Michel (1980). "Exemplary Pornography: Barres, Loyola and the Novel" in Suleiman and Crosman (eds) *Reader in the Text.* Pp. 325–49.

Becker, Edith, Michelle Citron, Julia Lesage, and B. Ruby Rich (1981). "Lesbians and Film" rpt. in Steven (ed) *Jump Cut.* Pp. 296–314.

Becker, Samuel L. (1984). "Marxist Approaches to Media Studies: The British Experience," *Critical Studies in Mass Communication* 1: 66–80.

Benjamin, Walter (1935). "The Work of Art in the Age of Mechanical Reproduction" in *Illuminations,* trans. Harry Zohn. New York: Schocken Books, 1969. Pp. 217–51.

Bennett, Tony (1982). "Text and Social Process: The Case of James Bond," *Screen Education,* no. 41 (Winter/Spring): 3–14.

—— (1996). "Figuring Audiences and Readers" in Hay, Grossberg, and Wartella (eds) *Audience and Its Landscape.* Pp. 145–59.

Bennett, Tony, and Janet Woollacott (1987). *Bond and Beyond: The Political Career of a Popular Hero.* New York: Methuen.

Berenstein, Rhona J. (1996). *Attack of the Leading Ladies: Gender, Sexuality, and Spectatorship in Classic Horror Cinema.* New York: Columbia University Press.

Bergman, David (1991). "Strategic Camp: The Art of Gay Rhetoric" rpt. in Bergman (ed) *Camp Grounds.* Pp. 92–109.

—— (ed) (1993). *Camp Grounds: Style and Homosexuality.* Amherst: University of Massachusetts Press.

—— (1993). "Introduction" in Bergman (ed) *Camp Grounds.* Pp. 3–16.

Berlant, Lauren (1998). "Intimacy: A Special Issue," *Critical Inquiry* 24, no. 2 (Winter): 281–88.

Bernardi, Daniel (ed) (1996). *The Birth of Whiteness: Race and the Emergence of U.S. Cinema.* New Brunswick, NJ: Rutgers University Press.

Bernstein, Matthew (1999). "'Floating Triumphantly': The American Critics on *Titanic*" in Sandler and Studlar (eds) *Titanic.* Pp. 14–28.

Bielby, Denise, and C. Lee Harrington (1993). "Reach Out and Touch Someone: Viewers, Agency, and Audiences in the Televisual Experience" in Cruz and Lewis (eds) *Viewing, Reading, Listening.* Pp. 81–100.

Bigsby, C. W. E. (ed) (1976). *Approaches to Popular Culture.* Bowling Green, OH: Bowling Green University Press.

Bird, S. Elizabeth (1997). "What a Story! Understanding the Audience for Scandals" in Lull and Hinerman (eds) *Media Scandals.* Pp. 99–121.

Birtha, Rachel Roxanne (1977). *Pluralistic Perspectives on the Black-Directed, Black-Oriented Feature Film: A Study of Content, Intent and Audience Response.* Unpublished PhD dissertation: University of Minnesota.

Blumenthal, Ralph (1973). "Porno Chic," *New York Times Magazine,* 21 January, 28+.

Blumer, Jay (1996). "Recasting the Audience in the New Television Marketplace?" in Hay, Grossberg, and Wartella (eds) *Audience and Its Landscape.* Pp. 97–111.

Bobo, Jacqueline (1988). "*The Color Purple*: Black Women's Responses," *Jump Cut*, no. 33: 43–51.

——— (1995). *Black Women as Cultural Readers.* New York: Columbia University Press.

Boddy, William (1996). "Approaching *The Untouchables*: Social Science and Moral Panics in Early Sixties Television," *Cinema Journal* 35, no. 4: 70–87.

Bodroghkozy, Aniko (1992). "'Is This What You Mean by Color TV?': Race, Gender, and Contested Meanings in NBC's *Julia*" in Spigel and Mann (eds) *Private Screenings.* Pp. 143–68.

Bordo, Susan (1990). "Material Girl: The Effacements of Postmodern Culture," *Michigan Quarterly Review* 29, no. 4 (Fall): 655–77.

Bordwell, David (1971). "*Citizen Kane*" rpt. in Nichols (ed) *Movies and Methods,* vol. I. Pp. 273–90.

——— (1979). "The Art Cinema as a Mode of Film Practice," *Film Criticism* 4, no. 1 (Fall): 56–63.

——— (1985). *Narration in the Fiction Film.* Madison: University of Wisconsin Press.

Bordwell, David, and Kristin Thompson (1979). *Film Art: An Introduction.* Reading, MA: Addison-Wesley.

Bowser, Pearl, Jane Gaines, and Charles Musser (2001). *Oscar Micheaux and His Circle: African American Filmmaking and Race Cinema of the Silent Era.* Bloomington: Indiana University Press.

Branigan, Edward (1984). *Point of View in the Cinema: A Theory of Narration and Subjectivity in Classical Film.* Berlin and New York: Mouton.

——— (1992). *Narrative Comprehension and Film.* London: Routledge.

Brasell, R. Bruce (1992). "My Hustler: Gay Spectatorship as Cruising," *Wide Angle* 14, no. 2 (April): 54–64.

Braudy, Leo (1986). *Frenzy of Renown: Fame & Its History.* New York: Oxford University Press.

Britton, Andrew (1978/79). "For Interpretation—Notes against Camp," *Gay Left*, no. 7 (Winter): 11–14.

Brooks, Cleanth (1947). *The Well Wrought Urn: Studies in the Structure of Poetry.* New York: Harcourt, Brace & World.

Brower, Sue (1992). "Fans as Tastemakers: Viewers for Quality Television" in Lewis (ed) *Adoring Audience.* Pp. 163–84.

Brown, Beverley (1981). "A Feminist Interest in Pornography: Some Modest Proposals," *m/f*, nos. 5/6: 5–18.

Brown, Jane, and Laurie Schulze (1990). "The Effects of Race, Gender, and Fandom on Audience Interpretations of Madonna's Music Videos," *Journal of Communication* 40, no. 2 (Spring): 88–102.

Brown, Jeffrey A. (1997). "'They Can Imagine Anything They Want . . .': Identification, Desire and the Celebrity Text," *Discourse* 19, no. 3: 122–43.

Brown, Mary Ellen (1990a). "Conclusion: Consumption and Resistance—the Problem of Pleasure" in M. Brown (ed) *Television and Women's Culture*. Pp. 201–10.

—— (1990b). "Motley Moments: Soap Operas, Carnival, Gossip and the Power of the Utterance" in M. Brown (ed) *Television and Women's Culture*. Pp. 183–98.

—— (ed) (1990c). *Television and Women's Culture: The Politics of the Popular*. London: Sage.

Brown, Roger, and James Kulik (1977). "Flashbulb Memories," *Cognition* 5: 73–99.

Brownmiller, Susan (1975). *Against Our Will: Men, Women, and Rape*. New York: Simon and Schuster.

Bruner, Jerome (1993). "The Autobiographical Process" in Folkenflick (ed) *Culture of Autobiography*. Pp. 38–56.

—— (1994). "The 'Remembered' Self" in Neisser and Fivush (eds) *Remembering Self*. Pp. 41–54.

Brunsdon, Charlotte, and David Morley (1978). *Everyday Television: "Nationwide."* London: British Film Institute.

Bryant, Jennings, and Dolf Zillmann (1982). "Massive Pornography, Even If Noncoercive, Creates Callousness to Rape, Study Finds," *Media Report to Women* 10, nos. 11/12 (1 November/1 December): 4.

—— (eds) (1991). *Responding to the Screen: Reception and Reaction Processes*. Hillsdale, NJ: Erlbaum.

—— (eds) (1994). *Media Effects: Advances in Theory and Research*. Hillsdale, NJ: Erlbaum.

Buckingham, David (1996). *Moving Images: Understanding Children's Emotional Reactions to Television*. Manchester, UK: Manchester University Press.

—— (1997). "Electronic Child Abuse? Rethinking the Media's Effects on Children" in Barker and Petley (eds) *Ill Effects*. Pp. 32–47.

Buckland, Warren (ed) (1995). *The Film Spectator: From Sign to Mind*. Amsterdam: Amsterdam University Press.

Budd, Michael (1981). "*The Cabinet of Dr. Caligari*: Conditions of Reception," *Ciné-Tracts* 3, no. 4 (Winter): 41–49.

Burch, Noël (1969). *Theory of Film Practice*, trans. Annette Michelson. New York: Praeger, 1973.

Burgess, Marilyn (1990/91). "'Proudly She Marches': Wartime Propaganda and the Lesbian Spectator," *CineAction*, no. 23 (Winter): 22–27.

Burgin, Victor, James Donald, and Cora Kaplan (eds) (1986). *Formations of Pleasure*. London: Routledge.

Burt, Richard (1995). "Getting Off the Subject: Iconoclasm, Queer Sexuality, and the Celebrity Intellectual," *Performing Arts Journal* 50/51 (May/September): 137–50.

Butler, Cheryl B. (1991). "*The Color Purple* Controversy: Black Woman Spectatorship," *Wide Angle* 13, nos. 3/4: 62–69.

Butsch, Richard (ed) (1990). *For Fun and Profit: The Transformation of Leisure into Consumption.* Philadelphia: Temple University Press.

———— (2000). *The Making of American Audiences: From Stage to Television, 1750–1990.* New York: Cambridge University Press.

———— (2001). "A History of Research on Movies, Radio, and Television," *Journal of Popular Film and Television* 29, no. 3 (Fall): 112–20.

Cahiers du Cinéma editors (1970). "John Ford's *Young Mr. Lincoln*" rpt. in Nichols (ed) *Movies and Methods,* vol. I. Pp. 493–529.

Cairns, Robert B., J. C. N. Paul, and J. Wishner (1970). "Psychological Assumptions in Sex Censorship" in *Technical Report of the Commission on Obscenity and Pornography,* vol. I. Washington, DC: U.S. Government Printing Office. Pp. 5–21.

Campbell, Russell (1982). *Cinema Strikes Back: Radical Filmmaking in the United States, 1930–1942.* Ann Arbor, MI: UMI Research Press.

Cantor, Joanne (1991). "Fright Response to Mass Media Productions" in Bryant and Zillmann (eds) *Responding to the Screen.* Pp. 169–97.

Carbine, Mary (1990). "'The Finest Outside the Loop': Motion Picture Exhibition in Chicago's Black Metropolis, 1905–1928," *camera obscura,* no. 23 (May): 11–41.

Carey, James W. (1975a). "A Cultural Approach to Communication," *Communications* 2: 1–22.

———— (1975b). "Mass Communication and Cultural Studies" rpt. in *Communication as Culture: Essays on Media and Society.* Boston: Unwin Hyman, 1989. Pp. 37–68.

Carroll, Noël (1978). "Toward a Theory of Film Editing," *Millennium Film Journal,* no. 3: 79–99.

———— (1990). *The Philosophy of Horror, or Paradoxes of the Heart.* New York: Routledge.

———— (1998). *Interpreting the Moving Image.* Cambridge: Cambridge University Press.

———— (1999). "Horror and Humor," *Journal of Aesthetics and Art Criticism* 57, no. 2 (Spring): 145–60.

Carruthers, Fiona (2004). "Fanfic Is Good for Two Things—Greasing Engines and Killing Brain Cells," *Participations* 1, no. 2 (May): on-line, accessed 1 June 2004.

Carter, Angela (1978). *The Sadeian Woman and the Ideology of Pornography.* New York: Pantheon Books.

Cartmell, Deborah, I. Q. Hunter, Heidi Kaye, and Imelda Whelehan (eds)

(1997). *Trash Aesthetics: Popular Culture and Its Audience*. London: Pluto Press.

Castle, Terry (1993). *The Apparitional Lesbian*. New York: Columbia University Press.

Cavicchi, Daniel (1998). *Tramps Like Us: Music and Meaning among Springsteen Fans*. New York: Oxford University Press.

Cawelti, John G. (1975). "Myths of Violence in American Popular Culture," *Critical Inquiry* 1, no. 3: 521–41.

Chambers, Iain, John Clarke, Ian Connell, Lidia Curti, Stuart Hall, and Tony Jefferson (1977/78). "Marxism and Culture," *Screen* 18, no. 4 (Winter): 109–19.

Champagne, John (1997). "'Stop Reading Films!': Film Studies, Close Analysis, and Gay Pornography," *Cinema Journal* 36, no. 4 (Summer): 76–97.

Charney, Leo (2001). "The Violence of a Perfect Moment" in Slocum (ed) *Violence and American Cinema*. Pp. 47–62.

Charney, Leo, and Vanessa R. Schwartz (eds) (1995). *Cinema and the Invention of Modern Life*. Berkeley: University of California Press.

Chatman, Seymour (1990). *Coming to Terms: The Rhetoric of Narrative in Fiction and Film*. Ithaca, NY: Cornell University Press.

Cherry, Brigid (1999). "Refusing to Refuse to Look: Female Viewers of the Horror Film" in Stokes and Maltby (eds) *Identifying Hollywood's Audiences*. Pp. 187–203.

Cicioni, Mirna (1998). "Male Pair-Bonds and Female Desire in Fan Slash Writing" in Harris and Alexander (eds) *Theorizing Fandom*. Pp. 153–77.

Clarke, John, Chas. Critcher, and Richard Johnson (eds) (1979). *Working-Class Culture*. London: Hutchinson.

Clarke, John, Stuart Hall, Tony Jefferson, and Brian Roberts (1976). "Subcultures, Cultures and Class" in Hall and Jefferson (eds) *Resistance through Rituals*. Pp. 9–79.

Clifford, James, and George E. Marcus (eds) (1986). *Writing Culture: The Poetics and Politics of Ethnography*. Berkeley: University of California Press.

Clover, Carol J. (1987). "Her Body, Himself: Gender in the Slasher Film," *Representations*, no. 20 (Fall): 187–228.

——— (1992). *Men, Women, and Chain Saws: Gender in the Modern Horror Film*. Princeton, NJ: Princeton University Press.

Cohan, Steven (1997). *Masked Men: Masculinity and the Movies of the Fifties*. Bloomington: Indiana University Press.

——— (2001). "Judy on the Net: Judy, Garland Fandom and 'the Gay Thing' Revisited" in Tinkcom and Villarejo (eds) *Keyframes*. Pp. 119–36.

Coleman, Robin R. Means (2002). "Introduction" in Coleman (ed) *Say It Loud*. Pp. 1–26.

———— (ed) (2002). *Say It Loud: African-American Audiences, Media, and Identity.* New York: Routledge.

Colin, Michel (1992). "Film Semiology as a Cognitive Science," trans. Claudine Tourniaire in Buckland (ed) *Film Spectator.* Pp. 87–110.

Collins, Patricia Hill (2000). *Black Feminist Thought: Knowledge, Consciousness, and the Politics of Empowerment.* 2nd ed. New York: Routledge.

Comolli, Jean-Louis (1971–72). "Technique et idéologie: Caméra, perspective, profoundeur de champ," *Cahiers du Cinéma,* no. 229 (May 1971): 4–15; "Profondeur de champ: La double scène," no. 229 (May 1971): 16–21; "Profondeur de champ: La double scène (suite)," no. 230 (July 1971): 51–57; "Profondeur de champ: La double scène (suite)," no. 231 (August-September 1971): 42–49; "La profondeur de champ 'primitive,'" no. 233 (November 1971): 39–45; "Effacement de la profondeur/avènement de la parole," nos. 234–35 (December 1971/January–February 1972): 94–100; "Quelle parole?" no. 241 (September–October 1972): 20–24.

———— (1977). "Historical Fiction—A Body Too Much," trans. Ben Brewster, *Screen* 19, no. 2 (Summer 1978): 41–54.

Connerton, Paul (1989). *How Societies Remember.* Cambridge: Cambridge University Press.

Conway, Martin A. (1995). *Flashbulb Memories.* Hove, East Sussex, UK: Erlbaum.

Conway, Mary T. (1996). "Inhabiting the Phallus: Reading *Safe Is Desire,*" *camera obscura,* no. 38 (May): 132–61.

Cook, Bruce (1976). "Why TV Stars Don't Become Movie Stars," *American Film* 1, no. 8 (June): 58–61.

Cooper, Brenda (1998). "'The White-Black Fault Line': Relevancy of Race and Racism in Spectators' Experiences of Spike Lee's *Do the Right Thing,*" *Howard Journal of Communication* 9, no. 3: 105–28.

Copp, David, and Susan Wendell (ed) (1983). *Pornography and Censorship.* New York: Prometheus Books.

Cornell, Daniell (1998). "Stealing the Spectacle: Gay Audiences and the Queering of Douglas Fairbanks's Body," *Velvet Light Trap,* no. 42 (Fall): 76–90.

Cornwell, Nancy C., and Mark P. Orbe (2002). "'Keepin' It Real' and/or 'Sellin' Out to the Man': African-American Responses to Aaron McGruder's *The Boondocks,*" in Coleman (ed) *Say It Loud.* Pp. 27–43.

Couldry, Nick (2000a). *Inside Culture: Re-imagining the Method of Cultural Studies.* London: Sage.

———— (2000b). "What and Where Are Media Effects? New Answers to Old Questions." Unpublished paper.

Cowan, Gloria, and Margaret O'Brien (1990). "Gender and Survival vs. Death in Slasher Films: A Content Analysis," *Sex Roles* 23, nos. 3/4 (August): 187–96.

Coward, Rosalind (1982). "Sexual Violence and Sexuality," *Feminist Review*, no. 11 (June): 9–21.

Coward, Rosalind, and John Ellis (1977). *Language and Materialism: Developments in Semiology and the Theory of the Subject*. London: Routledge & Kegan Paul.

Cowie, Elizabeth (1984). "Fantasia," *m/f*, no. 9: 71–104.

—— (1997). *Representing the Woman: Cinema and Psychoanalysis*. Minneapolis: University of Minnesota Press.

Crary, Jonathan (1995). "Unbinding Vision: Manet and the Attentive Observer in the Late Nineteenth Century" in Charney and Schwartz (eds) *Cinema and the Invention of Modern Life*. Pp. 46–71.

Crawford, June, Susan Kippax, Jenny Onyx, Una Gault, and Pam Benton (1992). *Emotion and Gender: Constructing Meaning from Memory*. London: Sage.

Crawford, Mary, and Roger Chaffin (1986). "The Reader's Construction of Meaning: Cognitive Research on Gender and Comprehension" in Flynn and Schweickart (eds) *Gender and Reading*. Pp. 3–30.

Creed, Barbara (1995). *The Monstrous-Feminine: Film, Feminism, Psychoanalysis*. New York: Routledge.

Crenshaw, Kimberlé Williams (1993). "Beyond Racism and Misogyny: Black Feminism and 2 Live Crew," in Matsuda (ed) *Words That Wound*. Pp. 111–32.

Cressey, Paul G. (1932). "The Community—A Social Setting for the Motion Picture" in Jowett, Jarvie, and Fuller (eds) *Children and the Movies*. Pp. 133–219.

Cripps, Thomas (1983). "*Amos 'n' Andy* and the Debate over American Racial Integration" in O'Connor (ed) *American History/American Television*. Pp. 33–54.

Crofts, Stephen (1992). "Cross-Cultural Reception" rpt. in *Film/Literature Quarterly* 21, no. 2 (1993): 157–68.

Cruz, Jon, and Justin Lewis (eds) (1993). *Viewing, Reading, Listening: Audiences and Cultural Reception*. Boulder, CO: Westview Press.

Culler, Jonathan (1981). *The Pursuit of Signs: Semiotics, Literature, Deconstruction*. Ithaca, NY: Cornell University Press.

—— (1982). *On Deconstruction: Theory and Criticism after Structuralism*. Ithaca, NY: Cornell University Press.

Cumberbatch, Guy (1989). "Violence and the Mass Media: The Research Evidence" in Cumberbatch and Howitt, *Measure of Uncertainty*. Pp. 31–59.

Cumberbatch, Guy, and Dennis Howitt (1989). *A Measure of Uncertainty: The Effects of the Mass Media*. London: John Libbey.

Curran, James, and Michael Gurevitch (eds) (1991). *Mass Media and Society*. London: Arnold.

Curran, James, Michael Gurevitch, and Janet Wollacott (eds) (1982). "The Study of the Media: Theoretical Approaches" in Gurevitch et al. (eds) *Culture, Society and the Media*. Pp. 11–28.

Curry, Ramona (1996). *Too Much of a Good Thing: Mae West as Cultural Icon*. Minneapolis: University of Minnesota Press.

D'Acci, Julie (1994). *Defining Women: Television and the Case of* Cagney & Lacey. Chapel Hill: University of North Carolina Press.

Dahlgren, Peter (1985). "The Modes of Reception: For a Hermeneutics of TV News" in Drummond and Paterson (eds) *Television in Transition*. Pp. 235–49.

Damasio, Antonio R. (1994). *Descartes' Error: Emotion: Reason, and the Human Brain*. New York: HarperCollins.

Damico, James (1975). "Ingrid from Lorraine to Stromboli: Analyzing the Public's Perception of a Film Star," *Journal of Popular Film* 4, no. 1: 3–19.

Davis, Reid (2001–2). "What WOZ: Lost Objects, Repeat Viewings, and the Sissy Warrior," *Film Quarterly* 55, no. 2 (Winter): 2–13.

Dayan, Daniel (1998). "Particularistic Media and Diasporic Communication" in Liebes and Curran (eds) *Media, Ritual, Identity*. Pp. 103–13.

Dayan, Daniel, and Elihu Katz (1992). *Media Events: The Live Broadcasting of History*. Cambridge, MA: Harvard University Press.

de Certeau, Michel (1984). *The Practice of Everyday Life,* trans. Steven Rendall. Berkeley: University of California Press, 1984.

de Lauretis, Teresa (1984). *Alice Doesn't: Feminism, Semiotics, Cinema*. Bloomington: Indiana University Press.

———— (1994). *The Practice of Love: Lesbian Sexuality and Perverse Desire*. Bloomington: Indiana University Press.

de Saussure, Ferdinand (1916). *Course in General Linguistics,* trans. Wade Baskin. New York: McGraw-Hill, 1966.

DeAngelis, Michael (1999). "Art Cinema Hits the Suburbs: Exhibition Practices of the 1960s and 1970s," unpublished paper presented at the Society for Cinema Studies conference, West Palm Beach, FL.

———— (2001). *Gay Fandom and Crossover Stardom: James Dean, Mel Gibson, and Keanu Reeves*. Durham, NC: Duke University Press.

deCordova, Richard (1990). *Picture Personalities: The Emergence of the Star System in America*. Urbana: University of Illinois Press.

DeGeorge, Richard, and Fernande DeGeorge (eds) (1972). *The Structuralists: From Marx to Lévi-Strauss*. Garden City, NY: Doubleday.

Dell, Chad (1998). "'Lookit That Hunk of Man!': Subversive Pleasures, Female Fandom, and Professional Wrestling" in Harris and Alexander (eds) *Theorizing Fandom*. Pp. 87–108.

Dembo, Richard (1973). "Gratifications Found in Media by British Teenage Boys," *Journalism Quarterly* 50, no. 3 (Autumn): 517–26.

Desjardins, Mary (1995). "Meeting Two Queens: Feminist Film-Making, Identity Politics, and the Melodramatic Fantasy," *Film Quarterly* 48, no. 3 (Spring): 26–33.

Diawara, Manthia (1990). "Black British Cinema: Spectatorship and Identify Formation in 'Territories,'" *Public Culture* 3, no. 1 (Fall): 33–47.

——— (ed) (1993). *Black American Cinema*. New York: Routledge.

Dickinson, Roger, Ramaswami Harindranath, and Olga Linné (eds) (1998). *Approaches to Audiences: A Reader*. London: Arnold.

Dickstein, Morris (1980). "The Aesthetics of Fright" rpt. in Grant (ed) *Planks of Reason*. Pp. 65–78.

Dines, Gail, and Jean M. Humez (eds) (1995). *Gender, Race and Class in Media: A Text-Reader*. Thousand Oaks, CA: Sage.

Dines, Gail, Robert Jensen, and Anne Russo (1998). *Pornography: The Production and Consumption of Inequity*. New York: Routledge.

Doane, Mary Ann (1982). "Film and the Masquerade—Theorizing the Female Spectator," *Screen* 23, nos. 3–4: 74–88.

——— (1993). "Technology's Body: Cinematic Vision in Modernity," *Differences* 5, no. 2: 1–23.

Dobinson, Cheryl, and Kevin Young (2000). "Popular Cinema and Lesbian Interpretative Strategies," *Journal of Homosexuality* 40, no. 2: 97–122.

Dollimore, Jonathan (1991). *Sexual Dissidence: Augustine to Wilde, Freud to Foucault*. Oxford: Oxford University Press.

Donnerstein, Edward I., and Daniel G. Linz (1986). "The Question of Pornography," *Psychology Today* 20, no. 12 (December): 56–59.

Doss, Erika (1999). *Elvis Culture: Fans, Faith and Image*. Lawrence: University Press of Kansas.

Doty, Alexander (1993). *Making Things Perfectly Queer: Interpreting Mass Culture*. Minneapolis: University of Minnesota Press.

Douglas, Mary (1980). "Introduction: Maurice Halbwachs (1877–1945)" in Halbwachs (1950) *Collective Memory*. Pp. 1–21.

Doyle, Jennifer, Jonathan Flatley, and José Esteban Muñoz (eds) (1996). *Pop Out: Queer Warhol*. Durham, NC: Duke University Press.

Drummond, Phillip, and Richard Paterson (eds) (1985). *Television in Transition*. London: British Film Institute.

Duberman, Martin (ed) (1997). *A Queer World: The Center for Lesbian and Gay Studies Reader*. New York: New York University Press.

duCille, Ann (1998). "The Shirley Temple of My Familiar," *Transition*, no. 73: 10–34.

Dunbar, Roxanne (1969). "'Sexual Liberation': More of the Same Thing," *No More Fun and Games*, no. 3 (November): n.p.

Duncombe, Stephen (2002). "'I'm a Loser Baby': Zines and the Creation of Underground Identity" in Jenkins, McPherson, and Shattuck (eds) *Hop on Pop*. Pp. 227–50.

Durkin, Kevin (1985). *Television, Sex Roles and Children: A Developmental Social Psychological Account*. Milton Keys, UK: Open University Press.

Dworkin, Andrea (1974). *Woman Hating*. New York: Dutton.

Dyer, Richard (ed) (1977). *Gays & Film*. London: British Film Institute.

—— (1977–78). "Lana: Four Films of Lana Turner," *Movie*, no. 35 (Winter): 30–52.

—— (1979). *Stars*. London: British Film Institute.

—— (1982). "*A Star Is Born* and the Construction of Authenticity" rpt. in Gledhill (ed) *Stardom*. Pp. 132–40.

—— (1985). "Coming to Terms: Male Gay Porn," *Jump Cut*, no. 30: 27–29.

—— (1986). *Heavenly Bodies: Film Stars and Society*. New York: St. Martin's Press.

—— (1990). *Now You See It: Studies on Lesbian and Gay Film*. New York: Routledge.

Eagleton, Terry (1983). *Literary Theory: An Introduction*. Minneapolis: University of Minnesota Press.

Echols, Alice (1989). *Daring to Be Bad: Radical Feminism in America, 1967–1975*. Minneapolis: University of Minnesota Press.

Eco, Umberto (1984). "*Casablanca*: Cult Movies and Intertextual Collage," trans. William Weaver, rpt. in *Travels in Hyperreality*. San Diego, CA: Harcourt Brace Jovanovich, 1986. Pp. 197–211.

Ehrenreich, Barbara, Elizabeth Hess, and Gloria Jacobs (1992). "Beatlemania: Girls Just Want to Have Fun" in L. Lewis (ed) *Adoring Audience*. Pp. 84–106.

Eisenstein, Sergei (1924). "The Montage of Film Attractions," trans. Jay Leyda, in Leyda and Voynow (eds) *Eisenstein at Work*. Pp. 17–20.

Eitzen, Dirk (1995). "Against the Ivory Tower: An Apologia for 'Popular' Historical Documentaries," *Film Historia 5*, no. 1: 25–34.

Elliott, William R., and William J. Schenk-Hamlin (1979). "Film, Politics and the Press: The Influence of 'All the President's Men,'" *Journalism Quarterly* 56, no. 3 (Autumn): 546–53.

Ellis, John (1980). "Photography, Pornography, Art Pornography," *Screen* 21, no. 1 (Spring): 81–108.

—— (1982). *Visible Fictions: Cinema, Television, Video*. Boston: Routledge & Kegan Paul.

Ellison, Julie (1999). *Cato's Tears and the Making of Anglo-American Emotion*. Chicago: University of Chicago Press.

Ellsworth, Elizabeth (1986). "Illicit Pleasures: Feminist Spectators and *Personal Best*," *Wide Angle* 8, no. 2: 45–56.

Elsaesser, Thomas (1976). "Screen Violence: Emotional Structure and Ideological Function in *A Clockwork Orange*" in Bigsby (ed) *Approaches to Popular Culture*. Pp. 171–200.

Epstein, Julia, and Kristina Straub (eds) (1991). *Body Guards: The Cultural Politics of Gender Ambiguity*. New York: Routledge.

Erb, Cynthia (1998). *Tracking King Kong: A Hollywood Icon in World Culture*. Detroit: Wayne State University Press.

Everett, Anna (2000). "Lester Walton's *Écriture Noir*: Black Spectatorial Transcodings of 'Cinematic Excess,'" *Cinema Journal* 39, no. 3 (Spring): 30–52.

——— (2001). *Returning the Gaze: A Genealogy of Black Film Criticism, 1909–1949*. Durham, NC: Duke University Press.

Farmer, Brett (2000). *Spectacular Passions: Cinema, Fantasy, Gay Male Spectatorship*. Durham, NC: Duke University Press.

Faulstich, Werner, and Helmut Korte (eds) (1997). *Der Star: Geschichte, Rezeption, Bedeutung*. Munich: Wilhelm Fink.

Ferguson, Marjorie, and Peter Golding (1997a). "Cultural Studies and Changing Times: An Introduction" in Ferguson and Golding (eds) *Cultural Studies in Question*. Pp. xiii–xxvii.

——— (eds) (1997b). *Cultural Studies in Question*. London: Sage.

Feuer, Jane (1995). "Nancy and Tonya and Sonja: The Figure of the Figure Skater in American Entertainment" in Baughman (ed) *Women on Ice*. Pp. 3–21.

Fiske, John (1986). "Television: Polysemy and Popularity," *Critical Studies in Communication* 3, no. 4 (December): 391–408.

——— (1987). *Television Culture*. London: Methuen.

——— (1989). *Understanding Popular Culture*. Boston: Unwin Hyman.

——— (1992). "The Cultural Economy of Fandom" in L. Lewis (ed) *Adoring Audience*. Pp. 30–49.

Flinn, Caryl (1995). "The Deaths of Camp," *camera obscura*, no. 35 (May): 52–84.

Flynn, Elizabeth A., and Patrocinio P. Schweickart (eds) (1986). *Gender and Reading: Essays on Readers, Texts, and Contexts*. Baltimore: Johns Hopkins University Press.

Folkenflick, Robert (ed) (1993). *Culture of Autobiography: Constructions of Self-Representation*. Stanford, CA: Stanford University Press.

Forman, Henry J. (1933). *Our Movie Made Children*. New York: Macmillan.

Fowles, Jib (1992). *Starstruck: Celebrity Performers and the American Public*. Washington, DC: Smithsonian Institution Press.

Fox, Stephen (1984). *The Mirror Makers: A History of American Advertising and Its Creators*. New York: William Morrow.

Freedman, Jonathan (1984). "Effects of Television Violence on Aggressiveness," *Psychological Bulletin* 96, no. 2 (September): 227–46.

—— (1986). "Television Violence and Aggression: A Rejoinder," *Psychological Bulletin* 100, no. 3 (November): 372–78.

Freeland, Cynthia A. (1999). "Cognitive Science and Film Theory." Unpublished paper circulated on H-Net listserv (June 3).

—— (2000). *The Naked and the Undead: Evil and the Appeal of Horror.* Boulder, CO: Westview Press.

Fregoso, Rosa Linda (ed) (2001). *Lourdes Portillo:* The Devil Never Sleeps *and Other Films.* Austin: University of Texas Press.

Friedberg, Anne (1993). *Window Shopping: Cinema and the Postmodern.* Berkeley: University of California Press.

Friedman, Norman F. (1978). "Responses of Blacks and Other Minorities to Television Shows of the 1970s about Their Groups," *Journal of Popular Film and Television* 7, no. 1: 85–102.

Friedrich-Cofer, Lynette, and Aletha C. Huston (1986). "Television Violence and Aggression: The Debate Continues," *Psychological Bulletin* 100, no. 3 (November): 364–71.

Frijda, Nico H. (1997). "Commemorating" in Pennebaker et al. (eds) *Collective Memory of Political Events.* Pp. 103–27.

Frissen, Valerie (1996). "Heavy Viewing as Social Action" in Renckstorf, Mc-Quail, and Jankowski (eds) *Media Use as Social Action.* Pp. 53–70.

Fung, Richard (1991). "Looking for My Penis: The Eroticized Asian in Gay Video Porn" in Bad Object-Choices (ed) *How Do I Look?* Pp. 146–60.

Gabriel, John (1996). "What Do You Do When Minority Means You? *Falling Down* and the Construction of 'Whiteness'," *Screen* 37, no. 2 (Summer): 129–51.

Gaines, Jane (2001a). *Fire & Desire: Mixed-Race Movies in the Silent Era.* Chicago: University of Chicago Press.

—— (2001b). "'Green Like Me'" in Stokes and Maltby (eds) *Hollywood Spectatorship.* Pp. 105–20.

Gamson, Joshua (1994). *Claims to Fame: Celebrity in Contemporary America.* Berkeley: University of California Press.

—— (1997). "The Organizational Shaping of Collective Identity: The Case of Lesbian and Gay Film Festivals in New York" in Duberman (ed) *Queer World.* Pp. 526–43.

Garrison, Lee C. (1972). "The Needs of Motion Picture Audiences," *California Management Review* 15, no. 2 (Winter): 144–52.

Gauntlett, David (1995). *Moving Experiences: Understanding Television's Influences and Effects.* London: John Libbey.

—— (1996). *Video Critical: Children, the Environment and Media Power.* Bedfordshire, UK: University of Luton.

Geertz, Clifford (1973). *Interpretation of Culture: Selected Essays.* New York: Basic Books.

Gelder, Ken (1997). "Introduction to Part Three" in Gelder and Thornton (eds) *Subcultures Reader*. Pp. 145–48.

Gelder, Ken, and Sarah Thornton (eds) (1997). *The Subcultures Reader*. London: Routledge.

Geraghty, Christine (2000). "Re-examining Stardom: Questions of Text, Bodies and Performance" in Gledhill and Williams (eds) *Reinventing Film Studies*. Pp. 183–201.

Gergen, Kenneth J. (1994). "Mind, Text, and Society: Self-Memory in Social Context" in Neisser and Fivush (eds) *Remembering Self*. Pp. 78–104.

Gilbert, James (1986). *A Cycle of Outrage: America's Reaction to the Juvenile Delinquent in the 1950s*. New York: Oxford University Press.

Giles, Dennis (1977). "Pornographic Space: The Other Place" in Lawton and Staiger (eds) *1977 Film Studies Annual*. Pp. 52–65.

—— (1984). "Conditions of Pleasure in Horror Cinema" in Grant (ed) *Planks of Reason*. Pp. 38–52.

Glander, Timothy (2000). *Origins of Mass Communication Research during the American Cold War: Educational effects and Contemporary Implications*. Mahwah, NJ: Erlbaum.

Gledhill, Christine (1991a). "Introduction" in Gledhill (ed) *Stardom*. Pp. xiii–xx.

—— (ed) (1991b). *Stardom: Industry of Desire*. London: Routledge.

Gledhill, Christine, and Linda Williams (eds) (2000). *Reinventing Film Studies*. London: Arnold. Pp. 183–201.

Glynn, Kevin (1996). "Bartmania: The Social Reception of an Unruly Image," *camera obscura*, no. 38 (May): 61–91.

Goldstein, Richard (1984). "Pornography and Its Discontents," *Village Voice*, 16 October. Pp. 19–22, 44.

Grant, Barry K. (ed) (1984). *Planks of Reason: Essays on the Horror Film*. Metuchen, NJ: Scarecrow Press.

—— (1991). "Science Fiction Double Feature: Ideology in the Cult Film" in Telotte (ed) *Cult Film Experience*. Pp. 122–37.

Green, Shoshanna, Cynthia Jenkins, and Henry Jenkins (1998). "Normal Female Interest in Men Bonking: Selections from *The Terra Nostra Underground* and *Strange Bedfellows*" in Harris and Alexander (eds) *Theorizing Fandom*. Pp. 9–38.

Greenberg, Clement (1939). "Avant-Garde and Kitsch," *Partisan Review* 6, no. 5 (Fall): 34–49.

Gregory, Stanford W., Jr., and Jerry M. Lewis (1988). "Symbols of Collective Memory: The Social Process of Memorializing May 4, 1970, at Kent State University," *Symbolic Interaction* 11, no. 2 (Fall): 213–33.

Griffiths, Alison, and James Latham (1999). "Film and Ethnic Identity in

Harlem, 1896–1915" in Stokes and Maltby (eds) *American Movie Audiences*. Pp. 46–63.

Grodal, Torben (1997). *Moving Pictures: A New Theory of Film Genres, Feelings, and Cognition*. New York: Oxford University Press.

Gross, Larry (1991). "Out of the Mainstream: Sexual Minorities and the Mass Media" in Wolf and Kielwasser (eds) *Gay People, Sex, and the Media*. Pp. 19–46.

—— (1996). "Marginal Texts, Marginal Audiences" in Hay, Grossberg, and Wartella (eds) *Audience and Its Landscape*. Pp. 161–76.

—— (1998). "Minorities, Majorities and the Media" in Liebes and Curran (eds) *Media, Ritual, Identity*. Pp. 87–102.

Grossberg, Lawrence (1992). "Is There a Fan in the House? The Affective Sensibility of Fandom" in L. Lewis (ed) *Adoring Audience*. Pp. 50–65.

Gunning, Tom (1986). "The Cinema of Attraction: Early Film, Its Spectator and the Avant-Garde," *Wide Angle* 8, nos. 3–4: 63–70.

—— (1995). "Tracing the Individual Body: Photography, Detectives, and Early Cinema," in Charney and Schwartz (eds) *Cinema and the Invention of Modern Life*. Pp. 15–45.

Gunter, Barrie (1991). "Responding to News and Public Affairs" in Bryant and Zillmann (eds) *Responding to the Screen*. Pp. 229–60.

—— (1994). "The Question of Media Violence" in Bryant and Zillmann (eds) *Media Effects*. Pp. 163–211.

Gurevitch, Michael, Tony Bennett, James Curran, and Janet Woollacott (eds) (1982). *Culture, Society and the Media*. London: Methuen.

Halberstam, Judith (1998). *Female Masculinity*. Durham, NC: Duke University Press.

Halbwachs, Maurice (1950). *The Collective Memory*, trans. Francis Ditter Jr. and Vida Yazdi. New York: Harper and Row, 1980.

Hall, Stuart (1980a). "Cultural Studies and the Centre: Some Problematics and Problems" in Hall et al. (eds) *Culture, Media, Language*. Pp. 15–47.

—— (1980b). "Cultural Studies: Two Paradigms," *Media, Culture and Society* 2: 57–72.

—— (1980c). "Encoding/Decoding" in Hall et al. (eds) *Culture, Media, Language*. Pp. 128–39.

—— (1989). "Reflections upon the Encoding/Decoding Model: An Interview with Stuart Hall" in Cruz and Lewis (eds) *Viewing, Reading, Listening*. Pp. 253–74.

Hall, Stuart, Dorothy Hobsen, Andrew Lowe, and Paul Willis (eds) (1980). *Culture, Media, Language*. London: Hutchinson.

Hall, Stuart, and Tony Jefferson (eds) (1976). *Resistance through Rituals: Youth Subcultures in Post-war Britain*. London: Hutchinson.

214 | *Selected Bibliography*

Handel, Leo A. (1950). *Hollywood Looks at Its Audience: A Report of Film Audience Research*. Urbana: University of Illinois Press.

Hansen, Christian, Catherine Needham, and Bill Nichols (1991). "Pornography, Ethnography, and the Discourses of Power" in Nichols (ed) *Representing Reality*. Pp. 201–28.

Hansen, Miriam (1991). *Babel and Babylon: Spectatorship in American Silent Film*. Cambridge, MA: Harvard University Press.

Harbord, Victoria (1997). "*Natural Born Killers*: Violence, Film and Anxiety" in Sumner (ed) *Violence, Culture and Censure*. Pp. 137–58.

Harper, Sue, and Vincent Porter (1996). "Moved to Tears: Weeping in the Cinema in Postwar Britain," *Screen* 37, no. 2 (Summer): 152–73.

Harris, Cheryl (1998). "A Sociology of Television Fandom" in Harris and Alexander (eds) *Theorizing Fandom*. Pp. 41–54.

Harris, Cheryl, and Alison Alexander (eds) (1998). *Theorizing Fandom: Fans, Subculture and Identity*. Cresskill, NJ: Hampton Press.

Hartley, John (1996). "Power Viewing: A Glance at Persuasion in the Postmodern Perplex" in Hay, Grossberg, and Wartella (eds) *Audience and Its Landscape*. Pp. 221–33.

Haskell, Molly (1973). *From Reverence to Rape: The Treatment of Women in the Movies*. Chicago: University of Chicago Press.

Hay, James, Lawrence Grossberg, and Ellen Wartella (eds) (1996). *The Audience and Its Landscape*. New York: Westview Press.

Hayward, Jennifer (1997). *Consuming Pleasures: Active Audiences and Serial Fictions from Dickens to Soap Opera*. Lexington: University Press of Kentucky.

Heath, Stephen (1975–76). "Film and System: Terms of Analysis," *Screen* 16, no. 1 (Spring 1975): 7–77; 16, no. 2 (Summer 1975): 91–113; 17, no. 1 (Spring 1976): 115–17.

——— (1978). "Difference," *Screen* 19, no. 3 (Autumn): 51–112.

Hebdige, Dick (1979). *Subculture: The Meaning of Style*. London: Methuen.

——— (1988). *Hiding in the Light*. London: Routledge.

Hennegan, Alison (1988). "On Becoming a Lesbian Reader" in Radstone (ed) *Sweet Dreams*. Pp. 165–91.

Herman, David (1997). "Scripts, Sequences, and Stories: Elements of a Postclassical Narratology," *PMLA* 112, no. 5 (October): 1046–59.

Hermans, Liesbeth, and Leo van Snippenburg (1996). "Women's Use of TV News" in Renckstorf, McQuail, and Jankowski (eds) *Media Use as Social Action*. Pp. 139–50.

Hermes, Joke (1995). *Reading Women's Magazines: An Analysis of Everyday Media Use*. Cambridge, UK: Polity Press.

Herzog, Charlotte Cornelia, and Jane Marie Gaines (1985). "'Puffed Sleeves before Tea-Time': Joan Crawford, Adrian and Women Audiences" rpt. in Gledhill (ed) *Stardom*. Pp. 74–91.

Hess, John (1974). "La politique des auteurs: World View as Aesthetic" (part I), *Jump Cut*, no. 1 (May–June): 19–22.

Hill, Annette (1997). *Shocking Entertainment: Viewer Response to Violent Movies*. Luton, UK: University of Luton Press.

Hills, Matt (2002). *Fan Cultures*. London: Routledge.

———— (2003). "Putting Away Childish Things: Jar Jar Binks and the 'Virtual Star' as an Object of Fan Loathing" in T. Austin and Barker (eds) *Contemporary Hollywood Stardom*. Pp. 74–89.

Hinerman, Stephen (1992). "'I'll Be Here with You': Fans, Fantasy and the Figure of Elvis" in L. Lewis (ed) *Adoring Audience*. Pp. 107–34.

———— (1997). "'Don't Leave Me Alone': Tabloid Narrative and the Michael Jackson Child-Abuse Scandal" in Lull and Hinerman (eds) *Media Scandals*. Pp. 143–63.

Hoberman, J., and Jonathan Rosenbaum (1983). *Midnight Movies*. New York: Harper & Row.

Hobson, Dorothy (1990). "Women Audiences and the Workplace" in M. Brown (ed) *Television and Women's Culture*. Pp. 61–71.

Hodge, Bob, and David Tripp (1986). "Ten Theses on Children and Television" rpt. in Dickinson et al. (eds) *Approaches to Audiences*. Pp. 146–50.

Höijer, Birgitta (1992). "Reception of Television Narration as a Socio-cognitive Process: A Schema-Theoretical Outline," *Poetics* 21: 283–304.

Hollinger, Karen (1998). "Theorizing Mainstream Female Spectatorship: The Case of the Popular Lesbian Film," *Cinema Journal* 37, no. 2 (Winter): 3–17.

Holmes, Diane, and Belinda Budge (eds) (1994). *The Good, the Bad, and the Gorgeous: Popular Culture's Romance with Lesbianism*. London: Pandora.

hooks, bell (1982). "The Oppositional Gaze: Black Female Spectators" revised and reprinted in Diawara (ed) *Black American Cinema*. Pp. 288–302.

Howitt, Dennis (1989). "Pornography: The Recent Debate" in Cumberbatch and Howitt (eds) *Measure of Uncertainty*. Pp. 61–80.

Hunter, I. Q., and Heidi Kaye (1997). "Introduction—Trash Aesthetics: Popular Culture and Its Audience" in Cartmell et al. (eds) *Trash Aesthetics*. Pp. 1–13.

Ignatiev, Noel (1995). *How the Irish Became White*. New York: Routledge.

Iser, Wolfgang (1972). *The Implied Reader: Patterns of Communication in Prose Fiction from Bunyan to Beckett*. Baltimore: Johns Hopkins University Press, 1974.

———— (1976). *The Act of Reading: A Theory of Aesthetic Response*. Baltimore: Johns Hopkins University Press, 1978.

Jacobs, Lea (1990). "Reformers and Spectators: The Film Education Movement in the Thirties," *camera obscura*, no. 22 (January): 28–49.

Jaggar, Alison M. (1989). "Love and Knowledge: Emotion in Feminist Epistemology" in Jaggar and Bordo (eds) *Gender/Body/Knowledge*. Pp. 145–71.

Jaggar, Alison M., and Susan R. Bordo (eds) (1989). *Gender/Body/Knowledge:
Feminist Representations of Being and Knowing*. New Brunswick, NJ: Rutgers University Press.

Jahn, Manfred (1997). "Frames, Preferences, and the Reading of Third-Person
Narratives: Toward a Cognitive Narratology," *Poetics Today* 18, no. 4 (Winter): 441–68.

Jakobson, Roman (1960). "Linguistics and Poetics," rpt. in DeGeorge and De-
George (eds) *Structuralists*. Pp. 85–122.

Jauss, Hans Robert (1974). "Levels of Identification of Hero and Audience,"
trans. Benjamin Bennett and Helga Bennett, *New Literary History* 5 (Winter):
283–317.

Jay, Martin (1973). *The Dialectical Imagination: A History of the Frankfurt
School and the Institute of Social Research, 1923–1950*. Boston: Little,
Brown.

Jenkins, Henry (1988). "*Star Trek* Rerun, Reread, Rewritten: Fan Writing as
Textual Poaching," *Critical Studies in Mass Communication* 5, no. 2 (June):
85–107.

——— (1992a). "'Strangers No More, We Sing': Filking and the Social Construction of the Science Fiction Fan Community" in L. Lewis (ed) *Adoring
Audience*. Pp. 208–36.

——— (1992b). *Textual Poachers: Television Fans & Participatory Culture*.
New York: Routledge.

——— (1992c). *What Made Pistachio Nuts? Early Sound Comedy and the
Vaudeville Aesthetic*. New York: Columbia University Press.

——— (1995). "'Do You Enjoy Making the Rest of Us Feel Stupid?': Alt.tv.twin-
peaks, the Trickster Author, and Viewer Mastery" in Lavery (ed) *Full of Secrets*. Pp. 51–69.

Jenkins, Henry, Tara McPherson, and Jane Shattuck (eds) (2002). *Hop on Pop:
The Politics and Pleasures of Popular Culture*. Durham, NC: Duke University
Press.

Jensen, Joli (1992). "Fandom as Pathology: The Consequences of Characterization" in L. Lewis (ed) *Adoring Audience*. Pp. 9–29.

Jensen, Klaus Bruhn (1987). "Qualitative Audience Research: Toward an Inte-
grative Approach to Reception," *Critical Studies in Mass Communication* 4,
no. 1 (March): 21–36.

Johnson, Claudie L. (1996). "The Divine Miss Jane: Jane Austen, Janeites, and
the Discipline of Novel Studies" rpt. in Machor and Goldstein (eds) *Reception Study*. Pp. 118–32.

Johnson, Mark (1987). *The Body in the Mind: The Bodily Basis of Meaning,
Imagination, and Reason*. Chicago: University of Chicago Press.

Johnson, Richard (1979a). "Culture and the Historians" in Clarke et al. (eds) *Working-Class Culture*. Pp. 41–71.

———— (1979b). "Three Problematics: Elements of a Theory of Working-Class Culture" in Clarke, Critcher, and Johnson (eds) *Working-Class Culture*. Pp. 201–37.

Johnston, Deirdre D. (1995). "Adolescents' Motivations for Viewing Graphic Horror," *Human Communication Research* 21, no. 4 (June): 522–52.

Jones, Harold Ellis, and Herbert S. Conrad (1930). "Rural Preferences in Motion Pictures," *Journal of Social Psychology* 1: 419–23.

Jowett, Garth S. (1971). "Books," *Film Comment* 7, no. 2 (Summer): 70–72.

———— (1985). "Giving Them What They Want: Movie Audience Research before 1950," in B. Austin (ed) *Current Research in Film*, vol. I. Pp. 19–35.

Jowett, Garth S., Ian C. Jarvie, and Kathryn H. Fuller (1996). *Children and the Movies: Media Influence and the Payne Fund Controversy*. Cambridge: Cambridge University Press.

Joyrich, Lynne (1993). "Elvisophilia: Knowledge, Pleasure and the Cult of Elvis," *Differences* 5, no. 1: 73–91.

Kaplan, E. Ann (1987). *Rocking around the Clock: Music Television, Postmodernism, and Consumer Culture*. New York: Routledge.

Kapsis, Robert E. (1992). *Hitchcock: The Making of a Reputation*. Chicago: University of Chicago Press.

Katriel, Tamar, and Thomas Farrell (1991). "Scrapbooks as Cultural Texts: An American Art of Memory," *Text and Performance Quarterly* 11, no. 1 (January): 1–17.

Katz, Elihu (1959). "Mass Communications Research and the Study of Popular Culture," *Studies in Public Communication* 2: 1–6.

Katz, Elihu, and Paul F. Lazarsfeld (1955). *Personal Influence: The Part Played by People in the Flow of Mass Communication*. Glencoe, IL: Free Press.

Katz, Elihu, and Tamar Liebes (1984). "Decoding *Dallas*: Notes from a Cross-Cultural Study" rpt. in Newcomb (ed) *Television*. Pp. 419–32.

Kawin, Bruce (1991). "After Midnight" in Telotte (ed) *Cult Film Experience*. Pp. 18–25.

Kehr, David (1986). "A Star Is Made," *Film Comment* 15, no. 1 (January/February): 7–12.

King, Barry (1987). "The Star and the Commodity: Notes Toward a Performance Theory of Stardom," *Cultural Studies* 1 (May): 145–61.

King, Neal (1999). *Heroes in Hard Times: Cop Action Movies in the U.S.* Philadelphia: Temple University Press.

King, Nicola (2000). *Memory, Narrative, Identity: Remembering the Self*. Edinburgh: Edinburgh University Press.

King, Thomas A. (1994). "Performing 'Akimbo': Queer Pride and Epistemological Prejudice" in Meyer (ed) *Politics and Poetics of Camp*. Pp. 23–50.

Kipnis, Laura (1996). *Bound and Gagged: Pornography and the Politics of Fantasy in America.* New York: Grove Press.

Klapper, Joseph T. (1963). "Mass Communications Research: An Old Road Revisited," *Public Opinion Quarterly* 27, no. 4 (Winter): 515–27.

Kleinhans, Chuck, and Julia Lesage (1984). "The Politics of Sexual Representation," *Jump Cut*, no. 30: 24–26.

Klenow, Daniel J., and Jeffrey L. Crane (1977). "Selected Characteristics of the X-Rated Movie Audience: Toward a National Profile of the Recidivist," *Sociological Symposium*, no. 20 (Fall): 73–83.

Klinger, Barbara Gail (1986). *Cinema and Social Process: A Contextual Theory of the Cinema and Its Spectators.* Unpublished PhD dissertation: University of Iowa.

—— (1994). *Melodrama and Meaning: History, Culture, and the Films of Douglas Sirk.* Bloomington: Indiana University Press.

—— (2001). "The Contemporary Cinephile: Film Collecting in the Post-video Era" in Stokes and Maltby (eds) *Hollywood Spectatorship.* Pp. 132–51.

Knapp, Steven (1989). "Collective Memory and the Actual Past," *Representations*, no. 26 (Spring): 123–49.

Knee, Adam (1985). "Notions of Authorship and the Reception of *Once Upon a Time in America*," *Film Criticism* 10, no. 1 (Fall): 3–17.

Knight, Arthur, and Hollis Alpert (1967). "The History of Sex in Cinema: Part 15: Experimental Films," *Playboy* 14, no. 4 (April): 136+.

Kolodny, Annette (1980). "A Map for Rereading: Gender and the Interpretation of Literary Texts" rpt. in Showalter (ed) *New Feminist Criticism.* Pp. 46–62.

Kracauer, Siegfried (1942). *Propaganda and the Nazi War Film.* New York: Museum of Modern Art Film Library [rpt. in *From Caligari to Hitler*].

—— (1947). *From Caligari to Hitler: A Psychological History of the German Film.* Princeton, NJ: Princeton University Press.

—— (1960). *Theory of Film: The Redemption of Physical Reality.* New York: Oxford University Press.

Kracklauer, Mary Elizabeth (2000). *Jeanette's Girls: Fan Clubs in the 1930s, '40s, and '50s.* Unpublished master's thesis: University of Texas at Austin.

Krippendorff, Klaus (1980). *Content Analysis: An Introduction to Its Methodology.* Beverly Hills, CA: Sage.

Kuentz, Pierre (1976). "A Reading of Ideology or an Ideology of Reading," trans. Wayne Gymon, *Sub-stance* 15: 82–93.

Kuhn, Annette (1984). "Women's Genres," *Screen* 25, no. 1 (January–February): 18–28.

—— (1988). *Cinema, Censorship and Sexuality, 1909–1925.* London: Routledge.

—— (2002). *Dreaming of Fred and Ginger: Cinema and Cultural Memory.*

New York: New York University Press. [In Britain as *An Everyday Magic: Cinema and Cultural Memory.*]

Lakoff, George, and Mark Johnson (1980). *Metaphors We Live By.* Chicago: University of Chicago Press.

Lancaster, Kurt (2001). *Interacting with "Babylon 5."* Austin: University of Texas Press.

Lane, Jim (1994). "Critical and Cultural Reception of the European Art Film in 1950s America: A Case Study of the Brattle Theatre (Cambridge, Massachusetts)," *Film & History* 24, nos. 3/4: 48–64.

Langellier, Kristin M. (1999). "Personal Narrative, Performance, Performativity: Two or Three Things I Know for Sure," *Text and Performance Quarterly* 19: 125–44.

Langer, John (1981). "Television's 'Personality' System," *Media, Culture, Society* 3, no. 4 (October): 351–65.

Lashley, Karl S., and John B. Watson (1922). *A Psychological Study of Motion Pictures in Relation to Venereal Disease.* Washington, DC: Interdepartmental Social Hygiene Board.

Lasswell, Harold D. (1948). "The Structure and Function of Communication in Society" rpt. in Schramm (ed) *Mass Communications.* Pp. 117–30.

Lavery, David (ed) (1995a). *Full of Secrets: Critical Approaches to* Twin Peaks. Detroit, MI: Wayne State University Press.

——— (1995b). "The Semiotics of Cobbler: *Twin Peaks'* Interpretive Community" in Lavery (ed) *Full of Secrets.* Pp. 1–21.

Lawrence, Patricia A., and Philip C. Palmgreen (1996). "A Uses and Gratifications Analysis of Horror Film Preference" in Weaver and Tamborini (eds) *Horror Films.* Pp. 161–78.

Lawton, Ben, and Janet Staiger (eds) (1977). *1977 Film Studies Annual.* Pleasantville, NY: Redgrave.

Lazarsfeld, Paul F., and Robert K. Merton (1948). "Mass Communication, Popular Taste, and Organized Social Action" rpt. in Schramm and Roberts (eds) *Process and Effects of Mass Communication.* Pp. 554–78.

Leckenby, John D., and Stuart H. Surlin (1976). "Incidental Social Learning and Viewer Race: *All in the Family* and *Sanford and Son,*" *Journal of Broadcasting* 20, no. 4 (Fall): 481–94.

Levine, Lawrence W. (1988). *Highbrow/Lowbrow: The Emergence of Cultural Hierarchy in America.* Cambridge, MA: Harvard University Press.

Lewis, Howard T. (1933). *The Motion Picture Industry.* New York: D. Van Nostrand.

Lewis, Justin (1991). *The Ideological Octopus: An Exploration of Television and Its Audience.* New York: Routledge.

——— (1994). "The Meaning of Things: Audiences, Ambiguity, and Power" in Cruz and Lewis (eds) *Viewing, Reading, Listening.* Pp. 19–32.

Lewis, Lisa (ed) (1992). *The Adoring Audience: Fan Culture and Popular Media*. New York: Routledge.

Leyda, Jay, and Zina Voynow (eds) (1983). *Eisenstein at Work*. New York: Pantheon Books and Museum of Modern Art.

Liebes, Tamar (1988). "Cultural Differences in the Retelling of Television Fiction," *Critical Studies in Mass Communication* 5, no. 4 (December): 277–92.

Liebes, Tamar, and James Curran (eds) (1998). *Media, Ritual, Identity*. New York: Routledge.

Liebes, Tamar, and Elihu Katz (1990). *The Export of Meaning: Cross-Cultural Readings of Dallas*. 2nd ed. Cambridge, UK: Polity Press, 1993.

Linné, Olga, and Ellen Wartella (1998). "Research about Violence in the Media: Different Traditions and Changing Paradigms" in Dickinson, Harindranath, and Linné (eds) *Approaches to Audiences*. Pp. 104–19.

Livingstone, Sonia (1990). "Interpreting a Television Narrative: How Different Viewers See a Story," *Journal of Communication* 40, no. 1 (Winter): 72–85.

——— (1991). "Audience Reception: The Role of the Viewer in Retelling Romantic Drama" in Curran and Gurevitch (eds) *Mass Media and Society*. Pp. 285–306.

——— (1998). "Relationships between Media and Audiences" in Liebes and Curran (eds) *Media, Ritual, Identity*. Pp. 237–55.

Livingstone, Sonia, and Peter Lunt (1994). *Talk on Television: Audience Participation and Public Debate*. London: Routledge.

Long, Elizabeth (1993). "Textual Interpretation as Collective Action" in Cruz and Lewis (eds) *Viewing, Reading, Listening*. Pp. 181–211.

Lotman, Jurij (1970). *The Structure of the Artistic Text*, trans. Ronald Vroon. Ann Arbor: Michigan Slavic Contributions, 1977.

——— (1973). *Semiotics of Cinema*, trans. Mark E. Suino. Ann Arbor: University of Michigan Press, 1976.

Lowenthal, David (1975). "Past Time, Present Place: Landscape and Memory," *Geographical Review* 65, no. 1 (January): 1–36.

Lowenthal, Leo (1944). "The Triumph of Mass Idols" rpt. in Lowenthal (ed) *Literature, Popular Culture, and Society*. Pp. 109–40.

——— (ed) (1961). *Literature, Popular Culture, and Society*. Englewood Cliffs, NJ: Prentice-Hall.

Lucaites, John Louis, and Celeste Michelle Condit (1985). "Reconstructing Narrative Theory: A Functional Perspective," *Journal of Communication* 35, no. 4 (Autumn): 90–108.

Lull, James and Stephen Hinerman (eds) (1997a). *Media Scandals: Morality and Desire in the Popular Culture Marketplace*. Cambridge, UK: Polity Press.

——— (1997b). "The Search for Scandals" in Lull and Hinerman (eds) *Media Scandals*. Pp. 1–33.

Lutz, Catherine A. (1990). "Engendered Emotion: Gender, Power, and the

Rhetoric of Emotional Control in American Discourse" in Lutz and Abu-Lughod (eds) *Language*. Pp. 69–91.

Lutz, Catherine A., and Lila Abu-Lughod (1990). *Language and the Politics of Emotion*. Cambridge, MA: Cambridge University Press.

Lynd, Robert S., and Helen Merrell Lynd (1929). *Middletown: A Study in American Culture*. New York: Harcourt, Brace.

MacDonald, Andrea (1998). "Uncertain Utopia: Science Fiction Media Fandom and Computer Mediated Communication" in Harris and Alexander (eds) *Theorizing Fandom*. Pp. 131–52.

MacDonald, Dwight (1938a). "The Soviet Cinema: 1930–1938" (part I), *Partisan Review 5*, no. 2 (July): 37–50.

——— (1938b). "The Soviet Cinema: 1930–1938" (part II), *Partisan Review 5*, no. 3 (August–September): 35–62.

——— (1939). "Soviet Society and Its Cinema," *Partisan Review 6*, no. 2 (Winter): 80–95.

——— (1966). "The American Stasis" rpt. in *On Movies*. New York: Berkeley Medallion Books, 1971.

MacDonald, Paul (2000). *The Star System: Hollywood's Production of Popular Identities*. London: Wallflower.

——— (2003). "Stars in the Online Universe: Promotion, Nudity, Reverence" in T. Austin and Barker (eds) *Contemporary Hollywood Stardom*. Pp. 29–61.

Macherey, Pierre (1966). *A Theory of Literary Production*, trans. Geoffrey Wall. London: Routledge & Kegan Paul, 1978.

Machor, James L., and Philip Goldstein (eds) (2001). *Reception Study: From Literary Theory to Cultural Studies*. New York: Routledge.

Maltby, Richard (1986). "'Baby Face' or How Joe Breen Made Barbara Stanwyck Atone for Causing the Wall Street Crash," *Screen 27*, no. 2 (March–April): 22–45.

——— (2001). "The Spectacle of Criminality" in Slocum (ed) *Violence and American Cinema*. Pp. 117–52.

Mann, Denise (1989). "The Spectacularization of Everyday Life: Recycling Hollywood Stars and Fans in Early Television Variety Shows," *camera obscura*, no. 16 (January): 49–77.

Mann, Jay, Leonard Berkowitz, Jack Sidman, Sheldon Starr, and Stephen West (1974). "Satiation of the Transient Stimulating Effect of Erotic Films," *Journal of Personality and Social Psychology 30*, no. 6 (December): 729–35.

Maranda, Pierre (1980). "The Dialectic of Metaphor: An Anthropological Essay on Hermeneutics" in Suleiman and Crosman (eds) *Reader in the Text*. Pp. 183–204.

Marchetti, Gina (1986). "Subcultural Studies and the Film Audience: Rethinking the Film Viewing Context" in B. Austin (ed) *Current Research in Film*, vol. II. Pp. 62–79.

Marshall, P. David (1997). *Celebrity and Power: Fame in Contemporary Culture.* Minneapolis: University of Minnesota Press.

Matsuda, Mari J. (ed) (1993). *Words That Wound: Critical Race Theory, Assaultive Speech, and the First Amendment.* Boulder, CO: Westview Press.

Mayne, Judith (1982). "Immigrants and Spectators," *Wide Angle* 5, no. 2: 32–41.

――― (1993). *Cinema and Spectatorship.* New York: Routledge.

McCombs, Maxwell E., and Donald L. Shaw (1972). "The Agenda-Setting Function of Mass Media," *Public Opinion Quarterly* 36, no. 2 (Summer): 176–87.

McConachie, Bruce A. (1990). "Pacifying Theatrical Audiences, 1820–1900" in Butsch (ed) *For Fun and Profit.* Pp. 47–70.

McLean, Adrienne L. (2001). "Introduction" in McLean and Cook (eds) *Headline Hollywood.* Pp. 1–26.

McLean, Adrienne L., and David A. Cook (eds). *Headline Hollywood: A Century of Film Scandal.* New Brunswick, NJ: Rutgers University Press.

McLeland, Susan (1996). *Fallen Stars: Femininity, Celebrity and Scandal in Poststudio Hollywood.* Unpublished PhD dissertation: University of Texas at Austin.

McNair, Brian (1996). *Mediated Sex: Pornography and Postmodern Culture.* London: Arnold.

McQuail, Denis (ed) (1972). *Sociology of Mass Communications.* Harmondsworth, UK: Penguin Books.

――― (1984). "With the Benefit of Hindsight: Reflections on Uses and Gratifications Research" rpt. in Dickinson, Harindranath, and Linné (eds) *Approaches to Audiences.* Pp. 151–65.

――― (1987). *Mass Communication Theory: An Introduction,* 2nd ed. London: Sage.

McRobbie, Angela, and Jenny Garber (1976). "Girls and Subcultures: An Exploration" in Hall and Jefferson (eds) *Resistance through Rituals.* Pp. 209–22.

Medhurst, Andy (1991). "That Special Thrill: *Brief Encounter*, Homosexuality and Authorship," *Screen* 32, no. 2 (Summer): 197–208.

Merton, Robert K. (1946). *Mass Persuasion: The Social Psychology of a War Bond Drive.* New York: Harper & Brothers.

Metz, Christian (1971a). *Film Language: A Semiotics of the Cinema,* trans. Michael Taylor. New York: Oxford University Press, 1974.

――― (1971b). *Language and Cinema,* trans. Donna Jean Umiker-Sebeok. The Hague: Mouton, 1974.

――― (1975a). "History/Discourse: Note on Two Voyeurisms," trans. Susan Bennett, *Edinburgh '76 Magazine,* no. 1 (1976): 21–25.

――― (1975b). "The Imaginary Signifier," trans. Ben Brewster in *The Imagi-*

nary Signifier: Psychoanalysis and the Cinema. Bloomington: Indiana University Press, 1981. Pp. 3–87.

Meyer, Moe (1994a). "Introduction: Reclaiming the Discourse of Camp" in Meyer (ed) *Politics and Poetics of Camp*. Pp. 1–22.

—— (ed) (1994b). *The Politics and Poetics of Camp*. New York: Routledge.

Michelson, Peter (1970). *The Aesthetics of Pornography*. New York: Herder and Herder.

Middleton, Russell (1960). "Ethnic Prejudice and Susceptibility to Persuasion," *American Sociological Review* 25, no. 5 (October): 679–86.

Mikulak, Bill (1998). "Fans versus Time Warner: Who Owns Looney Tunes?" in Sandler (ed) *Reading the Rabbit*. Pp. 193–208.

Mills, C. Wright (1956). *The Power Elite*. New York: Oxford University Press.

Mitchell, Alice Miller (1929). *Children and Movies*. Chicago: University of Chicago Press.

Modleski, Tania (1979). "The Search for Tomorrow in Today's Soap Operas" rpt. in *Loving with a Vengeance*. Pp. 85–109.

—— (1984). *Loving with a Vengeance: Mass-Produced Fantasies for Women*. New York: Methuen.

Molitor, Fred, and Barry S. Sapolsky (1993). "Sex, Violence and Victimization in Slasher Films," *Journal of Broadcasting & Electronic Media* 37, no. 2 (Spring): 233–42.

Morgan, Robin (1974). "Theory and Practice: Pornography and Rape" rpt. in *Going Too Far: The Personal Chronicle of a Feminist*. New York: Random House, 1977. N.p.

Morin, Edgar (1957). *The Stars: An Account of the Star-System in Motion Pictures*, trans. Richard Howard. New York: Grove Press, 1960.

Morley, David (1980a). *The "Nationwide" Audience: Structure and Decoding*. London: British Film Institute.

—— (1980b). "Texts, Readers, Subjects" in Hall et al. (eds) *Culture, Media, Language*. Pp. 163–73.

—— (1986). *Family Television*. London: Comedia.

—— (1992). *Television, Audiences, and Cultural Studies*. New York: Routledge.

Morreale, Joanne (1998). "*Xena: Warrior Princess* as Feminist Camp," *Journal of Popular Culture* 32, no. 2 (Fall): 79–86.

Morrill, Cynthia (1994). "Revamping the Gay Sensibility: Queer Camp and Dyke Noir" in Meyer (ed) *Politics and Poetics of Camp*. Pp. 110–29.

Morris, Mitchell (1993). "Reading as an Opera Queen" in Solie (ed) *Musicology and Difference*. Pp. 184–200.

Morrison, David, with Brent MacGregor, Michael Svennevig, and Julie Firmston (1999). *Defining Violence: The Search for Understanding*. Luton, UK: University of Luton Press.

Mulvey, Laura (1975). "Visual Pleasure and Narrative Cinema," *Screen* 16, no. 3 (Autumn): 6–18.

——— (1977–78). "Notes on Sirk & Melodrama," *Movie*, no. 25 (Winter): 53–56.

——— (1981). "On *Duel in the Sun*: Afterthoughts on 'Visual Pleasure and Narrative Cinema,'" *Framework*, nos. 15–17 (Summer): 12–15.

Mumford, Louis (1938). *The Culture of Cities*. New York: Harcourt, Brace.

Muñoz, José Esteban (1996). "Famous and Dandy Like B. 'n' Andy: Race, Pop, and Basquiat" in Doyle, Flatley, and Muñoz (eds) *Pop Out*. Pp. 144–79.

Münsterberg, Hugo (1916). *The Film, A Psychological Study: The Silent Photoplay in 1916*. Rpt., New York: Dover, 1970.

Murdock, Graham (1997). "Reservoirs of Dogma: An Archaeology of Popular Anxieties" in Barker and Petley (eds) *Ill Effects*. Pp. 67–86.

Mykerji, Chandra, and Michael Schudson (eds) (1991). *Rethinking Popular Culture*. Berkeley: University of California Press.

Nakayama, Thomas K., and Lisa N. Peñaloza (1993). "Madonna T/Races: Music Videos through the Prism of Color" in Schwichtenberg (ed) *Madonna Connection*. Pp. 39–55.

Nash, Melanie (1999). "'Beavis Is Just Confused': Ideologies, Intertexts, Audiences," *Velvet Light Trap*, no. 43 (March): 4–22.

Nash, Melanie, and Martti Lahti (1999). "'Almost Ashamed to Say I Am One of Those Girls': *Titanic*, Leonardo DiCaprio, and the Paradoxes of Girls' Fandom" in Sandler and Studlar (eds) *Titanic*. Pp. 64–88.

Neale, Steve (1981). "*Halloween*: Suspense, Aggression and the Look" rpt. in Grant (ed) *Planks of Reason*. Pp. 331–45.

Nehring, Neal (1997). *Popular Music, Gender and Postmodernism: Anger Is an Energy*. Thousand Oaks, CA: Sage.

Neisser, Ulric (1967). *Cognitive Psychology*. New York: Appleton-Century-Crofts.

——— (1981). "John Dean's Memory: A Case Study," *Cognition* 9: 1–22.

——— (1994). "Self-Narratives: True and False" in Neisser and Fivush (eds) *Remembering Self*. Pp. 1–18.

Neisser, Ulric, and Robyn Fivush (eds) (1994). *The Remembering Self: Construction and Accuracy in the Self-Narrative*. New York: Cambridge University Press.

Nelsen, Anne K., and Hart M. Nelsen (1970). "The Prejudicial Film: Progress and Stalemate, 1915–1967," *Phylon* 31, no. 2 (Summer): 142–49.

"New Department Installed" (1917). *Motography* 18, no. 2 (14 July): 98.

Newcomb, Horace (1974). *TV: The Most Popular Art*. Garden City, NY: Anchor Books.

——— (ed) (1987). *Television: The Critical View*, 4th ed. New York: Oxford University Press.

Newcomb, Horace, and Paul M. Hirsch (1983). "Television as a Cultural Forum: Implications for Research," *Quarterly Review of Film Studies* 8, no. 3 (Summer): 45–55.

Newton, Esther (1972). *Mother Camp: Female Impersonators in America.* Chicago: University of Chicago Press.

Nichols, Bill (ed) (1976). *Movies and Methods*, vol. I. Berkeley: University of California Press.

——— (ed) (1985). *Movies and Methods*, vol. II. Berkeley: University of California Press.

——— (ed) (1991). *Representing Reality.* Bloomington: Indiana University Press.

Norden, Martin F., and Kim Wolfson (1986). "Cultural Influences on Film Interpretation among Chinese and American Students" in B. Austin (ed) *Current Research in Film*, vol. II. Pp. 21–34.

Noriega, Chon (2001). "'Waas Sappening?': Narrative Structure and Iconography in *Born in East L.A.*" in Tinkcom and Villarejo (eds) *Keyframes.* Pp. 187–202.

O'Connor, John E. (ed) (1983). *American History/American Television: Interpreting the Video Past.* New York: Ungar.

Ohmer, Susan (1991). "Measuring Desire: George Gallup and Audience Research in Hollywood," *Journal of Film and Video* 43, nos. 1–2 (Spring–Summer): 3–28.

Oliver, Mary Beth (1993). "Adolescents' Enjoyment of Graphic Horror: Effects of Viewers' Attitudes and Portrayals of Victims," *Communication Research* 20, no. 1 (February): 30–50.

——— (1994). "Contributions of Sexual Portrayals to Viewers' Responses to Graphic Horror," *Journal of Broadcasting & Electronic Media* 38, no. 1 (Winter): 1–17.

Ortiz, Christopher (1994). "Hot and Spicy: Representation of Chicano/Latino Men in Gay Pornography," *Jump Cut*, no. 39 (June): 83–90.

Ortony, Andrew, Gerald L. Clore, and Allan Collins (1988). *The Cognitive Structure of Emotions.* Cambridge: Cambridge University Press.

Packard, Vance (1957). *The Hidden Persuaders.* New York: McKay.

Pagliaro, Harold E. (1972). "The Affective Question," *Bucknell Review* 20, no. 1 (Spring): 3–20.

Pajaczkowska, Claire (1981). "The Heterosexual Presumption: A Contribution to the Debate on Pornography," *Screen* 22, no. 1: 79–94.

Paletz, David L., Judith Koon, Elizabeth Whitehead, and Richard B. Hagens (1972). "Selective Exposure: The Potential Boomerang Effect," *Journal of Communication* 22, no. 1 (March): 48–53.

Parkin, Frank (1971). *Class Inequality and Political Order: Social Stratification in Capitalist and Communist Societies.* London: MacGibbon & Kee.

Pavletich, JoAnn (1998). "Emotions, Experience, and Social Control in the Twentieth Century," *Rethinking Marx*ism 10, no. 2 (Summer): 51–64.

Pearson, Roberta E., and William Uricchio (eds) (1991). *The Many Lives of Batman: Critical Approaches to a Superhero and His Media*. New York: Routledge.

Penley, Constance (1991). "Brownian Motion: Women, Tactics, and Technology" in Penley and Ross (eds) *Technoculture*. Pp. 135–62.

——— (1993). "The Cabinet of Dr. Pee Wee: Consumerism and Sexual Terror" in Penley and Willis (eds) *Male Trouble*. Pp. 121–41.

——— (1997). "Crackers and Whackers: The White Trashing of Porn" in Wray and Newitz (eds) *White Trash*. Pp. 89–112.

Penley, Constance, and Andrew Ross (eds) (1991). *Technoculture*. Minneapolis: University of Minnesota Press.

Penley, Constance, and Sharon Willis (eds) (1993). *Male Trouble*. Minneapolis: University of Minnesota Press.

Pennebaker, James W., and Becky L. Banasik (1997). "On the Creation and Maintenance of Collective Memories: History as Social Psychology" in Pennebaker, Paez, and Rimé (eds) *Collective Memory of Political Events*. Pp. 3–19.

Pennebaker, James W., Dario Paez, and Bernard Rimé (eds) (1997). *Collective Memory of Political Events: Social Psychological Perspectives*. Mahwah, NJ: Erlbaum.

Peterson, James (1994). *Dreams of Chaos, Visions of Order: Understanding the American Avant-Garde Cinema*. Detroit, MI: Wayne State University Press.

Petro, Patrice (1983). "From Lukács to Kracauer and Beyond: Social Film Histories and the German Cinema," *Cinema Journal* 22, no. 3 (Spring): 47–70.

Phelan, Rev. J. L. (1919). "Motion Pictures as a Phase of Commercialized Amusement in Toledo, Ohio," rpt. in *Film History* 13, no. 3 (2001): 238–328.

Piccone, Paul (1978). "General Introduction" in Arato and Gebhardt (eds) *Essential Frankfurt School Reader*. Pp. xi–xxiii.

Pillemer, David B. (1998). *Momentous Events, Vivid Memories*. Cambridge, MA: Harvard University Press.

Pinedo, Isabel Cristina (1997). *Recreational Terror: Women and the Pleasures of Horror Film Viewing*. Albany: State University of New York Press.

Plantinga, Carl, and Greg M. Smith (1999a). "Introduction" in Plantinga and Smith (eds) *Passionate Views*. Pp. 1–17.

——— (eds) (1999b). *Passionate Views: Film, Cognition, and Emotion*. Baltimore: Johns Hopkins University Press.

Poe, G. Tom (2001). "Historical Spectatorship around and about Stanley Kramer's *On the Beach*" in Stokes and Maltby (eds) *Hollywood Spectatorship*. Pp. 91–102.

Pope, Daniel (1983). *The Making of Modern Advertising*. New York: Basic Books.

Potamianos, George (1998). "Movie Mad: Audiences and Censorship in a California Town, 1916–1926," *Velvet Light Trap*, no. 42 (Fall): 62–75.

Press, Andrea (1990). "Class, Gender and the Female Viewer: Women's Responses to *Dynasty*" in M. Brown (ed) *Television and Women's Culture*. Pp. 158–80.

——— (1991). *Women Watching TV: Gender, Class, and Generation in the American Television Experience*. Philadelphia: University of Pennsylvania Press.

Press, Andrea, and Elizabeth Cole (1993). "Women Like Us: Working-Class Women Respond to Television Representations of Abortion" in Cruz and Lewis (eds) *Viewing, Reading, Listening*. Pp. 55–80.

Preston, Catherine L. (2000). "In Retrospect: The FSA-OWI Photographic Collection and the Contingencies of American Visual Memory." Unpublished ms.

Prince, Stephen (1988). "The Pornographic Image and the Practice of Film Theory," *Cinema Journal* 27, no. 2 (Winter): 27–39.

——— (1990). "Power and Pain: Content Analysis and the Ideology of Pornography," *Journal of Film and Video* 42, no. 2 (Summer): 31–41.

Projansky, Sarah (2001). "The Elusive/Ubiquitous Representation of Rape: A Historical Survey of Rape in U.S. Film, 1903–1972," *Cinema Journal* 41, no. 1 (Fall): 63–90.

Propp, Vladimir (1928). *Morphology of the Folktale*, trans. Laurence Scott, 2nd rev. ed. Austin: University of Texas Press, 1968.

Puri, Jyoti (1997). "Reading Romance Novels in Postcolonial India," *Gender & Society* 11, no. 4 (August): 434–52.

Radstone, Susannah (1988). *Sweet Dreams: Sexuality, Gender and Popular Fiction*. London: Lawrence & Wishart.

Radway, Janice (1984a). "Interpretive Communities and Variable Literacies: The Functions of Romance Reading" rpt. in Mykerji and Schudson (eds) *Rethinking Popular Culture*. Pp. 465–86.

——— (1984b). *Reading the Romance: Women, Patriarchy, and Popular Literature*. Chapel Hill: University of North Carolina Press.

"Rampage Killers in 100 Cases" (2000). *New York Times*, 10 April. P. A13.

Reeves, Bryon (1996). "Hemispheres of Scholarship: Psychological and Other Approaches to Studying Media Audiences" in Hay, Grossberg, and Wartella (eds) *Audience and Its Landscape*. Pp. 265–79.

Regester, Charlene (2001). "The African-American Press and Race Movies, 1909–1929" in Bowser, Gaines, and Musser (eds) *Oscar Micheaux and His Circle*. Pp. 34–49.

Reid, Roddey (1993). *Families in Jeopardy: Regulating the Social Body in France, 1750–1910*. Stanford, CA: Stanford University Press.

Renckstorf, Karsten, and Denis McQuail (1996). "Social Action Perspectives in Mass Communication Research: An Introduction" in Renckstorf, McQuail, and Jankowski (eds) *Media Use as Social Action*. Pp. 1–17.

Renckstorf, Karsten, Denis McQuail, and Nicholas Jankowski (eds) (1996). *Media Use as Social Action: A European Approach to Audience Studies*. London: John Libbey.

Rentschler, Eric (1981–82). "American Friends and New German Cinema: Patterns of Reception," *New German Critique*, nos. 24–25 (Fall/Winter): 7–35.

Riesman, David, with Reuel Denney and Nathan Glazer (1950). *The Lonely Crowd: A Study of the Changing American Character*. New Haven, CT: Yale University Press.

Riggs, Karen E. (1996). "The Case of the Mysterious Ritual: Murder Dramas and Older Women Viewers," *Critical Studies in Mass Communication* 13, no. 4: 309–23.

——— (1998). *Mature Audiences: Television in the Lives of Elders*. New Brunswick, NJ: Rutgers University Press.

Robertson, Pamela (1996). *Guilty Pleasures: Feminist Camp from Mae West to Madonna*. Durham, NC: Duke University Press.

Rogers, Everett M. (1994). *A History of Communication Study: A Biographical Approach*. New York: Free Press.

Rollin, Roger B. (1982). "Triple-X: Erotic Movies and Their Audiences," *Journal of Popular Film and Television* 10, no. 1 (Spring): 2–21.

Rosen, Marjorie (1973). *Popcorn Venus*. Rpt., New York: Avon Books, 1974.

Rosenfield, Israel (1985). "The New Brain," *New York Review of Books*, 14 March. Pp. 34–38.

Ross, Andrew (1989). *No Respect: Intellectuals & Popular Culture*. New York: Routledge.

Ross, Sharon (2002). *Super(natural) Women: Female Heroes, Their Friends, and Their Fans*. Unpublished PhD dissertation: University of Texas at Austin.

Ross, Steven J. (1999). "The Revolt of the Audience: Reconsidering Audiences and Reception during the Silent Era" in Stokes and Maltby (eds) *American Movie Audiences*. Pp. 92–111.

Rowland, Willard D., Jr. (1983). *The Politics of TV Violence: Policy Uses of Communication Research*. Beverly Hills, CA: Sage.

——— (1997). "Television Violence Redux: The Continuing Mythology of Effects" in Barker and Petley (eds) *Ill Effects*. Pp. 102–24.

Rubin, Gayle S. (1984). "Thinking Sex: Notes for a Radical Theory of the Politics of Sexuality" rpt. in Vance (ed) *Pleasure and Danger*. Pp. 267–319.

Sanbonmatsu, David M., and Russell H. Fazio (1991). "Construct Accessibility: Determinants, Consequences, and Implications for the Media" in Bryant and Zillmann (eds) *Responding to the Screen*. Pp. 45–62.

Sandler, Kevin S. (ed) (1998). *Reading the Rabbit: Explorations in Warner Bros. Animation.* New Brunswick, NJ: Rutgers University Press.

Sandler, Kevin S., and Gaylyn Studlar (eds) (1999). Titanic: *Anatomy of a Blockbuster.* New Brunswick, NJ: Rutgers University Press.

Sapolsky, Barry S., and Fred Molitor (1996). "Content Trends in Contemporary Horror Films" in Weaver and Tamborini (eds) *Horror Films.* Pp. 33–48.

Schauber, Ellen, and Ellen Spolsky (1986). *The Bounds of Interpretation: Linguistic Theory and Literary Text.* Stanford, CA: Stanford University Press.

Scheiner, Georganne (1998). "The Deanna Durbin Devotees: Fan Clubs and Spectatorship" in J. Austin and Willard (eds) *Generations of Youth.* Pp. 81–95.

——— (2000). *Signifying Female Adolescence: Film Representations and Fans, 1920–1950.* Westport, CT: Praeger.

Schickel, Richard (1985). *Intimate Strangers: The Culture of Celebrity.* Garden City, NY: Doubleday.

Schlesinger, Phillip, R. Emerson Dobash, Russell P. Dobash, and C. Kay Weaver (1992). *Women Watching Violence.* London: British Film Institute.

Schramm, Wilbur (ed) (1960). *Mass Communications: A Book of Readings*, 2nd ed. Urbana: University of Illinois Press.

——— (1963a). "Communication Research in the United States" in Schramm (ed) *Science of Human Communication.* Pp. 1–16.

——— (ed) (1963b). *The Science of Human Communication: New Directions and New Findings in Communication Research.* New York: Basic Books.

Schramm, Wilbur, and Donald F. Roberts (eds) (1971). *The Process and Effects of Mass Communication*, rev. ed. Urbana: University of Illinois Press.

Schulze, Laurie (1999). "Not an Immaculate Reception: Ideology, the Madonna Connection, and Academic Wannabes," *Velvet Light Trap*, no. 43 (March): 37–50.

Schulze, Laurie, Anne Barton White, and Jane D. Brown (1993). "'A Sacred Monster in Her Prime': Audience Construction of Madonna as Low-Other" in Schwichtenberg (ed) *Madonna Connection.* Pp. 15–37.

Schwartz, Barry (1982). "The Social Context of Commemoration: A Study in Collective Memory," *Social Forces* 61, no. 2 (December): 374–402.

——— (1996). "Introduction: The Expanding Past," *Qualitative Sociology* 19, no. 3: 275–82.

Schweickart, Patrocinio P. (1986). "Reading Ourselves: Toward a Feminist Theory of Reading" in Flynn and Schweickart (eds) *Gender and Reading.* Pp. 31–62.

Schwichtenberg, Cathy (ed) (1993). *The Madonna Connection: Representational Politics, Subcultural Identities, and Cultural Theory.* Boulder, CO: Westview Press.

Sconce, Jeff (1995). "'Trashing the Academy': Taste, Excess, and an Emerging Politics of Cinematic Style," *Screen* 36, no. 4 (Winter): 371–93.

Sebastian, Richard J., Ross D. Parke, Leonard Berkowitz, and Stephen G. West (1978). "Violence on the Screen: Film Violence and Verbal Aggression: A Naturalistic Study," *Journal of Communication* 28, no. 3 (Summer): 164–71.

Segal, Lynne (1990). "Pornography and Violence: What the 'Experts' Really Say," *Feminist Review*, no. 36 (Autumn): 29–41.

Seiter, Ellen, Hans Borchers, Gabriele Kreutzner, and Eva-Maria Warth (eds) (1989). *Remote Control: Television, Audiences, and Cultural Power.* London: Routledge.

—— (1989). "'Don't Treat Us Like We're So Stupid and Naive': Toward an Ethnography of Soap Opera Viewers" in Seiter et al. (eds) *Remote Control.* Pp. 223–47.

Sheldon, Caroline (1977). "Lesbians and Film: Some Thoughts" in Dyer (ed) *Gays & Film.* Pp. 5–26.

Shingler, Martin (2001). "Interpreting *All about Eve*: A Study in Historical Reception" in Stokes and Maltby (eds) *Hollywood Spectatorship.* Pp. 46–62.

Showalter, Elaine (ed) (1985). *The New Feminist Criticism: Essays on Women, Literature and Theory.* New York: Pantheon Books.

Signorielli, Nancy, and George Gerbner (1988). *Violence and Terror in the Mass Media: An Annotated Bibliography.* New York: Greenwood Press.

Silberman, Marc (1984). "[Review of] Holub's *Reception Theory*," *New German Critique*, no. 33 (Fall): 249–54.

Siomopoulos, Anna (1999). "Entertaining Ethics: Technology, Mass Culture and American Intellectuals of the 1930s," *Film History* 11, no. 1: 45–54.

Slade, Joseph W. (1984). "Violence in the Hard-Core Pornographic Film: A Historical Survey," *Journal of Communication* 34, no. 3 (Summer): 148–63.

—— (1993). "Bernard Natan: France's Legendary Pornographer," *Journal of Film and Video* 14, nos. 2–3 (Summer–Fall): 72–90.

Slocum, J. David (ed) (2001). *Violence and American Cinema.* New York: Routledge.

Smith, Greg M. (2002). "The Critical Reception of *Rashomon* in the West," *Asian Cinema* 13, no. 2 (Fall/Winter): 115–28.

Smith, Murray (1995). *Engaging Characters: Fiction, Emotion, and the Cinema.* New York: Oxford University Press.

Smoodin, Eric (1996). "'This Business of America': Fan Mail, Film Reception and *Meet John Doe*," *Screen* 37, no. 2 (Summer): 111–29.

—— (1998). "'The Moral Part of the Story Was Great': Frank Capra and Film Education in the 1930s," *Velvet Light Trap*, no. 42 (Fall 1998): 20–35.

Smythe, Dallas W., John R. Gregory, Alvin Ostrin, Oliver P. Colvin, and William Moroney (1955). "Portrait of a First-Run Audience," *Quarterly of Film, Radio, and Television* 9, no. 4 (Summer): 390–409.

Smythe, Dallas W., Parker B. Lusk, and Charles A. Lewis (1953). "Portrait of an Art-Theater Audience," *Quarterly of Film, Radio, and Television* 8, no. 1 (Fall): 28–50.

Sobchack, Vivian (ed) (1996). *The Persistence of History: Cinema, Television, and the Modern Event.* New York: Routledge.

Solie, Ruth A. (ed) (1993). *Musicology and Difference: Gender and Sexuality in Music Scholarship.* Berkeley: University of California Press.

Sontag, Susan (1964). "Notes on 'Camp,'" rpt. in *Against Interpretation.* New York: Dell, 1968. Pp. 275–92.

—— (1967). "The Pornographic Imagination," rpt. in *Styles of Radical Will.* New York: Dell, 1969. Pp. 35–73.

Sparks, Glenn G. (1991). "The Relationship between Distress and Delight in Males' and Females' Reactions to Frightening Films," *Human Communication Research* 17, no. 4 (June 1991): 625–37.

Spigel, Lynn, and Henry Jenkins (1991). "Same Bat Channel, Different Bat Times: Mass Culture and Popular Memory" in Pearson and Uricchio (eds) *Many Lives of Batman.* Pp. 117–48.

Spigel, Lynn, and Denise Mann (eds) (1992). *Private Screenings: Television and the Female Consumer.* Minneapolis: University of Minnesota Press.

Spivak, Gayatri Chakravorty (1985). "Subaltern Studies: Deconstructing Historiography," rpt. in *In Other Worlds: Essays in Cultural Politics.* London: Routledge, 1987. Pp. 197–221.

Spoehr, Kathryn T., and Stephen W. Lehmkuhle (1982). *Visual Information Processing.* San Francisco: Freeman.

Stacey, Jackie (1994). *Star Gazing: Hollywood Cinema and Female Spectatorship.* London: Routledge.

Staiger, Janet (1983). "Seeing Stars," rpt. in Gledhill (ed) *Stardom.* Pp. 3–16.

—— (1985). "The Politics of Film Canons," *Cinema Journal* 24, no. 3 (Spring): 4–23.

—— (1990). "Announcing Wares, Winning Patrons, Voicing Ideals: Thinking about the History and Theory of Film Advertising," *Cinema Journal* 29, no. 3 (Spring): 3–31.

—— (1992). *Interpreting Films: Studies in the Historical Reception of American Cinema.* Princeton, NJ: Princeton University Press.

—— (1995). *Bad Women: Regulating Sexuality in Early American Cinema.* Minneapolis: University of Minnesota Press.

—— (1997). "Das Starsystem und der Classische Hollywoodfilm" in Faulstich and Korte (eds) *Star.* Pp. 48–59.

—— (2000a). *Blockbuster TV: Must-See Sitcoms in the Network Era.* New York: New York University Press.

—— (2000b). *Perverse Spectators: The Practices of Film Reception.* New York: New York University Press.

—— (forthcoming). "Cabinets of Transgression: Collecting and Arranging Hollywood Images," *Participations* (on-line journal).

Stallybrass, Peter, and Allon White (1986). *The Politics and Poetics of Transgression*. London: Methuen.

Stern, Lesley (1982). "The Body as Evidence," *Screen* 23, no. 5 (November–December): 38–60.

Steven, Peter (ed) (1985). *Jump Cut: Hollywood, Politics and Counter Cinema*. New York: Praeger.

Stevenson, Jack (1997). "From the Bedroom to the Bijou: A Secret History of American Gay Sex Cinema," *Film Quarterly* 51, no. 1 (Fall): 24–31.

Stewart, Jacqueline (2003). "Negroes Laughing at Themselves? Black Spectatorship and the Performance of Urban Modernity," *Critical Inquiry* 29, no. 4 (Summer): 650–77.

Stockbridge, Sally (1990). "Rock Video: Pleasure and Resistance" in M. Brown (ed) *Television and Women's Culture*. Pp. 102–13.

Stokes, Melvyn, and Richard Maltby (eds) (1999a). *American Movie Audiences: From the Turn of the Century to the Early Sound Era*. London: British Film Institute.

—— (eds) (1999b). *Identifying Hollywood's Audiences: Cultural Identity and the Movies*. London: British Film Institute.

—— (eds) (2001). *Hollywood Spectatorship: Changing Perceptions of Cinema Audiences*. London: British Film Institute.

Streible, Dan (1996). "Race and the Reception of Jack Johnson Fight Films" in Bernardi (ed) *Birth of Whiteness*. Pp. 170–200.

Studlar, Gaylyn (1996). *This Mad Masquerade: Stardom and Masculinity in the Jazz Age*. New York: Columbia University Press.

Suleiman, Susan, and Inge Crosman (eds) (1980). *The Reader in the Text: Essays on Audience and Interpretation*. Princeton, NJ: Princeton University Press.

Sullivan, K. E. (1997). "[Review of] *Attack of the Leading Ladies: Gender, Sexuality, and Spectatorship in Classic Horror Cinema*," *Film Quarterly* 50, no. 4 (Summer): 40–42.

Sumner, Colin (1997a). "Introduction: The Violence of Censure and the Censure of Violence" in Sumner (ed) *Violence, Culture and Censure*. Pp. 1–6.

—— (ed) (1997b). *Violence, Culture and Censure*. London: Taylor and Francis.

Tamborini, Ron (1991). "Responding to Horror: Determinants of Exposure and Appeal" in Bryant and Zillmann (eds) *Responding to the Screen*. Pp. 305–28.

Tan, Ed S. (1996). *Emotion and the Structure of Narrative Film: Film as an Emotion Machine*. Mahwah, NJ: Erlbaum.

Taylor, Greg (1999). *Artists in the Audience: Cults, Camp, and American Film Criticism*. Princeton, NJ: Princeton University Press.

Taylor, Helen (1989). *Scarlett's Women: Gone with the Wind and Its Female Fans.* New Brunswick, NJ: Rutgers University Press.

Telotte, J. P. (1991a). "Beyond All Reason: The Nature of the Cult," in Telotte (ed) *Cult Film Experience.* Pp. 5–17.

——— (ed) (1991b). *The Cult Film Experience: Beyond All Reason.* Austin: University of Texas Press.

Thornton, Sarah (1997). "Introduction to Part One" in Gelder and Thornton (ed) *Subcultures Reader.* Pp. 11–15.

Thorp, Margaret (1939). *America at the Movies.* Rpt., New York: Arno Press and the New York Times, 1970.

Thouard, Sylvie (2001). "Performances of *The Devil Never Sleeps/Eldiablo nunca duerme*" in Fregoso (ed) *Lourdes Portillo.* Pp. 119–43.

Thrasher, Frederic M. (1949). "The Comics and Delinquency: Cause or Scapegoat," *Journal of Educational Sociology* 23, no. 4 (December): 195–206.

Thrupkaew, Noy (2003). "Fan/tastic Voyage," *Bitch,* no. 20 (Spring): 40–45, 92.

Tinkcom, Matthew, and Amy Villarejo (eds) (2001). *Keyframes: Popular Cinema and Cultural Studies.* London: Routledge.

Torres, Sasha (1996). "The Caped Crusader of Camp: Pop, Camp, and the *Batman* Television Series" in Doyle, Flatley, and Muñoz (eds) *Pop Out.* Pp. 238–55.

Traub, Valerie (1991). "The Ambiguities of 'Lesbian' Viewing Pleasure: The (Dis)Articulations of *Black Widow*" in Epstein and Straub (eds) *Body Guards.* Pp. 305–28.

Tulloch, John, and Henry Jenkins (1995). *Science Fiction Audiences: Watching Dr. Who and Star Trek.* London: Routledge.

Tulloch, John, and Marian Tulloch (1992). "Discourses about Violence: Critical Theory and the 'TV Violence' Debate," *Text* 12, no. 2: 183–231.

Turner, Graeme (1990). *British Cultural Studies: An Introduction.* Boston: Unwin Hyman.

Twitchell, James B. (1985). *Dreadful Pleasures: An Anatomy of Modern Horror.* New York: Oxford University Press.

Vance, Carole S. (ed) (1989). *Pleasure and Danger: Exploring Female Sexuality.* London: Routledge & Kegan Paul.

Vine, Ian (1997). "The Dangerous Psycho-Logic of Media 'Effects'" in Barker and Petley (eds) *Ill Effects.* Pp. 125–46.

Von Feilitzen, Cecilia (1998). "Media Violence: Four Research Perspectives" in Dickinson, Harindranath, and Linné (eds) *Approaches to Audiences.* Pp. 88–103.

Vorse, Mary Heaton (1911). "Some Picture Show Audiences," *Collier's,* 24 June. Pp. 441–47.

Waits, Jennifer C. (1997). "United We Dish: The Construction of Reality in the

Melrose Update Community." Unpublished paper, Popular Culture Association conference, San Antonio, Texas.

Walker, Alexander (1966). *The Celluloid Sacrifice: Aspects of Sex in the Movies*. New York: Hawthorn Books.

—— (1970). *Stardom: The Hollywood Phenomenon*. New York: Stein and Day.

Walkerdine, Valerie (1986). "Video Replay: Families, Films and Fantasy" in Burgin, Donald, and Kaplan (eds) *Formations of Pleasure*. Pp. 167–99.

Wallace, Michelle (1993). "Race, Gender, and Psychoanalysis in Forties Film: *Lost Boundaries, Home of the Brave*, and *The Quiet One*" in Diawara (ed) *Black American Cinema*. Pp. 257–71.

Wallen, Jeffrey (1998). *Closed Encounters: Literary Politics and Public Culture*. Minneapolis: University of Minnesota Press.

Waugh, Tom (1985). "Gay vs. Straight: Men's Pornography," *Jump Cut*, no. 30: 30–35.

—— (1992). "Homoerotic Representation in the Stag Film, 1920–1940," *Wide Angle* 14, no. 2 (Summer): 4–21.

Weaver, James B., III (1991). "Are 'Slasher' Horror Films Sexually Violent? A Content Analysis," *Journal of Broadcasting & Electronic Media* 35, no. 3 (Summer): 385–92.

Weaver, James B., III, and Ron Tamborini (eds) (1996). *Horror Films: Current Research on Audience Preferences and Reactions*. Mahwah, NJ: Erlbaum.

Weiss, Andrea (1991). "'A Queer Feeling When I Look at You': Hollywood Stars and Lesbian Spectatorship in the 1930s," rpt. in Gledhill (ed) *Stardom*. Pp. 283–99.

Wells, Paul (2003). "To Affinity and Beyond: Woody, Buzz and the New Authenticity" in T. Austin and Barker (eds) *Contemporary Hollywood Stardom*. Pp. 99–102.

Wertham, Fredric (1954). *Seduction of the Innocent*. New York: Rinehart.

West, Mark I. (1988). *Children, Culture and Controversy*. Hamden, CT: Archon.

Whatling, Clare (1997). *Screen Dreams: Fantasizing Lesbian in Film*. Manchester, UK: Manchester University Press.

White, Hayden (1996). "The Modernist Event" in Sobchack (ed) *Persistence of History*. Pp. 17–38.

Wilinsky, Barbara (2000). *Sure Seaters: The Emergence of Art House Cinema*. Minneapolis: University of Minnesota Press.

Willeman, Paul (1980). "Letter to John," *Screen* 21, no. 2 (Summer): 53–66.

Williams, Linda (1989). *Hard Core: Power, Pleasure, and the "Frenzy" of the Visible*. Berkeley: University of California Press.

———— (1991). "Film Bodies: Gender, Genre, and Excess," *Film Quarterly* 44, no. 4 (Summer): 2–13.

Williams, Raymond (1977). *Marxism and Literature.* Oxford: Oxford University Press.

———— (1981). *Culture.* Glasgow, UK: Fontana.

Winick, Charles (1963). "Tendency Systems and the Effects of a Movie Dealing with a Social Problem," *Journal of General Psychology* 68, no. 2 (April): 289–305.

———— (1970). "A Study of Consumers of Explicitly Sexual Materials" in *Technical Report of the Commission on Obscenity and Pornography*, vol. IV. Washington, DC: U.S. Government Printing Office, 1970. Pp. 245–62.

Wolf, Michelle A., and Alfred P. Kielwasser (eds) (1991). *Gay People, Sex, and the Media.* New York: Harrington Park Press.

Wolfenstein, Martha, and Nathan Leites (1950). *Movies: A Psychological Study.* Glencoe, IL: Free Press.

Wollen, Peter (1972). *Signs and Meaning in the Cinema*, rev. ed. Bloomington: Indiana University Press.

Wong, Cindy Hing-Yuk (1998). "Understanding Grassroots Audiences: Imagination, Reception, and Use in Community Videography," *Velvet Light Trap*, no. 42 (Fall): 91–102.

Wood, Jennifer F. (2002). "House Negro versus Field Negro: The Inscribed Image of Race in Television News Representations of African-American Identity" in Coleman (ed) *Say It Loud.* Pp. 95–114.

Wood, Robin (1979). "An Introduction to the American Horror Film," rpt. in Nichols (ed) *Movies and Methods*, vol. II. Pp. 195–220.

Wray, Matt, and Annalee Newitz (eds) (1997). *White Trash: Race and Class in America.* New York: Routledge.

Zelizer, Barbie (1995). "Reading the Past against the Grain: The Shape of Memory Studies," *Critical Studies in Mass Communication* 12 (June): 214–32.

Zillmann, Dolf (1991a). "Empathy: Affect from Bearing Witness to the Emotions of Others" in Bryant and Zillmann (eds) *Responding to the Screen.* Pp. 135–67.

———— (1991b). "The Logic of Suspense and Mystery" in Bryant and Zillmann (eds) *Responding to the Screen.* Pp. 281–303.

Zillmann, Dolf, and James B. Weaver III (1996). "Gender-Socialization Theory of Reactions to Horror" in Weaver and Tamborini (eds) *Horror Films.* Pp. 81–101.

Zillmann, Dolf, James B. Weaver, Norbert Mundorf, and Charles F. Aust (1986). "Effects of an Opposite-Gender Companion's Affect to Horror on Distress, Delight, and Attraction," *Journal of Personality and Social Psychology* 51, no. 3 (September): 586–94.

Zillmann, Dolf, and Jennings Bryant (1991). "Responding to Comedy: The Sense and Nonsense in Humor" in Bryant and Zillmann (eds) *Responding to the Screen*. Pp. 261–79.

Zillmann, Dolf, and Rhonda Gibson (1996). "Evolution of the Horror Genre" in Weaver and Tamborini (eds) *Horror Films*. Pp. 15–31.

Zimmerman, Bonnie (1981). "What Has Never Been: An Overview of Lesbian Feminist Literary Criticism," rpt. in Showalter (ed) *New Feminist Criticism*. Pp. 200–224.

Index

About the Author

Janet Staiger is William P. Hobby Centennial Professor of Communication and former director of the Center for Women's and Gender Studies at the University of Texas, Austin. She is the author of numerous books, including *Perverse Spectators: The Practices of Film Reception* and *Blockbuster TV: Must-See Sitcoms in the Network Era*, both available from NYU Press.